THE SAILOR AND THE DANCING GIRL

The Campaigns of General George Thomas, the Begum Somru, and the Twilight of the Mughal Empire, 1760–1836

Andy Copestake

Helion & Company Limited

Another For Carole.
Still putting up with it all.

Helion & Company Limited
Unit 8 Amherst Business Centre
Budbrooke Road
Warwick
CV34 5WE
England
Tel. 01926 499619
Email: info@helion.co.uk
Website: www.helion.co.uk
X (formerly Twitter): @Helionbooks
Facebook: @HelionBooks
Visit our blog at http://blog.helion.co.uk/

Published by Helion & Company 2026
Designed and typeset by Mach 3 Solutions (www.mach3solutions.co.uk)
Cover designed by Paul Hewitt, Battlefield Design (www.battlefield-design.co.uk)

ISBN 978-1-806722-55-6

British Library Cataloguing-in-Publication Data.
A catalogue record for this book is available from the British Library.

For details of other military history titles published by Helion & Company Limited, contact the above address, or visit our website: http://www.helion.co.uk

We always welcome receiving book proposals from prospective authors.

Contents

Preface

A few years ago, I wrote and had published by Helion my first book, *Their Infantry and Guns Will Astonish You*,[1] which told the story of Benoît de Boigne, the greatest of the 'European Military Adventurers', and the army he raised, trained and commanded in eighteenth-century India. In some of the many campaigns undertaken by elements of this, the 'Army of Hindustan', they encountered two of the most unlikely mercenary commanders that even the anarchy of eighteenth-century India could produce.

The first, a widow lady, who had once been a dancing girl, and was now the Mughal Emperor's adopted daughter, the other, an Irish sailor who had deserted from the Royal Navy and would, in time, rule his own city state. Even more unlikely, their stories were intertwined with a series of 'plot twists' that even Hollywood might find unbelievable. Yet their careers are documented fact. Indeed, one dictated his memoirs before he died, the other retained the state she ruled until the 1830s and was, in the way of such things back then, something of a celebrity, with her own army still guarding her lands and palace. I thought it was time to tell their stories.

To do that, we must go back to the middle of the eighteenth century and the wars in Northern India, particularly Bengal, which gave rise to the mercenary forces there. This is a story that begins with greed and perfidy on all sides, both accidental and with deliberate design, but there were also good and honourable men on all sides too, as no true story is ever purely black or white.

In particular, the early history of the Somru Brigade and its founder, the German mercenary Walter Reinhardt, who would marry the dancing girl, is covered in some depth to put the existence of this formation into historical context. Indeed, it was apparent during my research for this book that the story of the 'European Military Adventurers' and their mercenary forces began somewhat earlier in the eighteenth century than Lewis Ferdinand Smith declares.[2]

Much of the background in my previous book will be relevant. Shah Alam, the Mughal Emperor, sat uneasily on his somewhat threadbare throne, surrounded by greedy and often murderous courtiers. Plots and intrigue were constant, and failure

1 A. Copestake, *Their Infantry and Guns Will Astonish You: The Army of Hindustan and European Mercenaries in Maratha Service, 1780–1803* (Warwick: Helion, 2021).

2 L.F. Smith, Major, *A Sketch of the Rise, Progress and Termination of the Regular Corps Formed and Commanded by Europeans in the Service of the Native Princes of India* (Calcutta: J. Greenway, 1805), p.2.

often meant a painful death. Warfare was almost constant as the once mighty Mughal Empire fell apart and the various successor states fought for either mastery or survival. Into this mix, the European trading companies and their armies introduced technological and military improvements, which were eagerly adopted by many Indian rulers and caused 'European Military Experts' to be in high and constant demand by those rulers.

In some ways, this book is *Their Infantry and Guns – Part two*, as both General George Thomas, the Sailor, and Farzana, the Begum Somru, and one-time dancing girl, appear within the pages of that book. Yet only parts of their story appear there insofar as they each interacted with the Army of Hindustan and its commanders.

Therefore, this book will tell the rest of their remarkable stories.

Acknowledgements

As always, my thanks and first thoughts must go to my wife Carole for putting up with the disorder caused by this writing bug of mine. I also gratefully thank Stanley Agar, an old friend, for his photographs of the Red Fort in Delhi. Next, my thanks to Helion the publisher, for allowing me to scratch the writing itch caused by the incredible stories of Jehazi Sahib and the Begum Somru.

Chronology of Events

1498	Portuguese explorer Vasco da Gama reaches India. The Portuguese begin trading. They are followed in the next century by the Dutch and later the French and the British.
1556	Akbar the Great becomes Mughal Emperor. His tolerant attitude to religion within his Empire institutes something of a Golden Age in much of the Indian subcontinent.
1600	The East India Company is founded by English merchants.
1642	The East India Company in Madras begins the building of Fort St. George, which has a garrison of 35 'Europeans' plus the same number of local 'peons'. The Council of Madras is given the legal right by local rulers to dispense justice within its boundaries.
1658	Aurungzeb becomes Mughal Emperor after killing his three brothers. His brutal and intolerant attitude begins the break-up of the Empire.
1670	The Maratha hero Shivaji begins a war of independence against the Mughals. His guerrilla tactics wear out and destroy Mughal armies.
1707	Emperor Aurungzeb dies.
1717	The Mughal Emperor allows the English East India Company to trade duty free and to buy land and villages around its trading factories.
1720s–1760	Maratha conquests of former imperial provinces continue. The Maratha Confederacy becomes supreme in much of Central India and reaches as far north as the Punjab.
1727	Madhaji Scindia born.
1739	Nadir Shah of Persia invades northern India, captures and loots Delhi. Thousands are killed in the ensuing massacre. Nadir Shah then returns home with the loot including the Peacock Throne of the Mughal Emperors.
1740–48	War of the Austrian Succession in Europe.

September 1746	Madras falls to the French after a short siege. This despite a theoretical non-aggression pact between the British in Madras and the French in Pondicherry and the express instructions of the Nawab of the Carnatic, the nominal overlord of both of the European settlements, to abstain from hostilities.
4 November 1746	Battle of St Thome. The Nawab of the Carnatic sends his son, Maphuz Khan, to recover Madras with a 10,000 strong army, including artillery. This army is destroyed by a French force consisting of 200 Europeans and around 800 trained sepoys. This is the first instance where the superiority of European military training is displayed on an Indian battlefield.
1750	Farzana, the girl who would become the Begum Somru, born.
1746–1755	The British and the French carry on a 'war by proxy' acting as allies to the various contenders battling to rule the Carnatic. Robert Clive learns his soldiering in this war. Both Walter Reinhardt and René Madec are soldiers in the French forces.
1756	George Thomas born in Roscrea, Tipperary Ireland.
14 January 1761	Third Battle of Panipat. Afghan invaders helped by local Muslim rulers smash the Maratha Confederacy armies 80km northwest of Delhi. The Marathas lose their hold on Northern India. Although seriously wounded Maratha leader Madhaji Scindia escapes capture.
1756–1763	The Seven Years War in Europe. In India, the British emerge victorious over the French. Groups and individual ex-French officers and soldiers take service with local rulers anxious to strengthen their own military forces as the Mughal Empire continues to disintegrate. Walter Reinhardt is one of these.
1762–3	Walter Reinhardt alias 'Somru' and a little later René Madec are employed to raise 'trained brigades', *compoos* for Mir Kassim of Bengal and Shuja-ud-Daulah of Oudh respectively.
22 October 1764	Battle of Buxar. British defeat Shuja-ud-Daulah of Oudh and his 'Trained Brigades' under Walter Reinhardt and René Madec.
1767–69	First Mysore War. Haidar Ali defeats the Madras presidency of the British East India Company.
1775–1782	First Maratha War ends in a stalemate for the East India Company despite tactical military victories, but Madhaji Scindia learns the value of European-trained infantry and artillery.
1775–1783	American War of Independence. In India, the French land a force under Bussy in the Carnatic to 'support' Haidar Ali but it arrives only after his death.
January 1778	Benoît de Boigne lands in Madras.

1780–84	Second Mysore War. Haidar Ali defeats the British at first but is then in turn defeated by Sir Eyre Coote. Ali's son Tipu Sultan continues the war with some French aid. The end of the war sees more French adventurers becoming mercenaries. Pierre Cuillier – alias Perron – arrives in India at this time, as does George Thomas.
1787	George Thomas arrives in Delhi and takes service in the *compoo* of the Begum Somru. Their remarkable relationship begins.

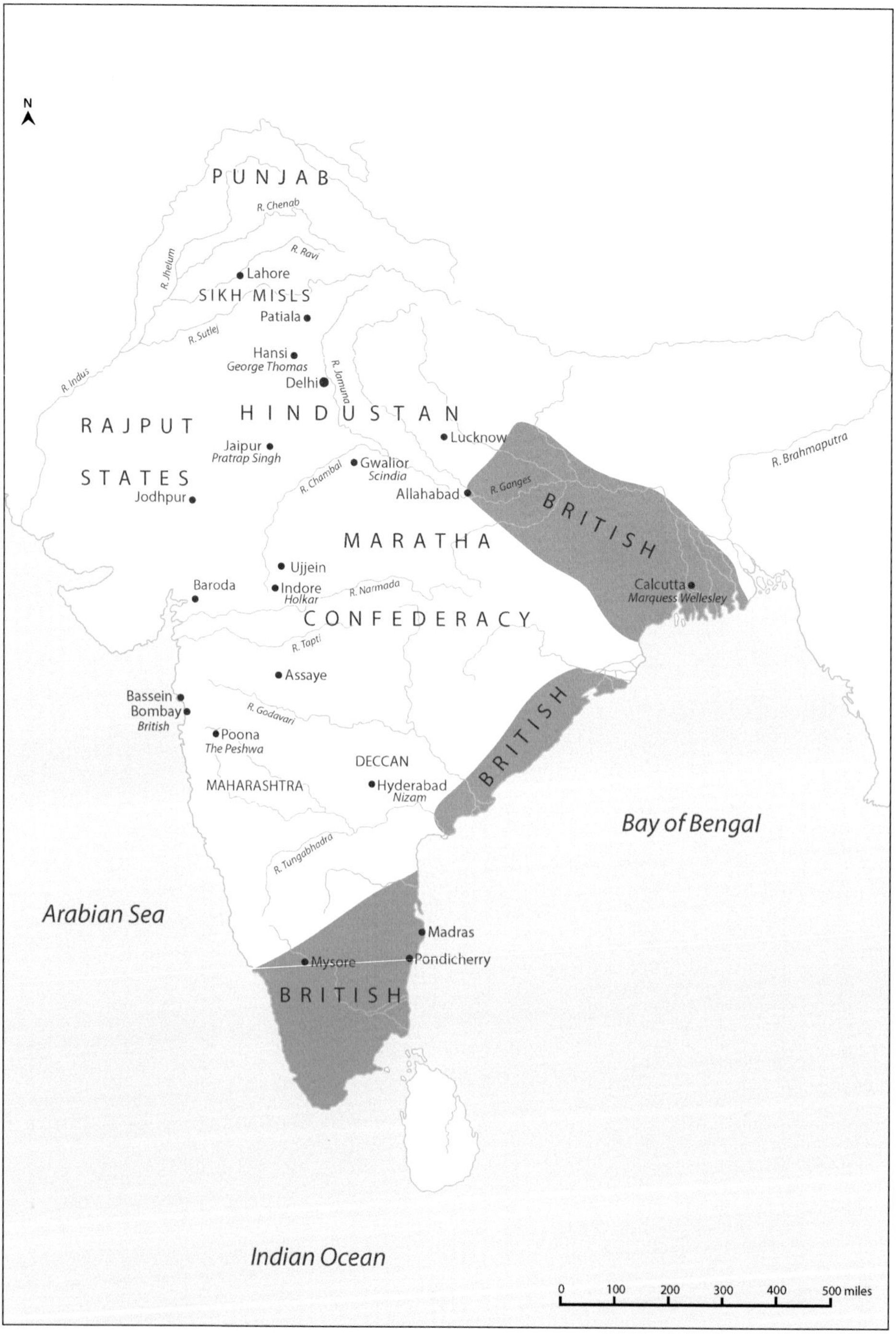

India, circa 1800. At this time, the British are by no means the supreme power in the subcontinent. That title belongs to the Maratha Confederacy. (George Anderson © Helion & Co)

1

The Mercenary Calling

In today's media-obsessed world, the term 'mercenary' has become, as often as not, a term of opprobrium, an insult to be flung about by assorted politicians and journalists to score points over their adversaries. This is largely because some governments and many people find the idea of fighting for pay distasteful, especially when the fighters in question are fighting for nations other than their own, but also because some of today's mercenaries behave as little more than brutal bandits. In the eyes of the media, this has become so bad that many 'modern mercenaries' now style themselves 'Private Military Companies' and strive to avoid the 'M' word altogether.

This was not always so. Mercenary soldiering was once an honoured profession. Alexander the Great used mercenaries, the Roman Empire employed them, and medieval and Renaissance Italy was virtually awash with them. At some point in their history, virtually every country or empire has used mercenary soldiers of one sort or another.

The Indian subcontinent was no different.

By the eighteenth century, the much-invaded Indian peninsula was in a more than usual state of turmoil. The most successful of its recent invaders, the Mughals, had first established an empire in the sixteenth century when Babur defeated the Muslim Sultan of Delhi at the first Battle of Panipat. Through the rest of the sixteenth and most of the seventeenth centuries, the Mughals had continued to expand their holdings in the subcontinent until they had displaced many of the native Hindu dynasties as well as the Muslim dynasties of previous invaders. For a time, the Mughal Empire glittered with magnificence, producing sublime art, such as the Taj Mahal. Yet, as always, there was a serpent in Eden, and while the Emperor Akbar the Great had practised religious tolerance and had Hindu ministers and scholars at his court in Agra, one of his successors, his great-grandson Aurungzeb, was the worst kind of religious bigot, persecuting non-Muslims and thereby encouraging revolt.

By 1707, when Aurungzeb died, the cracks in the magnificence were definitely beginning to show. In south-central India, the Marathas had won de facto independence under their great leader Shivaji and his successors. In the north-west, the once peaceful Sikhs had become militarised and were fighting a guerrilla war against their Mughal oppressors. They would become a serious threat by the middle of the century.

To the south-east of Delhi, those hardy Hindu farmers, the Jats, were becoming restive and would forge an independent state in the coming decades. The Mughal governors of provinces such as Bengal, Oudh or Hyderabad would become independent rulers by the middle of the century. The passes of the north-west, long an invasion route, would be trodden once again by Persian and Afghan invaders.

Delhi, now the seat of the Mughal Emperors, would be mercilessly sacked by both Persian and Afghan alike, so that by the last quarter of the eighteenth century it was a mere shadow of its former opulence. The Emperor still resided in the Red Fort in Delhi, no longer on the Peacock Throne as Nadir Shah, the Persian invader, had looted it. The Empire consisted of only the last province of Hindustan and such of the other provinces whose independent rulers chose to pay a nominal tribute for form's sake. In practice, the Empire had expired, but the assorted factions fought over the decomposing carcass like vultures. It is no wonder that the eighteenth century in Indian history is often referred to as the 'Time of Troubles' or 'the Anarchy'.[1]

The disintegration of the empire led to constant warfare. Each of the newly independent rulers needed troops to both defend his own territories and, when necessary, invade his neighbours' lands.

Into this heady and dangerous mix came the European trading companies: first the Portuguese, then the Dutch, followed by the English and the French. Their trading posts, known as 'factories' because the trading agent was called a 'factor', were, to begin with, very small and existed only with the consent of the local ruler. Indeed, the Portuguese had settlements on the south-west coast of the subcontinent before the Mughal invasion far to the north (Goa was established by 1510),[2] and by the end of the seventeenth century, they were selling cannon to the Marathas. The Marathas were also buying cannon and powder from both the English and French traders in their rather more recently established settlements.[3] They were eager to improve their military capabilities for their war of independence against the Mughal Empire.

All of the European settlements had a military presence, often quite small, to protect their factories and administer local justice in the name of the ruler who had consented to the factory's existence. For example, in 1655, Madras, a British East India Company post, had a paltry garrison of 25 officers and men.[4] In the late seventeenth century, the French in Pondicherry had a garrison of 40 or so Europeans and 400 locally recruited 'pions' – native mercenaries under their own leaders – with which to resist a Dutch onslaught.[5] All of the European factories recruited locally to bolster the often tiny numbers of European troops available to them.

It was not one-way traffic. Small numbers of European mercenaries had appeared in Mughal armies from the seventeenth century onwards. At first, these were almost

1 See W. Dalrymple, *The Anarchy: The Relentless Rise of the East India Company* (London: Bloomsbury, 2019).
2 P. Abbott, *Rivals of the Raj: Non-British Colonial Armies in Asia 1497–1941* (Nottingham: Foundry Books, 2010), p.116.
3 S.N. Sen, *The Military System of the Marathas* (Delhi: K.P. Bagchi, 1958; reprint, 1979), pp.96–100.
4 J.P. Lawford, *Britain's Army in India, From its Origins to the Conquest of Bengal* (London: George Allen & Unwin, 1978), p.31.
5 Abbott, *Rivals*, p.73.

exclusively Portuguese, usually sailors working for the local rulers as gunners, but there were, by the early eighteenth century, a few English, again sailors, working as gunners.[6]

But it was the middle years of the eighteenth century when Indian rulers began to realise that they were not the masters of warfare that they had previously supposed themselves to be. The practice and development of the art of war on the Indian subcontinent had stagnated and, in effect, halted during the seventeenth century. Indian armies in 1750 were much the same as they had been one hundred years previously: largely feudal in nature and often consisting of masses of undrilled but courageous cavalry, backed by often unenthusiastic and equally undrilled infantry and, by eighteenth-century European standards, overlarge, clumsy, and immobile artillery.[7] Such armies were, at best, polyglot formations with some troops owing allegiance to the commanding general and others to more local leaders further down what passed for the chain of command. This meant that Mughal and, indeed, the various similar successor-state armies could be very brittle formations indeed.

Battles, while often bravely fought, tended to follow a stereotypical pattern. First, both armies would advance to find each other with attendant skirmishing between their respective cavalries draining the locality of provisions and fodder as they moved. Once in reasonable proximity, they would encamp, often fortifying that camp. Not infrequently, negotiations, sincere or otherwise, would take place between the two sides. A battle, if it finally took place, would usually begin with a long, mutual cannonade before one side launched a series of cavalry charges, watched by their commander from the lofty height of his elephant. Were this general to be killed, or even to dismount from his elephant, there was a strong likelihood that his army would panic and flee the field.

Spying, assassination, and bribery were normal aspects of the Indian art of 'Treacherous War', and it was a rare Mughal general who could trust all of his troops. There was a decided lack of permanence and continuity in the empire from the top down. Intrigue ruled the Mughal court. There was no law of primogeniture to ensure a peaceful succession when an emperor died. This meant a period of instability and uncertainty, which percolated down the military hierarchy. Not infrequently, the intrigue and instability broke into open civil war as the various contenders for the imperial throne fought it out.

This was not confined to the imperial throne but also extended to those successor states ruled by officers of the empire who had made themselves independent. They, too, faced the same instability and the constant threat of assassination or open rebellion. Leadership was entirely personal and feudal, as each nobleman fought and schemed to increase his lands, and thus his revenue and therefore his power, at the expense of his rivals. Alliances were fluid, and today's enemy might well be tomorrow's needed friend and ally.

The British and the French were, of course, at war with each other throughout much of the eighteenth century. These Eurocentric conflicts were often reflected in the overseas

6 Copestake, *Their Infantry and Guns*, p.30.

7 For traditional Indian armies see P. Mason, *A Matter of Honour: An Account of the Indian Army, its Officers and Men* (London: Jonathan Cape, 1974), pp.39–55; or Copestake, *Their Infantry and Guns*, pp.16–35.

possessions of those European powers. Thus, the War of the Austrian Succession (1740–1748) had an Indian subsidiary conflict as the two rival companies fought it out for mastery of the south of India. Once peace returned to Europe in 1748, one might have thought that the two rivals in India would stop the fighting, but this was not so. Indeed, the fighting actually spread and intensified as each side continued its private war as 'auxiliaries' and allies of local rulers, who were themselves fighting for mastery over the successor states of southern India. In return, the European companies, commercial as ever, received payments from the rulers they chose to aid, in the form of land concessions and sometimes the payment in cash of the expenses of the campaign.

Thus, the Europeans, particularly the French and then later the British, would, in time, provide the military stability Indian rulers needed. The French were first off the mark. The military officers of the *Compagnie des Indes* had begun to train, arm, and discipline local recruits in the European manner by the 1730s, if not earlier. The Battle of St Thome on 4 November 1746 was only the first of a string of victories won by small French armies,[8] often as part of a larger Mughal force, against the enemies of their chosen client rulers.

Similarly, at the Battle of Ambur in August 1749, a French force of 400 Europeans and 2,000 sepoys – backed by perhaps 30,000 assorted Mughals commanded by Chunda Sahib and Muffazzar Jang, contenders for the rule of the Carnatic and the Deccan respectively – faced Anwar-ud-Din's 20,000 'picked troops' in their earthworks. Anwar's force had the assistance of a company of 60 European mercenaries who manned many of his guns. These men seem to have been assorted deserters from the ships of both the British and French companies, and may have included deserters from their military forces as well. They deserve notice simply because they are an early instance of a significant number of European mercenaries in Indian service.

Nevertheless, the French stormed the position, though it took three attempts, and routed the enemy, capturing their camp, 60 elephants, and all of Anwar-ud-Din's guns, Anwar himself being killed in the debacle.[9]

The contemporary historian Robert Orme gives us an account of another French victory over a Mughal army in the same campaign:

> As soon as they retreated, Mr Dupleix ordered the main body at Valdore to march and join the camp near Trivady: the whole force when united consisted of 1,800 Europeans, 2,500 sepoys and 1,000 horse levied by Chunda Sahib, together with twelve field pieces. The army of Muhammed Ali consisted of 5,000 foot and 15,000 horse variously armed: his camp extended between two villages which secured the flanks; the rear was defended by a river; in front were several entrenchments occupied by infantry; and in the other intervals where there were no entrenchments cannon were placed: the cavalry instead of being out on the plain, formed a second line within the camp. On 21st of August the French advanced to attack

8 Copestake, *Their Infantry and Guns*, pp.13–15.
9 Colonel G.B. Malleson, *History of the French in India: From the Founding of Pondicherry in 1674 to the Capture of that Place in 1761* (Edinburgh: John Grant, 1909), pp.237–238.

> this absurd disposition: their field pieces were distributed in front; the baggage carts were ranged in a regular line in the rear, the cavalry were on each wing; they made several halts during which they gave a general discharge of their artillery, which was answered by the enemy's cannon and musketry, not a shot of which did execution; but a rocket, which the Moors make use of to frighten cavalry, set fire to a tumbril, and this blowing up, wounded four of the Sepoys. As soon as the French troops were within 200 yards of the camp, they marched up briskly to the entrenchments, which were instantly abandoned, and the enemy at the same time deserted the cannon. The French, having entered the camp, formed again, brought up their artillery, and began to fire upon the cavalry, who were soon flung into confusion. The rout became general, and horse and foot promiscuously and with such precipitation, that many pushed directly into the river where they were drowned.[10]

By 1751, the French had won a string of seemingly impossible victories against Mughal and Maratha forces, which gave their client rulers the Carnatic and much of the Deccan. The Nizam of Hyderabad was completely in the power of Governor Dupleix and the French Company in Pondicherry. Such was the influence of the French Company that Dupleix was given the Mughal office of a Mansabdar of 7,000 horse as an honorific, as well as that of Nawab of the Carnatic by his supposed 'feudal overlord' Salabat Jang, the Mughal *subahdar* of the Deccan in 1752.[11] This prince, ostensibly ruling in the Emperor's name, was, in fact, all but independent and, although never officially recognised by the Emperor in Delhi, was the de facto Nizam of Hyderabad. To 'protect' the Nizam, a French army of 500 Europeans and 5,000 sepoys, paid for and sometimes uniformed by the Nizam, was stationed in Hyderabad state.

The commander of this army was one Charles-Joseph Patissier, Marquis de Bussy-Castelnau, who was, arguably, the best French soldier ever to serve in India. Bussy and his army kept the Nizam on his somewhat unsteady throne for four years, defeating rebellious vassals and, more importantly, a serious invasion by the Marathas led by the *Peshwa*, Balaji Baji Rao.

This invasion was the first time that a major Maratha army had encountered European-trained infantry and artillery. Balaji Baji Rao and his 40,000 cavalry had no answer to the French guns and disciplined musketry. As Bussy and Salabat Jang marched towards Poona, every Maratha attack was beaten off. On 22 November 1751, Salabat Jang and Bussy stormed the Maratha camp in a night attack, with Bussy's infantry taking the lead, and dispersed the Marathas almost without any serious fighting.[12]

The influence of Bussy's and the other French victories was far-reaching. In the beginning, it led to the employment of at least two Indian mercenary leaders who each

10 R. Orme, *A History of the Military Transactions of the British Nation in Indostan, from the Year MDCCXLV* (London, 1758; repr. New Delhi: Today and Tomorrow, 1985), vol.1, p.154.

11 Malleson, *The French in India*, p.337.

12 Malleson, *The French in India*, pp.362–363; J.G. Duff, *A History of the Mahrattas*, vol.1 (repr. New Delhi: Associated Publishing, 1982), pp.347–348.

recruited their own *compoo* – a brigade of regular infantry and artillery – and trained them in the French manner. These two, Muzuffir Khan and his kinsman Ibrahim Khan Gardi, took service with the Marathas. Both men had served in Bussy's army. Muzuffir Khan was in Maratha service by 1752 and Ibrahim may have been with him. Neither of these men, nor the troops they recruited, were Marathas. Muzuffir is described as a 'Deccani Muslim'[13] and many of his men must have been similar. He was implicated in a plot against the *Peshwa* in 1759 and executed, but the men of his *compoo* seem to have continued, joining the *compoo* of Ibrahim Khan. At the outset of the campaign of 1760–61, which led to the Third Battle of Panipat, Ibrahim Khan's *compoo* was noted as 10,000 infantry in 10 battalions with 50 guns.[14]

Although Ibrahim Khan Gardi's *compoo* was destroyed in this fateful battle and he was captured and killed by the Afghan victors, the seed had been sown. Khan's regular troops, trained in the European manner, had come close to being a battle-winning force. The battlefield effectiveness of European-trained troops was repeatedly shown on Indian battlefields during the 1750s and early 1760s. Other Indian princes were soon to realise that they also would need trained infantry and artillery. The time of the European 'free-lance' or 'military adventurer' was close at hand. These adventurers were many and various. To begin with, most were French – the flotsam of those French armies defeated by the British – including a few 'gentlemen' of sorts, such as Le Vassault or the Chevalier Dudrenec, both of whom play a part in our story. Others were ordinary soldiers or sailors who had deserted or been abandoned and had to survive as best they could. A few would rise to command a battalion or even a *compoo*, though most remained as junior officers or even gunners in the formations of other adventurers. A little later, more of these mercenaries would be British – again, sometimes sailors, but more often 'country-born' with British fathers and Indian mothers.

Many, perhaps most, would die in India. A very few would return to their native countries in Europe with a fortune. Others would remain in India and become part of Indian society, with their descendants living on in their adopted country.

13 Duff, *History of the Mahrattas*, vol.1, p.364.
14 Copestake, *Their Infantry and Guns*, pp.31–34 for an account of the third Battle of Panipat.

2

The British in Bengal

From Humiliation to Ascendency

By 1755, the war between the two trading companies, British and French, and their local allies in the south of the Indian peninsula had finally reached a temporary conclusion. While, territorially speaking, the position had not changed a great deal, militarily the superiority of European training and military methods had been proven beyond doubt. The string of victories won by often quite small European-led armies, both British and French, had caused Indian rulers to realise that they must strengthen their own military forces or perish. It quickly became apparent to these rulers that infantry and guns trained and organised on the European model were a possible way forward, both to confront future European encroachment and to further their own territorial ambitions.

As we have seen in the previous chapter, the first of these 'mercenary companies' appeared in Maratha service in 1752, commanded by one Muzuffir Khan and later by his more famous kinsman Ibrahim Khan Gardi. This *compoo*, eventually 10 battalions with 50 guns, was trained in the French style, as both of its founders had been part of Bussy's force in the Carnatic. Despite its destruction at the Third Battle of Panipat in 1761, it would become something of a model for the various mercenary *compoos* or brigades which would be seen as an essential part of any Indian army from the 1760s onwards.[1]

In Bengal, the position of the British and French trading companies was somewhat different. Unlike the south, there was no 'war by proxy', as in the 1740s, the Viceroy of Bengal, Alivardi Khan, was strong enough to enforce his rule over the foreign trading companies in his territory, be they British, French, or Dutch. Equally, there was more of a common enemy in the Marathas, who made large-scale raids into Bengal in 1742, 1743 and 1744. Alivardi Khan used a mixture of military action, bribery, and treachery – defeating the 1742 raid in battle (though not before it had devastated a swathe of the Burdwan district), buying the *Peshwa* off in 1743 with 22 lakhs of rupees, and in 1744 by the assassination of the Maratha leaders while supposedly negotiating a treaty with them. Alivardi Khan was not a man to be trifled with. The merchants of Calcutta were

1 For more details of this early *compoo* see Copestake, *Their Infantry and Guns*, pp.30–32.

even prevailed upon to build the 'Maratha Ditch' as a rudimentary defence against the raids of these predatory light cavalry.[2]

The forces available to Alivardi Khan were of the traditional Mughal type and had hardly changed for over a century. The organisation was essentially feudal, and leadership was very personal. First in importance was the cavalry, its significance stemming as much from social position as battlefield usage. Primary weapons were the lance and sabre. Although the composite bow was still in use, it was being steadily replaced by firearms. Armour was still worn by those who could afford it. Many of the available troops were Rohilla mercenaries. In 1745, around 9,000 cavalry and at least some infantry are described as 'local Afghans'[3] – in other words, Rohillas, who were Afghans and Pathans who had colonised parts of northern India and had carved out a nascent state, Rohlicund. They served in many of the armies of the various successor states that arose from the wreckage of the Mughal Empire.[4] Other cavalry were provided by local leaders in return for land grants – *jaghirs* – in the normal Mughal manner.

Infantry, although socially inferior, were still of some importance in Bengal because of the terrain, cavalry not being of great use in the more jungle-covered areas of the state. These were most usually musketeers armed with matchlock muskets, which did not carry bayonets and, while their longer barrels allowed them to outrange the British 'Brown Bess', they were much slower to load as the musketeers do not seem to have used prepared cartridges in the European manner. In addition, these musketeers knew nothing of drill or unit manoeuvre, so they were easy to panic when something untoward happened. However, they were the mainstay of the Bengali infantry, and their sheer numbers could make them formidable.

Artillery, when used, was highly primitive compared to that of the Europeans, being similar to that seen on European battlefields of the sixteenth century or even earlier. Guns were oversized, impossible to move on the battlefield, and slow to load and fire. The eighteenth century would see some improvements, but until the widespread arrival of mercenary *compoos* in the second half of the century, Indian artillery was still technologically behind that of the Europeans.

In 1756, Alivardi Khan died, and his eventual successor, Siraj-ud-Daulah, was a young man of a very different stamp: vain and capricious, self-indulgent, and sometimes cruel, ill-educated for the role of absolute ruler and fawned upon by sycophants whose main object was to increase their own power and wealth within the court.

The Viceroy or Nawab (the titles were used interchangeably) was, in theory, subject to the Mughal Emperor in Delhi. However, the frayed state of the Mughal Empire in the mid-eighteenth century meant that while imperial titles and favours from the Emperor might convey considerable status and political clout, most viceroys ignored whoever might be Emperor unless it was in their personal interest to do otherwise. Thus, despite not being confirmed as Viceroy of Bengal by the Emperor in Delhi, Siraj-ud-Daulah

2 P. Sensarma, *The Military History of Bengal* (Calcutta: Naya Prokash, 1977), pp.176–183.
3 Sensarma, *The Military History of Bengal*, p.181.
4 For more details of the armies of these successor states, see: Copestake, *Their Infantry and Guns*, pp.16–40.

ruled from his capital of Murshidabad, mistrusted by most of his nobles and generals who, over time, decided to look to their own survival.

In Calcutta, the Council of the East India Company (EIC) viewed the new Nawab with little more than contempt and neglected to offer the appropriate congratulations and gifts upon his accession in the usual manner. This was, at best, bad manners and, at worst, downright dangerous. This was largely because the assorted British traders and officials in Calcutta not infrequently combined their insatiable greed with huge arrogance and an equally huge military and political incompetence. This attitude would, in time, cost them very dear indeed.

This friction was intensified because there were also several outstanding areas of disagreement over trading rights and taxation between the Nawab (Nabob in contemporary English) and the Company. Siraj-ud-Daulah saw the company men as arrogant upstarts who needed to be put in their place. A clash of some kind became inevitable when the EIC council in Calcutta refused to hand over the son, wives and, most importantly, the accumulated wealth of Alivardi Khan's Prime Minister, who had fallen foul of the new ruler and had been dismissed and disgraced.

The Assault on Calcutta

The new Nawab was outraged by the Calcutta Council's attitude and set out with an army in early June 1756 to punish the upstart Europeans. The British in Calcutta refused to believe that their situation was dangerous until it was too late, and then acted with a mixture of cowardice and folly which might defy belief were it not a documented fact. Fort William in Calcutta was defensible, though the walls were in a parlous condition, and it was also overlooked by nearby houses, some of which were owned by the various European officials and merchants. Despite repeated previous orders from the Company in London, nothing had been done to remedy the numerous deficiencies in the fortifications. Captain Alexander Grant, an EIC officer, opined:

> By last year's shipping there was positive orders from the Company to execute a plan sent home by Colonel Scot for their approbation, but his death was thought too sufficient an excuse to postpone what they had so little inclination to have executed. By a later ship we were still further pressed by the Company to put our Settlement in the best state of defence possible as there was great appearance of a French war. Captain (Jasper Leigh) Jones of the artillery in September last thinking it more particularly his duty to represent the defenceless state the garrison was in and the situation of the cannon and ammunition gave in a representation to the Governor and Council of what was immediately necessary for the defence of the place in case of a French war; such as making outworks, mounting cannon which lay then useless for want of carriages, and putting their stores and ammunition in the best condition possible. The style and form of this paper and the manner of delivering it in, it seems, gave offence and Captain Jones was reprimanded for his irregularity in not delivering such representations first to the Commanding Officer of the troops.

> However though it contained many truths proper to be considered there was no further notice take of its contents, nor no orders given for any military preparations, trusting in the same kind fortune that has for so many years defended them in peace and security...[5]

The position had not changed by the time the Bengal forces advanced against the city.

Rather than defend Fort William, the garrison of some 500 or so Europeans and 1,500 'buxerries' (Indian irregular troops armed with matchlock muskets) were tasked to defend a number of redoubts covering the roads into Calcutta. None of these redoubts was in a position to support any of the others, so it came as no surprise that, despite repulsing an initial attack from Siraj-ud-Daulah's advance guard upon the northern redoubt on 16 June 1756, when the main attacks came in on the morning of 18 June, it did not take long before the garrison of each redoubt was bundled out of position and forced back into Fort William. This was despite sometimes sterling resistance from some parties of the garrison. During the night, some kind of evacuation was ordered for the European women and children, but numbers of soldiers, including the garrison commander and EIC officials, boarded the ships, and much of the now-demoralised garrison got drunk. By the afternoon of 19 June, the remaining troops were penned inside Fort William and in a state of panic. The following morning, efforts to contact EIC ships on the river proved unavailing, as the ships refused to come in and take off the panic-stricken Europeans.

Mr John Holwell, the senior magistrate and the highest-ranking official still within the fort, after making some efforts to continue the fight with his drunken and demoralised garrison, decided to treat for terms. While under a flag of truce, a party of the Nawab's matchlockmen burst through the open gate and the remaining garrison threw down its arms and surrendered. Calcutta had fallen. The European prisoners were jammed willy-nilly into a cell far too small for the 146 people. Most died of suffocation, and the 'Black Hole of Calcutta' became a byword for Siraj-ud-Daulah's cruelty, though there is considerable doubt that he even knew of it until it was too late.

Madras received the news of the fall of Calcutta on 16 August 1756, and other military operations were suspended in order to gather a force for the reconquest of the city. To that end, Robert Clive was given command of the land forces for the coming campaign. He had 570 Europeans and 1,000 sepoys,[6] a pretty slender force for the task in hand. It was not until 16 December that Clive and his tiny army, convoyed by the warships of the Royal Navy under Admiral Charles Watson, arrived at Fulta, a village on the banks of the River Hoogly, where the assorted escapees and deserters from Calcutta had gathered. The military capacity of this group was small. Despite pulling in outlying groups and even receiving an earlier reinforcement from Madras under Major Kilpatrick, they could muster little more than 100 fit troops, with around 200 sick,[7] to add to Clive's already slender command.

5 As quoted in S. Reid, *The Battle of Plassey 1757: The Victory That Won an Empire* (Barnsley: Frontline Books, 2017), p.26.

6 Lawford, *Britain's Army in India*, p.186.

7 Lawford, *Britain's Army in India*, pp.186–188.

Although difficult, the river Hoogly was navigable for the larger warships of the Royal Navy, so the land forces were assured of support and, at worst, a refuge if plans went awry. Thus, the first step in the recovery of Calcutta would be the taking of the mud-walled fort at Budge-Budge, some 15 miles to the north. There were three ships of the line – *Kent* (60), *Tyger* (50), and *Salisbury* (50) – as well as two smaller vessels each mounting 20 guns. This fleet, carrying Clive's force upriver, disembarked them at Mynapore, some five miles from Baj-baj (Anglicised as Budge-Budge). The plan was to assault the fort there from the landward side.

Robert Clive, the architect of the British victory over Siraj-ud-Daulah. He had won something of a reputation fighting in the south of India against the French. His reputation would be magnified by his victories in Bengal. (Public Domain)

Clive's reorganised force for the upcoming attack now consisted of the Bengal European Battalion under Major Kilpatrick, which was composed of all the remaining fit Europeans in EIC service currently in Bengal. It included the survivors from Calcutta, as well as the troops Clive had brought with him, and marked the first time that any higher permanent organisation other than the company had been used in the Bengal Presidency.[8] To this new battalion were added some 500 sepoys and two guns, crewed by Europeans. This force's only transport was a single cart or tumbril used to carry ammunition. Even this was moved by manpower, as there were no draught animals.

The night march to Baj-baj was slow and difficult, as much of the ground was covered in swamps and intersected by tributary streams to the Hoogly. By the time the British force came within striking distance of their objective, it was exhausted. Furthermore, the Nawab's governor of Calcutta, one Manikchand, was aware of the British presence and had gathered a force of 1,500 horse and 2,000 foot to oppose Clive's advance. Manikchand's scouts were well aware of the direction of the British approach, so much so that the Bengali commander planned to ambush the British force once it encamped.

Exhaustion had made the British force less than alert and no sentries had been posted as they slept, so Manikchand's initial assault with his matchlockmen overran the British guns and caused considerable confusion. Yet, despite this, the Bengal European Battalion rallied and recovered the guns, which then came into action, tipping the balance against the attackers. With the support of the sepoys, Clive restored order in the British camp and drove off the enemy infantry, though not without difficulty. Attempts by Manikchand's cavalry to intervene were forestalled by the British guns, and when a roundshot passed uncomfortably close to Manikchand himself, his forces drew off back into the jungle.

The British had been very close to defeat, but the superior training of their troops had allowed them to rally and continue the fight, despite initial confusion and surprise. Baj-baj was bombarded by HMS *Kent* and subsequently abandoned by the garrison. Further upriver, the various forts were abandoned by their garrisons, and Calcutta fell to Admiral Watson's fleet on 2 January 1757.

However, events in Europe now took a hand, for definite news arrived that Britain and France were at war once again. For Admiral Watson, the main task now became the destruction of his country's enemies. Yet he was not immediately able to undertake this task, as Siraj-ud-Daulah himself was once again advancing on Calcutta.

This was not entirely unexpected, and British preparations had been in hand for some days. A fortified camp was established about a mile to the north of Calcutta and half a mile from the riverbank. This camp's position made it impossible for an enemy to approach the town without passing in sight of the camp.[9] In addition, HMS *Marlborough*, separated from Watson's fleet by bad weather, had arrived with the remaining troops and artillery. However, there were still no draught animals to move the guns. Clive now had roughly 2,000 men, of whom 800 were Europeans, and 14

8 P.R. Innes, *The History of the Bengal European Regiment, now the Royal Munster Fusiliers, and How It Helped to Win India* (London: Simpkin, Marshall, 1885), pp.16–17.

9 Orme, *Military Transactions*, vol.2, p.128.

guns. He could call on support from Admiral Watson's fleet, so on 5 February 1757, Captain Warrick, RN, joined Clive with 569 seamen, for Clive had decided to take the offensive.[10]

The Nawab's army was huge, but the 40,000 horse and 60,000 foot mentioned by Sensarma[11] is surely a vast overestimate. More realistically, Harrington[12] gives a grand total of 40,000, but even this may be somewhat high. All we know for certain is that Clive was massively outnumbered by the Nawab's forces.

Siraj-ud-Daulah's unwieldy horde had moved past Clive's camp, despite a mutual cannonade on 2 February, and had encamped itself astride the Maratha Ditch with around one-third of its strength inside the ditch and the rest on the outside, and therefore outside of Calcutta proper. The camp was far from orderly, so a dawn attack seemed to have a good chance of putting these undisciplined warriors into a panic. Clive was emboldened by a report from some EIC emissaries, who had been negotiating with the Nawab, that the Bengali guns had not yet arrived.[13]

Robert Orme takes up the story:

> Their report determined Colonel Clive to attack the Nawab's camp in the morning. At midnight 600 sailors armed with firelocks were landed from the ships of war; the battalion of Europeans were 650, the artillerymen 100, the Sepoys 800, the field pieces 6 six pounders. The order of attack was a line advancing in half files that is three men abreast; half the Sepoys marched before and half behind the battalion of Europeans; in the rear were the field pieces and the artillerymen and Lascars and all the sailors.[14]

The *lascars* were labourers and, in this case, carried the ammunition for the guns. They were guarded by some of the sailors, while other sailors were used to pull the guns as, once again, no bullocks were available for this task.

As the column continued its march, it came upon an outlying guard of the Nawab's forces which, after firing a volley from their matchlocks, departed at speed towards the Bengali camp to their south. However, there was some confusion in the first division of Clive's column as the Bengalis had also fired some rockets, one of which exploded amongst the sepoys at the head of the column. It took Captain Eyre Coote some time to restore order before the column could begin its advance again.

Worse was to follow. As dawn came up, a thick fog blanketed the whole area, with visibility down to as little as 10 yards. A body of Pathan cavalry attacked the column but was beaten off by volleys of musketry and the column moved on slowly southward through the fog, firing more or less at random as bodies of enemy troops seemed to appear out of the murk.

10 Lawford, *Britain's Army in India*, p.198.
11 Sensarma, *Military History of Bengal*, p.181.
12 P. Harrington, *The Battle of Plassey: Clive of India's Finest Hour* (London: Osprey, 1994), p.25.
13 Orme, *Military Transactions*, vol.2, p.131.
14 Orme, *Military Transactions*, vol.2, p.131.

British troops under Clive in action. This Victorian illustration from a children's book shows impossibly heroic and well-dressed East India Company European troops. While the basic style of uniform is more or less correct, the rigours of campaigning would mean that such pristine uniformity would only be seen when the troops were in garrison. (Author's Collection)

Eventually, at around nine in the morning, the fog lifted, and Clive's column found itself in a parlous position. First, it was much closer to the Maratha Ditch than it expected to be, and worse, Bengali troops were now wide awake and belligerent. In particular, a body of Bengali infantry and guns ensconced within the walled enclosure of Omichand's garden within the Maratha Ditch were causing casualties by their fire. Assaulting this strong position was utterly out of the question. Indeed, it looked as if defeat was staring the British in the face. Two of the six guns had to be abandoned. Clive therefore decided to continue south and re-enter Calcutta by the Lal Bazar road. This was not accomplished without more fighting, as the British needed to storm a causeway across their front, which was held by the Nawab's matchlockmen and some guns with cavalry in support. However, the cavalry feared closing with the British column and were dispersed by artillery fire, and the position was taken, allowing the British to continue south until they turned west onto the Lal Bazar road and finally into Calcutta and safety.

This was no outright victory. Indeed, Clive had come close to defeat, yet despite this, his tiny force had held together and had caused around 1,000 casualties upon the Nawab's army.

Clive's command had suffered 157 casualties, which it could ill afford, but it had proved once again that European-trained infantry were superior, even in adverse circumstances, to the brave but undisciplined warriors which made up Siraj-ud-Daulah's army. The Nawab lost his nerve and, the following day, retreated north, away from Calcutta.

The Fall of Chandernagore

Events in other parts of India now became known to the Nawab. As he retreated, Siraj-ud-Daulah heard about the Afghan invasion far to his west. This invasion would eventually result in the Third Battle of Panipat and the temporary destruction of Maratha power in central India. However, the Nawab of Bengal was more concerned with the possible effect upon his own territories. To that end, he opened negotiations with the British, for might he not need allies against the fearsome Afghans and who better than the equally fearsome British? Consequently, the Nawab signed a treaty with the Calcutta council and Admiral Watson, restoring all of the Company's privileges in exchange for military assistance from the British.

This left the British free to deal with the French, with whom they were now officially at war once again following the outbreak of the Seven Years War in Europe.

Although reasonably well fortified, the main French factory in Bengal at Chandernagore on the River Hoogly was far less secure than it might appear. This was simply because the British factory at Calcutta was further down the river towards the coast and could, should war break out, blockade the French. Equally, the appearance of a British fleet could render the French position isolated.

In the event, Chandernagore fell to a combined force consisting of Royal Navy ships under Admiral Watson and a land force under Robert Clive. The brunt of the action was borne by the three ships of the Royal Navy: HMS *Tyger*, HMS *Kent*, and HMS

Salisbury. The artillery duel between the ships and the guns of Fort d'Orléans was so fierce that HMS *Kent* would never be seaworthy again. However, although the French position was captured, some 50 or so of the garrison made their escape and joined the small force under the command of Jean Law, who would in the coming years play some part in the mercenaries' story.

The Battle of Plassey and the Destruction of Siraj-ud-Daulah

That time was not quite yet, for in the normal run of Indian politics in the eighteenth century, intrigue was afoot. Once the Afghan threat proved illusory, Siraj-ud-Daulah went back to his capricious self, stirring up hatred amongst the prominent men of Bengal, Bihar, and Orissa. A plot to replace him was organised with Mir Jafar Ali Khan, the Nawab's military commander, as its titular head. The funds were provided by the Hindu banking house of Jagat Seth, which had previously been instrumental in helping Alivardi Khan to the throne.[15] However, this time the Seth family insisted that the plotters gain the support of the British. This move would have serious consequences for the whole of Bengal and, ultimately, the whole of India.

This plot put in train a series of events which would lead to the Battle of Plassey in June 1757 and to the death of Siraj-ud-Daulah. Mir Jafar would ascend the throne, propped up by British bayonets and beholden to the greedy merchants of the EIC, who would expect to extract their pound of flesh.

Militarily speaking, Plassey was much less of a battle than might be supposed from the bare facts. The intrigue and plotting which preceded it rather overshadowed the military action. Yet, this does not detract from the small British-Indian force's achievement. As Clive moved towards the Nawab's capital at Murshidabad, letters and messages assured him of the support of Mir Jafar and the rest of the conspirators. Yet, as the advance continued, none of this support appeared. Clive was understandably perturbed.

Lieutenant Colonel Robert Clive's army was some 3,000 strong, consisting mainly of EIC troops. The only King's troops were three companies of the 39th Foot, commanded respectively by Captains Grant, Weller, and Coote. Grant, as senior captain, commanded this detachment with the local rank of Major. Coote, who commanded the Grenadier company, would also be given a similar promotion before the battle and would command one of the 'grand divisions' into which each of the two European battalions was divided.[16] The detachment of the 39th numbered 238 officers and men in April 1757.[17] The rest of the European troops were from all three of the EIC presidencies. As noted above, the European infantry was divided into two battalions. One contained the men of the 39th and the Bengal Europeans, while the other held the Bombay and

15 G.B. Malleson, *The Decisive Battles of India from 1746–1849* (London: W.H. Allen & Co., 1883), p.41.

16 J. Corneille, *Journal of my Service in India*, edited by Michael Edwardes (London: The Folio Society, 1966), p.119.

17 Reid, *Plassey*, p.231.

Another illustration from the same Victorian children's book. This one purports to show Clive on the roof of the 'Hunting Lodge' in the mango grove. Again, the uniform style is vaguely correct, though it is unlikely that Clive's hat would be so small! (Author's Collection)

Madras detachments. Each of these battalions was further subdivided into two 'Grand Divisions' and would fight the battle this way. In total, there were around 700 European infantry.[18] The precise number of sepoys actually present is a little harder to assess. In his operational diary, Clive gives a figure of 2,200,[19] but also makes it clear that 500 of these were left as a garrison for the fort at Cutwa, which was taken by Coote on 18 June. Thus, there can have been no more than 1,700 sepoys at the battle. The same source tells us that there were also 190 artillerymen, with eight guns and a howitzer with the army. Some of the gunners were sailors from the naval squadron. All of Clive's eight guns were noted as 'short sixes', that is, short-barrelled 6-pounder guns.[20] Clive had no cavalry whatsoever.

With no recent word from the conspirators, Clive was in something of a quandary. After resting for two days at Cutwa, he continued the advance, but there was still no word from his supposed allies in the Nawab's camp.

On 21 June, Clive called a Council of War of the officers to decide what was to be done. After some discussion on the question of continuing the advance and giving battle to Siraj's army, a vote was taken. Of the 21 officers present, no less than 12 voted against attacking the Nawab. Clive, as chairman, did not vote, and Lieutenant Hater, RN, also abstained. Of the three majors, only Coote voted for an attack. Clive, 'informed the Council that he found he could not depend upon Meer Jaffier for anything more than his standing neuter in case we came to an action with the Nabob.'[21] Nevertheless, after some further thought and 'notwithstanding the resolution of the Council of War',[22] Clive decided to continue the march.

Major John Corneille – then a lieutenant (though given the temporary brevet rank of captain) in the detachment of the 39th – takes up the story: 'The city of Murshidabad is situated on a large island made by two branches of the Ganges. We had hitherto pursued our route on the opposite side but on the 22nd June after the aforementioned resolution we crossed the river and advanced to our enemy with no impediment in the way to hinder our meeting.'[23]

The advance continued, with the river now on the left flank of the British force.

> We made a forced march this day in order to reach a grove near which we were informed some of the nabob's army was encamped but our intelligence was very vague and little to be depended on. It was twelve at night before the first division of the army arrived, leaving a rear of upwards of three miles in length, our men fatigued to the last degree. Altogether we were in such a situation as would have made us an easy prey to four hundred men of any spirit that dared to have attacked us. But the enemy we had to encounter were luckily not of that stamp.[24]

18 Reid, *Plassey*, p.88.
19 As quoted in Reid, *Plassey*, pp.179–180.
20 As quoted in Reid, *Plassey*, p.179.
21 Eyre Coote's *Journal* as quoted in Reid, *Plassey*, p.199.
22 Eyre Coote's *Journal* as quoted in Reid, *Plassey*, p.200.
23 Corneille, *Journal*, p.120.
24 Corneille, *Journal*, p.120.

Clive's army now found itself in a large grove of trees as it bedded down for what remained of the night. The following morning, 23 June 1757, the tiny British army saw the enemy before it – all 50,000 of them.

Clive's official *Journal of Military Proceedings* takes up the story: 'June 23rd. At daybreak we discovered the Nabob's army at the distance of three miles in full march towards us, upon which the whole were ordered under arms. Being in two battalions the Europeans were told off in four grand divisions, the artillery distributed between them, and the sepoys on the right and left of the whole.'

In more detail, this meant that six of the artillery pieces, in two three-gun batteries, were placed with one battery at each end of the European part of the line. The sepoys in two battalions formed on the right and left of the European centre. The two remaining guns and the howitzer (Orme says two howitzers)[25] were pushed forward roughly 200 yards into the cover of some brick kilns on Clive's left, close to the riverbank. These guns were escorted by some 50 sailors.

Clive's journal continues:

> Our situation was very advantageous, being in a Grove surrounded by high mud banks, our right and front being entirely covered by the above mud banks, our left by Placis House, our rear by the Grove and a village. The enemy approached apace, covered a fine extensive plain in front of us as far as the eye could discern from right to left and consisted as we since learned of 15,000 horse and 35,000 foot with more than 40 pieces of cannon from 32 to 9 pounders.[26]

Initially, Clive's force formed up 'a few paces without the Grove',[27] that is, just in front of the mud bank, but once the Nawab's army began its cannonade, they quickly retired behind the mud banks to take shelter. Their own guns, short 6-pounders, could make no effective reply to the guns of the Bengali army, as they were significantly outranged by the Nawab's heavier pieces of artillery. Indeed, at least some of the Nawab's guns had attempted a rather novel solution to the problem of battlefield manoeuvrability:

> The cannon were mostly of the largest calibres 24 and 32 pounders and these were mounted on the middle of a large stage, raised six feet from the ground, carrying, beside the cannon, all the ammunition belonging to it and the gunners themselves who managed the cannon on the stage itself. These machines were drawn by 40 or 50 yoke of white oxen, of the largest size, bred in the country of Purnea; and behind each cannon walked an elephant trained to assist at difficult tugs by shoving with his forehead against the hinder part of the carriage.[28]

25 Orme, *Military Transactions*, vol.2, p.174.
26 As quoted in S. Reid, *Plassey*, p.180.
27 'Eyre Coote's Journal', as quoted in Reid, *Plassey*, p.200.
28 Orme, *Military Transactions*, vol.2, p.173.

Another picture from a Victorian children's book, this one showing French artillery under attack by British infantry. It is very unlikely that St Frais's 'vagabonds' were dressed this well, though some may have worn the French *Compagnie des Indes* blue uniform. (Author Collection)

Quite how effective these 'self-propelled guns' actually were, is, of course, another matter. Nevertheless, they were an ingenious attempt to solve the problem of manoeuvrability.

In addition to his 50,000 men and 50 guns, Siraj-ud-Daulah had the assistance of '40 vagabond Frenchmen under the command of one Sinfray... with four pieces of light cannon'.[29]

Actually, these Frenchmen, probably escapees from Chandernagore, were led by Monsieur de St Frais, who had been secretary to the Council at the French settlement. He and his 'vagabonds' were to conduct themselves rather well in the coming action.

The mass of the Nawab's army had debouched from their fortified camp to the north of Clive's position. The Bengali right under Mir Madan and Mohum Lal, faced Clive's position in the grove with St Frais's little command to their left protected somewhat by a 'tank' or open pond. St Frais had another smaller such tank to his rear. The rest of the Nawab's troops extended leftwards, moving south so that they curved around and almost surrounded the British position. The Nawab's left (which actually outflanked Clive's right wing) was, however, under the command of the chief conspirator, Mir Jafar, and would take no part in the ensuing action, despite Siraj-ud-Daulah's entreaties.

As noted above, the action opened with a cannonade, the Bengali guns firing at Clive's army as it was formed up in front of the mango grove. Clive's own guns could make no reply, his 'short sixes' being outranged by the Nawab's 24- and 32-pounders. In response to this cannonade, which had caused some casualties in his small army, Clive pulled his troops back into the grove and behind its protective banks. Interpreting this as a retreat, the Bengalis brought up more guns and began an intense bombardment. Most of the shot, however, flew too high, and as the enemy advanced, Clive's own guns, ensconced behind the banks of the grove, could now make some useful reply. The artillery exchange continued for some time, with the guns at the brick kilns seemingly concentrating upon St Frais's guns at the tank. 'About noon, a very heavy shower covered the plain and very soon damaged the enemy's powder so much that their fire slackened continually; but the English ammunition served on.'[30]

It was around this time that Mir Madan, one of those few commanders remaining faithful to the Nawab, was killed, and in the usual fashion of Indian warfare, his troops therefore began to retire to their camp. By around two in the afternoon, this retirement had become general, as the various contingents in Siraj's army began to fend for themselves. Mir Jafar remained inactive over on the left of the Bengali position, biding his time.

The British now went over to the offensive. First, Major Kilpatrick, on his own initiative, took the grenadier company of the 39th and some sepoys to attack St Frais's position at the tank. St Frais had sensibly pulled his command out and would redeploy them in a redoubt which was part of the Nawab's camp. Initially, Clive ordered Kilpatrick to return to the grove, but upon viewing the situation for himself, he ordered a general advance.

The crisis of the battle was now at hand.

29 Orme, *Military Transactions*, vol.2, p.173.
30 Orme, *Military Transactions*, vol.2, p.175.

> Colonel Clive advanced nearer and posted half his troops and artillery at the lesser tank and the other half at a rising ground about 200 yards to the left of it. From these stations the cannonade was renewed with more efficacy than before and killed many of the oxen which were drawing the artillery, which threw all the trains that were approaching into disorder. On the other hand the Frenchmen with Sinfray played their field-pieces from the redoubt; and matchlocks from the intrenchments, from ditches, hollows, and every hole or shelter; as also from bushes on the hillock east of the redoubt, they kept up a constant though irregular fire, while the cavalry advanced several times threatening to charge sword in hand, but were always stopped and repulsed by the quick firing of the field pieces.[31]

At this point, Mir Jafar, despite his troops' earlier being fired upon as they approached the grove, pulled his forces away from the action, remaining in much the same position as at the beginning of the battle.

This allowed the British the freedom to assault Siraj's fortified camp, and by five o'clock, the camp was occupied and the Bengali forces were in complete retreat. St Frais's handful of 'vagabonds' had manned their guns until the Nawab's men supporting them had departed, and with that, they had abandoned their guns and retired.

Once the fighting was over, Clive received a note from Mir Jafar which, though late, confirmed that Jafar and the conspirators were still intent on toppling Siraj-ud-Daulah and taking over the reins of power.

Yet, they could only do this at the behest of the British. The battle had been won more by political chicanery and plotting than by force of arms. Mir Jafar and his compatriots now ruled only through the power of the East India Company, and its merchants would expect their pound of flesh as payment.

The Council in Calcutta now had the role of 'kingmakers' for Bengal in the coming decades. This would become clear especially after the conclusion of the Seven Years War, which would put an end to French ambitions both in the south of India and in Bengal. There would be much more serious fighting than the Battle of Plassey before the British were entirely secure in their conquest, especially as Indian rulers sought to find a solution to the problem of British infantry and artillery.

31 Orme, *Military Transactions*, vol.2, pp.176–177.

3

Mercenary Commander

Walter Reinhardt and the Somru Brigade

The Battle of Plassey may have appeared to make the British paramount in Bengal, but the fighting was far from over. Mir Jafar, the new Nawab, propped up by British bayonets, soon began to regret the deal he had made for his throne. He intrigued with the Dutch in an attempt to replace the British in Bengal, but the Dutch invasion from their colonies in what is now Indonesia was defeated by Major Forde at the Battle of Bidarra on 25 November 1759. This occurred despite the fact that the British and Dutch were not actually at war at this time.

Prior to this unusual interlude, Mir Jafar and his British masters had other problems to contend with.

Jean Law – The Accidental Mercenary

In the previous chapter, mention was made of one Jean Law, a soldier and diplomat in the service of the French *Compagnie des Indes*. He is not to be confused with his brother Jacques, who served in the south of India and was repeatedly defeated by Stringer Lawrence and Clive. Jean had been in Bengal since 1744, managing the French settlement at Cossimbazar.[1] When Chandernagore fell to the British, he was left somewhat out on a limb. He had the dubious support of Siraj-ud-Daulah but very little force of his own. Nevertheless, the British saw him as a threat, so Clive sent Eyre Coote up the Ganges River after him in the aftermath of the Battle of Plassey. The Frenchman outdistanced Coote, who was forced to retire after his small force mutinied and refused to march further.

Before he left Cossimbazar to avoid the British, Law had increased his force with escapees from Chandernagore until he commanded a force of around 150 Europeans and 300 sepoys[2] with six field pieces. Chartrand puts his strength at 195 Europeans, of

1 R. Chartrand, *Armies and Wars of the French East India Company: European, Asian and African Soldiers in India, Africa, the Far East and Louisiana, 1664–1770* (Warwick: Helion, 2024), p.122.
2 Lawford, *Britain's Army in India*, p.218.

which many were deserters from the British service, and only 100 sepoys with 10 guns, these being two each of 2- and 3-pounders and six 1-pounders.[3]

Whatever the precise strength, this party left Cossimbazar in mid-April 1757 and marched westward, first reaching Patna and then Benares by 2 August. Law's objective, other than to avoid the British, was to reach Delhi, perhaps to elicit aid from the emperor. However, he was now entering an area of India which had never seen Europeans in any numbers. The little army was attacked by a force of Jats, reputedly a very unlikely 10,000 strong, whom Law drove off with regular volleys of musketry from his infantry and grape shot from the light field guns. This action seems to have greatly impressed the local Indian rulers, allowing Law to arrive in Delhi in early April 1758. He did not stay long, leaving for Agra to the south on 30 April.

In Delhi, the Emperor Alamgir II was little more than a prisoner of his vizier (prime minister) Imad-ul-Mulk, and indeed would fall to the assassin's knife on 29 November 1759 at the instigation of that minister. His son and heir, Ali Gauhar, who would in time become the Emperor Shah Alam II, had been banished from the imperial court (even personally cutting his way out when attacked in a house he was using in May 1758 and escaping with barely 100 followers),[4] though he does appear to have met Law sometime in April. However, the Shazada (heir to the throne) was in effect a landless wanderer through northern India. He spent much of the remaining months of 1758 campaigning to the south-west of Delhi, trying to raise support and money with very mixed success.

He was, however, not entirely without help and support. By March 1759, he appeared near the city of Patna in Bihar – which was part of the territory of Mir Jafar, the new Nawab of Bengal – with a considerable army, including some local rulers who were in rebellion against Mir Jafar. In the event, this was little more than a plundering expedition to raise money, and the appearance of a British force to support the local troops caused the Shazada to retire.

This would not be the end of the matter. In the following year, the Shazada – now Emperor Shah Alam II – appeared in arms again, in late January 1760, again marching on the city of Patna. As he was now the titular Emperor, Shah Alam's influence was something of consequence. Therefore, despite the usual lack of hard cash, his army was still considerable, though not well trained.

The governor of Patna, Ram Narian, with an army of supposedly 40,000 men, outnumbered the Emperor's forces. Against instructions from Mir Jafar – his overlord – he decided to fight. Despite the presence of a small British force consisting of a single company of the Bengal European Regiment, two guns and five companies of regular sepoys, he was beaten in the field by the imperial forces at the Battle of Masumpur on 9 February 1760, where at least some of Ram Narian's troops appear to have changed sides.[5] The small British force was roughly handled, losing all of its

3 Chartrand, *Armies and Wars*, p.122.
4 Jadunath Sarkar, *The Fall of the Mughal Empire*, vol.2: 1754–1771 (Hyderabad: Orient Blackswan, 1991), p.317.
5 Sarkar, *Mughal Empire*, vol.2, p.321.

officers and only regained the safety of Patna under the command of the contingent's surgeon, Dr Fullarton. The imperial army approached Patna on 17 February but made only a poor attempt to besiege the city. On 22 February, Major Caillaud – with an East India Company army of two battalions of sepoys, a battalion of the Bengal European Regiment and six guns – met the imperial army at the Battle of Seerpore. Major Caillaud had the doubtful support of Mir Jafar's son, Miran, with some 13,000 assorted cavalry which he deployed in a huge column to the right rear of the British line. This line was anchored on two villages, each occupied by British sepoys. The deployment of Miran's cavalry went directly against Major Caillaud's suggestion that they should be deployed as a second line behind the British troops. The gap between the two villages contained Caillaud's main line of battle, with the European troops in the centre flanked by three guns at each end of the battalion, followed on each flank of the guns by a battalion of sepoys. Caillaud's force in total was not more than 2,500 strong, and probably somewhat less.

In the late afternoon, Shah Alam launched 'a ferocious attack'[6] which Caillaud met with his infantry and guns in what was fast becoming the usual manner, fending off this assault with ease. However, over on the right, the imperials had attacked Miran's ridiculous column. Caillaud gave his account in a letter to Eyre Coote:

> He for some time stood the shock well but being wounded and turning his elephant – which in plain English is running away – the whole army in an instant was following his example. Luckily for him I brought up a battalion of sepoys which was on our right with which I flanked the body of horse which made the attack. The first fire threw them into confusion and the second fairly set them running. The Nabob's Dewan who was in the rear and not yet seized with panic came to support the runaways and thus ended the Battle of Seerpore with a loss of about 500 killed and wounded on both sides.[7]

Yet again, the value of steady infantry and well-served guns had been proved to Indian rulers. If even the emperor could be defeated by such small forces of European-trained soldiers, these rulers must have thought, then the answer must be to acquire their own Europeans to train their soldiers to fight this way.

The time was fast approaching when such thoughts would begin to bear fruit.

Meanwhile, Jean Law was striving to join the imperial army with a force that now numbered 150 Europeans and 150 sepoys.[8] He would finally join the emperor on 30 April as the imperial army was already in retreat once more.[9]

Law and his tiny command would be in imperial service for the next year or so. Of course, Law was not, strictly speaking, a mercenary. His little force was still fighting

6 Lawford, *Britain's Army in India*, p.297.
7 As quoted in Lawford, *Britain's Army in India*, p.298.
8 J. Law de Lauriston, *A Memoir of the Mughal Empire: Events of 1757–1761*, translated by G.S. Cheema (New Delhi: Manohar, 2014), p.258.
9 Sarkar, *Mughal Empire*, vol.2, p.323.

A raja on his elephant. This late-nineteenth-century illustration purports to show Siraj-ud-Daulah, but could equally be of any Indian ruler allowing his appearance on an elephant to emphasise his magnificence. (Author's Collection)

for France, at least in his own eyes, against the British. Yet, he was dependent on the largesse, or otherwise, of the emperor's commanders for food, for money to pay his men, and even for clothing. Chartrand shows an Indian watercolour painting, which he identifies as Law's Europeans being reviewed by Shah Alam. They are in red coats without cuffs, dark blue breeches and stockings, with black tricorn hats. They carry a colour which is plain violet without the usual white cross of France.[10] This uniform is very different in colour from the usual blue of the French Company European troops at this time.

The end would come for Jean Law early in 1761 when, once again, the Mughal emperor invaded Bengal. This time, however, the emperor was even shorter of money than usual, and treachery was in the air:

> On the other hand in the Emperors army everything was in short supply; without speaking of the suspicions of treason from the conduct of Kamgar Khan. It did not have any muskets or artillery apart from what I commanded – to wit 125 European soldiers 200 sepoys and 10 cannons.[11]

The British under Major Carnac caught the invaders in January 1761 and quickly put them to flight. The only effective resistance came from Law's command, which acted as an impromptu rearguard for the fleeing imperials. Law gallantly held his command together as the British closed in, but finally he could do no more and surrendered to Carnac with '3 or 4 Officers and about 40 soldiers who were with me'.[12]

The rest of Law's little force were either casualties or had dispersed. Though we have no way to be certain, at least some of these 'military experts' must have gravitated to the assorted mercenary *compoos*, which would be formed over the next few years.

A 'Military Revolution' in Northern India?

It may well be overstating the case to ascribe that much overused term 'military revolution' to the change that occurred in the forces of the new Nawab of Bengal, Mir Kassim Ali Khan. That potentate soon tired of being in thrall to the East India Company, which had placed him on his throne and now expected to reap the substantial financial rewards for its 'generosity'. It did not quite work out that way.

The new Nawab first moved his capital from Murshidabad to Monyghr, the latter place being further from Calcutta and the pernicious British interference in his rule. He made considerable strides in reforming his finances and was thus able to recruit 'European military advisors' – that is, mercenaries – to train new troops in the European style. One of these was Walter Reinhardt, alias 'Sombre' or 'Somru'.

10 Chartrand, *Armies and Wars*, p.xxvii.
11 Law de Lauriston, *Memoir*, p.299.
12 Law de Lauriston, *Memoir*, p.301.

Reinhardt's early life is something of a mystery. He was born in the village of Silbertal,[13] in western Austria, around 1720, though his family moved to Alsace soon afterwards. Later sources make much of his father being a butcher. He arrived in India sometime in 1750 or 1751 on a French frigate, and forthwith deserted his ship and joined the French *Compagnie des Indes* forces operating from Pondicherry. How long he remained there is unclear, for by 1756 he was in northern India and had changed sides, joining one of the 'Swiss' companies of the British East India Company[14] under the nom de guerre of 'Somers'. This name seems very quickly to have been corrupted to 'Sombre' on account of his morose disposition or, to Indian ears 'Somru'. It is as Somru that he would become infamous.

He did not stay long in British service. A mere 18 days later, he once again absconded and joined the French in Chandernagore,[15] where he seems to have been made a sergeant. This may have happened before Siraj-ud-Daulah took Calcutta,[16] but once again Reinhardt does not seem to have remained in French service for very long:

> But after the seizure of Chandernagar by the British (1757) he for a while wandered about in Bengal and was ultimately engaged by Gurgin Khan, the Armenian General of Mir Quasim the Nawab of Bengal who was the organising his forces on the European model.[17]

How he survived at this time is unknown, though he certainly adopted the customs and dress of the country during his wanderings. Quite when he deserted the French is also unknown. Did he perhaps serve, at least for a while, with Jean Law's little force before departing for pastures new? They were, after all, campaigning in roughly the same geographical area with which Somru was to become familiar in the service of Mir Kassim. The idea that he served as a 'simple trooper' in Siraj-ud-Daulah's forces[18] for a time is rather unlikely, though not impossible, simply because of the difficulty of passing himself off as one of the Nawab's Indian soldiers so soon after deserting the French. These difficulties arise because manners, language, and customs were so different, not only from the French but also from the people of southern India, where Somru had begun his 'Indian adventure'.

Whatever the details of Somru's life to this point, sometime in 1760 or 1761, he gravitated into the service of Mir Kassim Ali Khan, now Nawab, who had quite simply bribed the Calcutta Council to 'put away' Mir Jafar and make him the new Nawab of Bengal, Bihar, and Orissa. Needless to say, the British merchants of the EIC expected to be able to fill their pockets at the expense of the Nawab they had created, and doubtless

13 J. Lall, *Begam Samru: Fading Portrait in a Gilded Frame* (New Delhi: Roli Books, 1997), p.7.

14 H. Compton, *A Particular Account of the European Military Adventurers of Hindustan* (London: T. Fisher Unwin, 1892; repr. Karachi: Oxford University Press, 1976).

15 Compton, *Particular Account*, p.401.

16 Keay, J., *Farzana, the Woman who Saved an Empire* (London: I.B. Tauris, 2014), pp.39–40.

17 Banerji, B., *Begam Samru* (Calcutta: M.C. Sarkar & Sons, 1925), pp.4–5.

18 Compton, *Particular Account*, p.401.

rubbed their hands in greedy glee at the prospect. Their avariciousness would be amply rewarded, though not in the manner they expected.

To begin with, Somru, who had never held any rank higher than sergeant, gained command of two battalions in the *compoo* of Gurgin Khan, Mir Kassim's Armenian general, called Gregory by the Europeans.[19] Gurgin Khan also seems to have filled the office of 'Minister of War and Procurement', since his brother was a major merchant in Calcutta. There was another Armenian commander, Markar by name, who had a separate *compoo* of his own.[20] All of these battalions were trained in the French style as, seemingly, were the rest of Gurgin Khan's brigade. At this time, the new troops were mostly infantry or artillery. The cavalry remained somewhat more traditional but was still improved, being mostly Afghans or Rohillas with a reputation for courage: 'Within a year Meer Cossim had raised twenty-five thousand infantry and a regiment of excellent gunners the latter almost to a man European all equipped in every respect in the European fashion and fit for immediate service.'[21]

While we may doubt the hyperbole of Fortescue's claim, Mir Kassim's new army was, without question, far more efficient than the traditional Indian armies so often beaten by European-led forces. Doubtless, many of the Europeans in the Nawab's service were deserters, possibly from Jean Law's much-travelled command, but equally from the East India Company's forces. European 'military advisors' were in high demand and almost any European of whatever previous station in life was perceived by the Indian rulers to be knowledgeable in the art of war.

Mir Kassim's War (1763)

It would not be very long before Mir Kassim found a use for his new army. The politics need not weary us, except to say that the overweening greed of many of the EIC officials was the root cause of the Nawab's decision to fight. In essence, he had no choice if he wished to retain any independence from the grasping and venal Company officials.

Once again, the city of Patna was the centre of the conflict, though this time it was the British who began the violence.

A certain Mr Ellis, a member of the EIC council in Calcutta and company agent in Patna – a very important person, at least in his own eyes – decided to put pressure on Mir Kassim by seizing the city. While others of the Council were negotiating with the Nawab over certain trading rights, they were in effect pressurising the Nawab in order to fill their own pockets. Ellis's force, based in the fortified EIC factory just outside Patna, consisted of four companies of the Bengal European Regiment, totalling 19 officers and 220 NCOs and men.[22] There were also some European gunners and 2,500

19 Malleson, *Decisive Battles of India*, refers to this rather shadowy figure and Markar.
20 Arthur Broome, *History of the Rise and Progress of the Bengal Army*, vol.1 (London: Smith, Elder & Co., 1850, repr. Legare Street Press, [n.d.]), p.352.
21 J.W. Fortescue, *A History of the British Army* (London: Macmillan and Co., 1910), vol.3, p.64.
22 Innes, *The Bengal European Regiment*, p.128.

sepoys in three battalions. The force was under the military command of Captain Peter Carstairs of the Bengal European Regiment.

Early on the morning of 25 June 1763, the British force scaled the walls of Patna and took the city almost without firing a shot. They neglected, however, to take the citadel and one other large building called the Chetul Situn, which was used as a hospital. The governor of the city, Mir Medhie Khan, rode off to warn the Nawab of the situation. Once the city was occupied, the British officers of the force returned to the factory to take breakfast, leaving the troops, without control, to disperse and begin looting.

Medhie Khan met up with the advance guard of the Nawab's troops, who were advancing to reinforce the Patna garrison. Markar, the Armenian, in command of these troops, upon hearing the news, pushed on at speed and, catching the British by surprise, hustled them in panic, out of the town, with little resistance, back into the factory where they had begun that morning.

Markar then brought up his guns and began a siege of the factory. The British were in a parlous state and, frankly, Captain Carstairs was not up to the task of such a difficult command. On 29 June, the garrison took to boats and crossed the Ganges River and began to march roughly north towards the border of Oudh, where they thought they might find sanctuary. The march was made more difficult by the breaking of the monsoon, when the rain came down in torrents. Markar was soon in pursuit, and Somru, with his *compoo*, which now stood at four battalions plus a cavalry regiment and a company of artillery,[23] was moving east to cut them off, crossing the Ganges at Arah in order to do so. On 1 July, he caught the British at the village of Manjee. Carstairs formed his tired men into line, Europeans in the centre and a sepoy battalion on each flank with the third battalion in reserve behind his centre. They do not seem to have brought any guns from Patna. Despite the courage of the sepoys who drove back Reinhardt's first assault at bayonet point, the issue was never really in doubt. Once Carstairs and some of the other European officers had fallen, the remainder surrendered to Somru. Numbers of the sepoys took service with the victors, as did at least some of the Europeans. The remaining sepoys were relieved of their weapons and equipment and released, and the surviving Europeans were taken to Patna as prisoners. Somru's first major victory made his name, and he became something of a favourite of the Nawab. He had done what no other had done, defeated a British force in the open field. Doubtless, the story grew in the telling, but to the Nawab, the value of his new army had been proved.

Meanwhile, in Calcutta, the British had begun preparations for war as early as April, well before the fighting actually began. Troops were moved to the theatre of operations, but finding enough transport was a constant problem. The EIC Council in Calcutta decided to depose Mir Kassim and replace him with the previous Nawab, the now ageing Mir Jafar. Needless to say, they expected the old man to pay for his elevation to the tune of 30 lakhs of rupees (three million rupees) for war expenses, besides trade concessions and other 'donations' to the EIC army and navy. Mir Jafar was also supposed to maintain a force of 12,000 horse and 12,000 foot of his own.[24]

23 Broome, *Bengal Army*, p.353.
24 Broome, *Bengal Army*, p.370.

'So Gallant a Day's Work'

Mir Kassim's forces were not slow off the mark. A body of irregular troops put at a rather unlikely 17,000,[25] mostly cavalry, but without any artillery, attacked a convoy of cattle and grain destined for the British forces. The convoy escort consisted of a single battalion of sepoys and six guns crewed by Europeans. This little force cannot have numbered more than a thousand men all told and was probably less. They were also guarding some £20,000 in coin as pay for the main army. The escort was commanded by Lieutenant John Glenn, who drew up his men on a low hill in some broken ground and fought off the repeated cavalry assaults of the enemy. This action persisted for around four hours, by which time many of the European gunners were wounded or dead. Yet, despite the pressure, Glenn's command never faltered and the enemy drew off, nonplussed by their defeat. Glenn resumed his march and reached Cutwa, where he expected to join the main British army, but found the fort occupied by a small garrison of Mir Kassim's irregulars. Glenn forthwith stormed the fort, fortunately meeting little resistance, capturing it and the large quantity of grain and numbers of artillery bullocks it contained. Rightly does Fortescue refer to Glenn's actions as 'so gallant a day's work'[26] There would be gallantry enough, on both sides, in the days to come.

Mir Kassim's troops also captured Murshidabad from its weak British garrison and attacked and captured the factory at Cossimbazar. Once again, the sepoys were either taken into Mir Kassim's service or released without arms or equipment. The Europeans were taken prisoner and added to those taken when Patna fell.

When Glenn met the main army under Major Thomas Adams of HM 84th Foot, his corps brought the total strength of Adams's command to two small European battalions, HM 84th Foot at 400 men, four companies of the EIC's Bengal European Regiment, and a company of 'French Rangers', this second formation being around 350 men. The army also included 100 European cavalry, a company of artillery with 10 guns and a total of four battalions of sepoys.

On 19 July, Adams's army moved to encounter Mohammed Taki Khan, accounted one of Mir Kassim's best and bravest generals. His force did not contain any of Mir Kassim's new troops, but was still formidable with many Afghan, Pathan, Persian, and Rohilla mercenaries, both horse and foot. The foot included many *jezzailichis*, armed with the long-barrelled *jezzail*, a weapon which, although slower to load, significantly outranged the 'Brown Bess' of their British and Indian opponents. Taki Khan's army also contained a number of rocket men using the Indian war rocket, which here seems to have taken the place of artillery. He also had in his army those men who had been defeated by Lieutenant Glenn, but these declined to fight, even going so far as to deploy some distance behind the Khan's army, where they awaited events.

The British advance guard, which included all of the European cavalry, seems to have run into an ambush, for it was roughly handled by the *jezzailichis* and rocket men and

25 Broome, *Bengal Army*, p.370.
26 Fortescue, *British Army*, vol.3, pp.69–70.

retired in some disorder on the main body. Emboldened by this seeming success, Taki Khan's army:

> ...excited by this address of their favourite and gallant Commander loudly cheered him and rushed on boldly to the attack, vying with each other to get in advance and vowing either to sacrifice their lives or obtain the victory.[27]

The British now needed to stand firm to resist the furious cavalry charges of Taki Khan's men. This they did with the usual disciplined volleys of musketry and the rapid fire of their artillery. But Taki Khan was no mere reckless charger. He alternated his cavalry charges, which fixed the British line in place, with attacks from his rocket men and fire from his *jezzailichis*, which caused casualties in the smaller British force.

> and at length Muhammed Taki, observing some unsteadiness in the ranks of the Sepoys, rode off to lead a final and decisive attack. At that moment his foot was grazed and his horse killed under him by a cannon-shot but heedless of pain he mounted another horse and placed himself at the head of a choice corps of Afghan cavalry for a supreme effort against Adams right flank. That flank rested on a watercourse wherein Adams with excellent judgement had disposed a single company of sepoys *en potence*, concealing the men in the jungle upon the bank. To this point Mohammed Taki now led his Afghan squadrons with all the impetuosity of a dashing and intrepid cavalier. As he swept past the front of the British battalions he was struck by a bullet in the shoulder. He whirled the skirt of his garment over the wound in order to hide the blood, galloped on, followed by his men into the nullah and was ascending the opposite bank when up rose the hidden Sepoys from their ambush and poured a volley full into their faces.[28]

Despite Fortescue's purple prose, there is little doubt that the battle was hard-fought on both sides. Taki Khan was killed by that volley, and with the death of their general, Mir Kassim's adherents withdrew. The British, with no cavalry to speak of, could not pursue with any vigour, although they captured the enemy camp and stores. Many of Taki Khan's troops rallied on that contingent defeated by Glenn, who had watched the action from afar without aiding their compatriots.

The British halted for several days on the field of battle, which was in sight of the field of Plassey and the hunting lodge where Clive had rested almost seven years before. It was 25 July before Adams entered Murshidabad, escorting the reinstated Mir Jafar as Nawab.

27 Broome, *Bengal Army*, pp.372–373.
28 Fortescue, *British Army*, vol.3, pp.70–71; see also Broome, *Bengal Army*, pp.372–374.

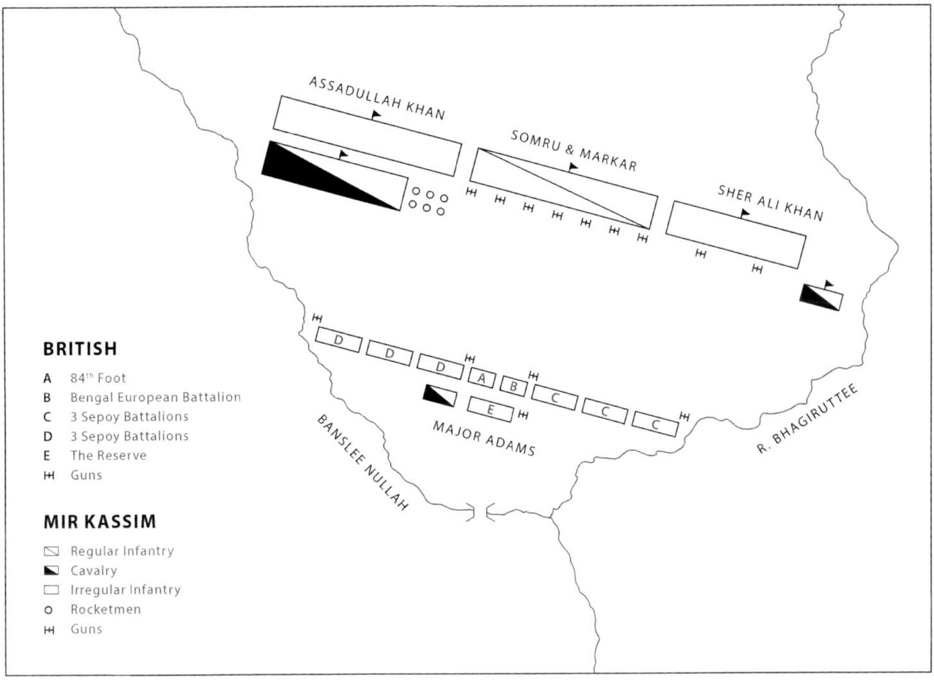

Plan of the dispositions of both armies at the Battle of Gheria. The engagement is sometimes referred to as the Battle of Sooty by some British sources (Gary Luxton © Helion & Co)

'Never Was a Battle More Fiercely Contested'[29] – The Battle of Gheria, 2 August 1763

Although Adams's campaign, despite some desperate and bloody fighting, had so far been successful, he had not yet encountered the new 'trained brigades' or mercenary *compoos* of Somru or Markar. These forces were part of Mir Kassim's main army encamped in the entrenchments at Sooty, some 37 miles (59.5km) from Murshidabad. Mir Kassim himself remained in his capital of Monyghr rather than in the field with his army. Despite his political and financial acumen, he does not seem to have had much talent as a military man and may not have realised that his mere presence would have given his army a boost to its morale. He left the fighting of the war to his generals.

Once Major Adams reached Murshidabad, he was joined by more troops which brought his strength up to just over 1,000 Europeans – two more companies of the Bengal European Regiment had joined under Captain Knox and some 4,000 sepoys in seven rather understrength battalions.[30] There were 10 guns crewed by Europeans, but with the aid of Indian *lascars* who would move the guns by manhandling on the

29 Malleson, *Decisive Battles of India*, p.154.
30 Innes, *Bengal European Regiment*, p.132.

battlefield. The artillery was commanded by Captain Jennings.[31] The cavalry stood at around 300 men in total, of whom 100 or fewer were the remaining Europeans who had been so roughly handled by Taki Khan the previous month. These had been joined by two *rissalahs* or troops of 'Mughal Horse', that is, Indian irregular cavalry in EIC service. These few were all of the cavalry that Major Adams could command.

Adams was opposed by a far larger force. Fortescue gives the enemy strength as 40,000 men,[32] which is surely far too high. Malleson calculates the total at a more reasonable 28,000.[33] The bulk of these were irregulars, some of whom had already fought and had been defeated twice. Many of these were cavalry and included those Afghans who had followed Taki Khan. The rocket men were also present and once again would prove to be something of a problem for the British.

The core of this army were the two 'trained brigades' of Somru and Markar, and these would now face the main British army for the first time. Together, they may have numbered perhaps 6,000–8,000 men, but in truth probably significantly less, with 16 guns. Broome gives 12,000 cavalry in the force, which he states was 'upwards of 40,000',[34] but as always, even if there were this many present in Mir Kassim's army, then numbers of the irregulars would take little or no part in the action. Those formations which would fight were most of the cavalry, the two trained *compoos*, the rocket men, and perhaps a minority of the irregular infantry, some of whom, at least, had some artillery of their own. Even if we calculate the number of actual combat troops as low as 20,000, this was still a formidable force for Adams's 5,000 to handle.

On 1 August 1763, Adams threw a bridge over the Banslee Nullah, which was a tributary of the Bhagiruttee River. The two streams formed a junction, so that once it had crossed the *nullah*, the British force was in effect surrounded by water on three sides with the open plain of Gheria to its front. Adams's flanks and rear might have been protected by these waterways, but were he to be defeated, there was nowhere for his army to run.

Major Adams formed his army in the conventional way. The two small European battalions formed the centre, with two guns on each flank of the European line. Next, on each flank of the Europeans, were three sepoy battalions and, on each outer flank of the three sepoy units, two more guns.

The reserve was formed from a single sepoy battalion, the cavalry, and the two remaining guns.

If we imagine for a moment that the British force were in a bottle formed by the two streams on their flanks and rear, then the cork in that bottle was Mir Kassim's army on the open plain to their front. Broome accuses the Nawab's commanders of making 'a grave error in advancing to meet the English',[35] but it was not quite as simple as that. Certainly, at first sight it would seem less than competent to abandon the safety of

31 E. Buckle, *Memoir of the Services of the Bengal Artillery* (London: W.H. Allen, 1852; repr. Uckfield: Naval & Military Press, 2021), p.21.
32 Fortescue, *British Army*, vol.3, p.72.
33 Malleson, *Decisive Battles of India*, p.150.
34 Broome, *Bengal Army*, p.377.
35 Broome, *Bengal Army*, p.377.

their earthworks at Sooty, yet they outnumbered their enemies by a significant margin and had a far superior cavalry force, which is of little use in earthworks. Furthermore, Adams, with rivers at his back, simply had nowhere to go and indeed was inviting the complete destruction of his army.

So, on the morning of 2 August 1763, Adams saw Mir Kassim's army advancing against him. The two regular *compoos* were in the centre, along with their artillery. On their right came Assadullah Khan with 8,000 cavalry supported by an unlikely 12,000 irregular foot. On the left of the regulars was another somewhat smaller division under Sher Ali Khan. This division rested its flank on the Bhagiruttee River.

The battle began with a mutual cannonade, with both armies advancing slowly towards each other. The two European battalions in Adams's centre and the sepoy battalions on their immediate flanks were opposite the *compoos* of Somru and Markar, and at first the mercenaries seem to have had marginally the advantage in the firefight.[36] The British centre, however, held its ground and slowly gained an equally marginal ascendancy.

Over on the British left, things were about to get very much worse. Assadullah Khan launched a furious cavalry charge from the Bengali right and smashed to pieces the left flank battalion of sepoys and pushed back the next in line on the centre, opening a gap in the British formation. More cavalry led by Mir Budruddin charged into this gap and 'made an intervention to favour Samru and Markar by attacking in the rear the troops with whom they were maintaining an almost equal combat'.[37]

This charge captured two of the British guns and caused considerable disorder in the ranks of the 84th Foot. This confusion was exacerbated by an almost simultaneous attack by the enemy rocket men, who threw their explosive missiles into the already disordered ranks.

Had the Nawab's left wing joined the battle at this point, it is hard to see how the British force could have avoided complete destruction. However, they did not, seemingly making only 'so feeble an attack'[38] that Major Adams was able to aid his hard-pressed centre with troops from his barely engaged right wing.

At this point, Adams also committed his reserves to restore the situation on his left. His few cavalry are not mentioned in the sources, but assuming they had not already fled, they must have been involved in this stage of the action, perhaps sealing off the break in the British line. At all events, Captain Carnac with the reserve sepoy battalion and two guns restored the British position, rallying the survivors of the left wing and recapturing the guns which had been on the flank of the 84th. This reserve sepoy battalion was a veteran unit having been first raised in late 1757 by Captain Mathews and had been on almost continuous service ever since, and even though Mathews was no longer in command, it was still known as 'Mathews ke Paltan' – The Mathews Battalion.[39]

36 Malleson, *Decisive Battles of India*, p.152.
37 Malleson, *Decisive Battles of India*, p.152.
38 Broome, *Bengal Army*, p.379.
39 J. Williams, *The Bengal Native Infantry. An Historical Account From its First Formation in 1757 to 1796, with supplementary notes to 1814*, (London: John Murray, 1817; reprint London: Frederick

With these reserves, Adams was able to restore the British line, especially as Budruddin Khan had been wounded, causing his troops to disengage and leave the field. This halted the enemy advance. Not only did Budruddin's troops halt and then retire, but so did his supports under Assadullah Khan. Adams saw his moment and ordered a general advance.

Only Somru's and Markar's brigades were still showing a front, but with the rest of the army falling into confusion, the best they could do was to retire, still in some kind of order and with at least some of their guns. Adams's force was too exhausted to mount a serious pursuit, but still captured 17 guns and 150 boats of assorted stores, which were moored in the Bhagiruttee River.

As for Somru, his new *compoo* had acquitted itself well enough in its second fight against the British, and true to his personality he had known the precise moment to pull out, preserving his major asset, his men.

The Battle of Gheria had been hard-fought by both sides. It demonstrated both the strengths and weaknesses of both the British and Indian armies. The British had a unified command structure, which made their smaller force much more resilient when under intense pressure. Many of the British sepoy battalions had been in existence for several years and had campaigned together, and in some cases, fought together in several previous actions. The major failing of the British army in India at this time was the lack of cavalry. The pathetic troop or two of Europeans, often infantrymen who might be able to ride, plus an occasional *rissalah* of 'Mughal Horse', were simply not sufficient or efficient. Yet, the Council in Calcutta seem to have seen permanent cavalry regiments as an expensive luxury until somewhat later in the century.

What may be seen as a 'reformed' Indian army – that of Mir Kassim – had problems of its own. The command was divided, as each of the generals looked for loyalty only from his own men. Equally, those men looked only to their own general for pay and subsistence. Most of the men were mercenaries of one sort or another, fighting primarily for pay. Loyalty was to their immediate commander, so armies, whichever part of the subcontinent they came from, tended to be fragile in combat. The death of a leader could be fatal to the whole army. In the same way, the men of the new *compoos*, or 'trained brigades' as the British would increasingly call them, owed their first loyalty to their commander. The European commander owed his loyalty to his paymaster. Thus, although the new *compoos* added some battlefield stability and better artillery to the usually unstable mixture within more traditional Indian armies, at this early period in their existence no Indian prince had gone so far as to give any European officer complete command of his forces. Mir Kassim's *compoo* commanders were still very definitely subordinates.

The Patna Massacre, 5 October 1763

The defeat at the Battle of Gheria did not end the campaign by any means. Mir Kassim had previously ordered his troops to fortify the pass at Udwah Nala. Here were not only some of the troops who had fought at Gheria, including Markar's *compoo*, but also a

Muller Ltd. 1970), p.15.

third 'trained brigade' commanded by another Armenian, Aratoon,[40] as well as other troops which may have brought the total back to a very unlikely 40,000. Of course, any cavalry would not be a great deal of use defending the fortifications, which would significantly lower the likely number of available troops even if some of the cavalry were prepared to fight dismounted.

The battle which followed was more of a siege and assault than a field action. The fortifications were truly formidable and were said to be 'impregnable'. Of course, there is no such thing as a truly impregnable fortress.

Adams took his time. It was not until 11 August that he arrived within four miles of the Udwah Nala position at the village of Palkipur.

The position he had to take was indeed formidable:

> The position selected by the enemy was one of exceeding strength to add to which no pains or expense had been spared. It commanded the main and only road, and extended across the gorge formed between the Ganges and the Rajmahal hills, a steep spur of which ran out and narrowed the pass at this particular point. A deep morass extended along the front of the lines from near the foot of the hills to less than 100 yards from the river, along which narrow strip ran the road. The left of the entrenchment rested on the river, from hence it ran in a south-westerly direction for about a mile, when it abutted on a steep isolated hill; from this it again branched off in a more southerly direction up to the main spur of the mountains, amongst the ravines and scarped precipices of which it finally terminated. The whole of this line of works was of recent construction, the ramparts were about 60 feet thick and 10 high surmounted by a parapet of 18 feet thick and seven high, and in front along the whole line of the plain, ran a deep ditch of 60 feet wide and about 12 deep. Batteries were erected at convenient intervals and upwards of 100 pieces of cannon were mounted upon them.[41]

Adams clearly had to consider his actions with some care. He was not without some advantages. His army had by now several victories over Mir Kassim's forces under its collective belt, and confidence must have been high. Adams moved his army within range of the enemy's works and began a regular siege by the middle of August 1763, erecting batteries for the heavy guns which he now had, and digging approach trenches. Yet, the enemy earthworks were barely scratched by his artillery, which managed only one small and impracticable breach by the beginning of September. This was on the left of the enemy works, close to the river, where the British had managed to advance their approach trenches to within 300 yards of the Bengali entrenchment.[42] In addition, his working parties were constantly harassed by parties of the Nawab's irregulars, who crossed the morass to raid the British positions.[43]

40 Broome, *Bengal Army*, p.382.
41 Broome, *Bengal Army*, pp.381–382.
42 Innes, *The Bengal European Regiment*, p.137.
43 Broome, *Bengal Army*, p.382.

Adams's luck changed when, on 4 September, a deserter from the enemy, one of the European mercenaries who had previously deserted from the EIC's service, came in to Adams's camp offering, 'on condition of pardon, to point out a ford through the morass by which the troops might cross and attack the left of the intrenchment'.[44]

In fact, the crossing of the morass would be vital to attack the enemy's right and the taking of 'the steep isolated hill' mentioned above.

Adams formulated his plan with some care. It involved one column under Captain Irving of the Bengal European Regiment, consisting of two companies of European grenadiers and two battalions of sepoys with scaling ladders. Their task was to take the 'isolated hill' before exploiting into the rest of the entrenchment. A second column under Captain Moran was to begin by launching a fake attack on the breach over at the other end of the entrenchment to fix the enemy's attention. This diversion could then become an attack in earnest if Irving's column was successful. Major Carnac commanded a third reserve column to act as circumstances might dictate, either reinforcing success or covering a failure.

Unusually for almost any military operation, the assault went in without a hitch. Irving's column overran the first enemy outpost, bayonetting the sleeping sentries, and stormed the hill without difficulty. The troops opposing him panicked and fled, 'for the enemy reckoned their position so strong as to need no watching, and the officers were more occupied with wine and dancing girls than with military vigilance'.[45]

Whatever the reason for this astonishing lack of preparedness, the panic quickly spread and it was with only a little more difficulty that the second column gained entry via the breach and then the main gate nearby, as the panic spread unchecked by any of Mir Kassim's officers, mercenary or otherwise.

However, worse was to come for Mir Kassim's army. Behind the entrenchment guarding the bridge over the *nullah*, and the only means of escape, was a body of troops who did not panic but carried out their orders to shoot any deserters or runaways. These draconian orders were carried out, and many of the Nawab's men died by their erstwhile comrades' hands. In the disaster that followed, some 15,000 of Mir Kassim's army became casualties and that army virtually ceased to exist. The British captured all of the guns in the entrenchment, as well as hundreds, perhaps thousands, of horses and cattle. The victory was truly astonishing, brought about by the sheer audacity of Adams's plan and the treachery of one of Mir Kassim's mercenaries.

Somru's command may not have been present with Mir Kassim's army at Udwah Nala, despite Broome's statement to the contrary,[46] and so avoided the debacle, but he was certainly in Patna some three or four weeks later, as events would show. The distance between the two places is roughly 198 miles (320 km), so it was going to take something close to three weeks or longer over the poor or non-existent roads of the time to travel such a distance with all the impedimenta of an army with bullock-hauled guns, elephants, and other baggage animals. Perhaps his uncanny ability to know when

44 Broome, *Bengal Army*, p.383.
45 Fortescue, *British Army*, vol.2, p.77.
46 Broome, *Bengal Army*, p.382.

to retreat served him well here, and if he was ever there at all, he may have moved to Patna before the battle began. We cannot know for certain. But it seems unlikely that his *compoo* was at Udwah almost 200 miles away on 5 September and in Patna with sufficient of his troops on 3 October to commit the deed which would blacken his name to the British for the rest of his life: 'Fortune smiled on Samru and he soon won the heart of his master and became a special favourite with him. But the manner in which he discharged the debt of gratitude to the Nawab has cast a slur on his character.'[47]

The string of defeats that Mir Kassim's army had suffered seems to have unhinged the normally sane Nawab. He wrote to Adams on 9 September after listing his many legitimate grievances, stating that, 'if you are resolved on your own authority to proceed in this business know for a certainty that I will cut off the heads of Mr Ellis and the rest of your chiefs and send them to you.'[48]

Adams wrote back in the strongest terms, 'if a hair of their heads is hurt you can have no title to mercy from the English and you may depend upon the utmost fury of their resentment.'[49]

Adams then continued his march, taking the Nawab's capital of Monyghr on 1 October when the governor of the place surrendered after taking a bribe to do so. Mir Kassim had already fled to Patna, where, as good as his word, he issued orders for the massacre of his prisoners.

Walter Reinhardt, alias Somru, would be the instrument of the Nawab's rage.

Some 150 Europeans, civilians and soldiers, were killed in the ensuing bloodbath, including Mr Ellis, who, above all, had begun the train of events which would lead to this point. Even Somru's sepoys baulked at such a deed, but fear of their commander drove them to complete the grisly task.[50] This event was to mark Somru until the end of his life and drove him to keep as far from British hands as he possibly could.

Mutiny in the Bengal Army

Although the immediate threat from Mir Kassim and his 'trained brigades' had been defeated, the Nawab was not quite finished. In his flight, he had managed to collect a sizeable amount of treasure, and he still had Somru's brigade and perhaps the remnants of Markar's *compoo* as well. He therefore threw himself on the dubious mercy of the Nawab-Vizier of Oudh, Shuja-ud-Daulah, crossing the border into Oudh in mid-November after a rather half-hearted attempt to relieve Patna, which was besieged by the British and had fallen to them on 6 November 1763.

There was now something of a hiatus in the campaign, but the British had other problems which would bear upon our story.

47 Banerji, *Begam Samru*, pp.5–6.
48 Broome, *Bengal Army*, p.389.
49 Broome, *Bengal Army*, p.390.
50 For details of the massacre see Broome, *Bengal Army*, pp.390–392.

When, far to the south, the French possession of Pondicherry fell to the British after a siege in 1761, many French prisoners taken there were given the chance to enter EIC service. Two companies were formed and shipped off to Calcutta to join the British forces in Bengal. One of these prisoners was René Madec, a Breton, a one-time French marine and later a sergeant of grenadiers.[51]

The campaign of 1763 had been a seriously testing affair. The men of Adams's army had done well against heavy odds and expected the rewards they had been promised for their exemplary service. However, Adams had left the army due to ill health, and his successor, Ranfurly Knox, was to do the same. Both would be dead before the end of the year.

So it was that Captain Jennings, the next senior present and an artillery officer, found himself in command of the army when the discontent over lack of pay erupted. This discontent, to begin with, only affected the European troops. By this time, the two French companies had joined the Bengal European Regiment and the discontent became such that on 30 January 1764 the Europeans refused to do duty until they were paid.[52] Jennings did his best to pacify the troops but had no ready money to hand and so promised to write to Calcutta for supplies of that commodity. He did so, but with no supplies forthcoming, on 11 February 1764 the army paraded without orders and declared through its apparent leader, a soldier called Straw, that they intended to march to Patna.[53] The bulk of the Bengal European Regiment then marched off in good order, despite all their officers could do to restrain them.

In fact, the Patna march was a ruse, and the root of the mutiny was in the two French companies, whose plan was decidedly different. The upshot of this was that the British mutineers, after discovering that the French companies planned to march into Oudh and join the enemy, returned to their colours. However, the French, led by René Madec, somewhere between 200 and 250 strong and with around 100 sepoys, joined Mir Kassim at his new base in Allahabad.[54]

A contemporary Indian source tells much the same story, but with somewhat different emphasis:

> Monshur Medec, a Frenchman, who served in the English army had come to some altercations with the English Commander on that failure; and the matter went so far, that the Frenchman at the head of above a hundred soldiers of his nation, quitted the camp with arms and baggage and I believe also, with a field piece, and marched into Raja Balwand Singh's country. A party of English pursued him for some time; but on reflecting the impropriety of lighting up the flames of dissension for so small a subject, and affording a matter of discontent to the Vizier, they returned back and the French took service with Shudjah-ud-Dualah.[55]

51 Emile Barbé, *Le Nabab René Madec* (Paris: Felix Alcan, 1894), translated by Yog Mehta as *The Nawab René Madec* (Privately Published, 2023), p.16.

52 Lawford, *Britain's Army in India*, pp.308–309.

53 Lawford, *Britain's Army in India*, p.309.

54 Fortescue, *British Army*, vol.2, p.87; Barbé, *René Madec*, p.29. Barbé provides the higher total and does not mention the sepoys at all.

55 Seid-Gholam Hossein Khan, *The Seir Mutaqherin, or Review of Modern Times*, vol.2 (Delhi: Low Price Publications, 1990), p.524.

This accession of strength to the ex-Nawab's force was, of course, welcome, though how he was to pay them was another matter. These men were seemingly the foundation of René Madec's own *compoo*, which was raised sometime in 1764:

> During the winter Madec increased his Corps by twenty-two companies of sepoys each sixty men strong. He trained his troops in the French style, and made them display the flag of the Nation.[56]

Somru was, in March 1764, conducting a minor campaign for the Nawab-Vizier of Oudh, Shuja-ud-Daulah. Mir Kassim seems to have offered the use of Somru's *compoo* as a gesture of friendship, though he probably had little choice. Somru scored an easy victory over the Raja of Bundlekhund, who had declared 'independence' from his over-lord, the Nawab-Vizier.[57] His irregulars were no match for Somru's now veteran brigade.

Shuja-ud-Daulah and Mir Kassim forged an alliance to put Mir Kassim back on the throne of Bengal, Orissa, and Bihar. Rather, it might be said that Mir Kassim had bought the support of the Nawab-Vizier and the emperor by paying them seventeen lakhs and 10 lakhs of rupees respectively.[58] As usual, the emperor was very short of money and relied on the Nawab-Vizier for almost everything. Indeed, this was why Shuja was the emperor's vizier, or chief minister, at this time. The emperor was little more than a puppet dancing to the Nawab-Vizier's tune in the so far vain hope of using the Nawab-Vizier as a stepping stone to his throne in Delhi.

The Battle of Patna, 3 May 1764

Thus it was that in 1764, Shuja-ud-Daulah and Mir Kassim, with the Emperor Shah Alam as a figurehead, invaded Bihar with a sizeable army of perhaps 35,000,[59] including Somru's brigade of regulars and René Madec's band of desperados, for the Breton leader had not yet had the time to add the '22 companies of sepoys' that he claims to have trained 'during the winter'. The men Madec had may have served the guns rather than fought as infantry. In addition, there were also the usual bands of irregular horse, of which the 3,000 Afghan and Rohilla cavalry were seen as the best,[60] matchlock-armed irregular infantry, some artillery in the older Mughal style, and 5,000 or so *goshains*, religious fanatics who went into battle naked and ash-smeared, with their uncut hair streaming behind them in their berserker charges.

The army which would face this host was not in the best condition. The new commander, Major Carnac, who replaced Jennings in early March,[61] seems to have

56 Barbé, *René Madec*, p.30.
57 Innes, *The Bengal European Regiment*, p.155.
58 Sarkar, *Mughal Empire*, vol.2, p.325. It is indicative of the Emperor's power that he received the smaller sum.
59 Fortescue, *British Army*, vol.2, p.90.
60 Innes, *Bengal European Regiment*, p.168.
61 Broome, *Bengal Army*, p.428.

dithered somewhat, and his indecision communicated itself to his troops. He began this phase of the new campaign with an army still simmering with assorted discontents over pay, which, while these had been mollified for the time being, would surface again later. Also, Major Carnac's manner towards his officers and soldiers was less than conducive to harmony. At this time, Carnac's force consisted of a single battalion of Europeans, which was around 650 strong, and seven battalions of sepoys. In addition, there was a single troop of European cavalry, 73 strong, plus two *rissalahs* of 'Mughal Horse' under their own officers. The strength of this body would shortly rise sharply to 1,200 men. Artillery consisted of two companies of European gunners and an unknown number of Indian *lascars*.[62] Carnac's total force was around 7,000 strong.

Carnac also had with him some 12,000 men of Mir Jafar's army, and for reasons best known to himself, he took to making his own camp with them, rather than with his own troops, which increased the undercurrents of discontent. Further, rather than advancing to meet the forces of the enemy alliance, he dithered and ordered entrenchments to be prepared at Buxar, while provisions were gathered. However, either through neglect or inability, nothing was done, and on 4 April 1764, a retreat to Patna was ordered.[63]

Indeed, at this point, the British force was in a somewhat perilous position. Carnac seems to have intended to deny the enemy the crossing of the Soane River, but again dithered and allowed the Nawab-Vizier's cavalry across the river:

> Carnac ordered Captain Hay with the European cavalry troop out to beat up the advance guard of the enemy's cavalry. The plan was to lure this body to a *tope* or grove of mango trees where a battalion of sepoys was to be concealed in ambush. These would then fire a volley at the enemy cavalry upon which Hay would about turn and charge the hopefully disordered enemy. Hay followed his orders but when he reached the *tope* as planned there were no sepoys to support him. The Captain and his dragoons had the greatest difficulty in regaining the British camp with the loss of several of his men. Carnac, it was discovered, had changed his mind about the ambush but had neglected to inform Captain Hay.[64]

At this point, it looked very much as if the allies' faster-moving cavalry would beat Carnac into Patna, but the British then had a piece of undeserved good fortune.

On 22 April, Captain Smith's battalion of sepoys and three guns was detached from the main force to secure a provision convoy coming to the army. Having met the convoy, Smith's command received warning of a body of enemy horse approaching. Smith placed the convoy and his troops in a nearby rectangular 'tank' or water reservoir, which was dry at that time of year. The embanked sides of the reservoir gave ample cover to his troops. 'He gave the enemy so warm and unexpected a reception, that they were glad to draw off as quickly as possible and left him to pursue his route to camp unmolested.'[65]

62 Broome, *Bengal Army*, p.428.
63 Innes, *The Bengal European Regiment*, p.164.
64 Broome, *Bengal Army*, p.438.
65 Broome, *Bengal Army*, p.438.

Had this chance encounter not taken place, it is quite likely that this body of cavalry would have reached Patna before the British.

Nevertheless, the British and Mir Jafar's troops reached Patna in the nick of time and occupied earthworks outside the town but beneath the walls, which Mir Jafar had prudently prepared some time previously. This meant that those troops outside the walls could be supported by the garrison and the guns on the walls of the fortress, as well as those on the walls of the city. The position had been cleverly chosen.

Once the British and Mir Jafar had taken up their positions around Patna, the 35,000 strong army of Shuja-ud-Daulah, Mir Kassim and the emperor arrived on 24 April and took up positions to the west and south of the city.

The positions of Carnac's army also on the western and southern faces of the city are described as:

> Our Europeans were encamped outside the west face and southwest angle of the fortress, their left resting on a mound occupied by some of our sepoy battalions. The south-west angle was considered the most likely point of attack, and Mir Jafar, therefore, had thoughtfully taken the precaution of clearing away a village and all the trees in front, so that the enemy might find no cover during his advance.
>
> In front of the position held by the Europeans the entrenchments were only partially completed, but the ground occupied was commanded by the south-west bastion of the fortress, the guns on which were worked by a British detachment sent by Carnac into the city to assist our army encamped without the walls.[66]

For almost a week, the two rival armies simply looked at each other, until on 2 May a report of British reinforcements coming to Patna reached Shuja's camp.

The Nawab-Vizier decided to act and prepared to attack the British position on 3 May. The plan appears to have been to use his irregulars to pin Mir Jafar's forces, while the best troops in the allied army would attack the British position outside the south-west corner of the fortress.

The battle began, as did most Indian battles, with a cannonade. The British replied with the guns on the walls and those of the fortress. Somru's brigade were first into action.

> Somru with five regiments of disciplined Telingas of Mir Kassim's, supported by some pieces of cannon mounted and served in the English manner,[67]
>
> …leading the assault, but being thrown back by the concentrated artillery fire from both the British line and the guns of the fort.[68]
>
> Sumroo next moved forward with his regular battalions in good order; but as they approached the entrenchment, they were received with so close and warm a fire, that after considerable loss, they drew off and took shelter in a hollow way

66 Innes, *The Bengal European Regiment*, p.167.
67 Khan, *Seir Mutaqherin*, vol.2, pp.531–532.
68 Fortescue, *British Army*, vol.2, p.91.

> about 80 yards in front of the entrenchment, where they remained inactive the greater part of the day.[69]

As for René Madec's conduct, Barbe says of this battle only that, 'For Twenty days Madec made the greatest efforts to take the city but was unable to succeed.'[70]

Whatever Madec's precise role in this battle actually was, all we can say for certain is that he was present. One might conjecture that the bulk of his followers were acting as gunners for the Nawab-Vizier's forces, as there were not yet enough of them to form an independent *compoo*.

The battle was certainly hard-fought. Mir Kassim's rocket men made strenuous efforts to turn the British right, putting some of the British sepoys under severe pressure. The Nawab-Vizier's Afghan and Rohilla cavalry made numerous charges, but they could neither intimidate nor break the steady infantry. Mir Kassim himself kept out of danger, as was his wont. This seemingly angered the Nawab-Vizier, who had led some of the attacks in person. Shuja sent messages to Mir Kassim, demanding that he support the Nawab-Vizier's attacks, but he received no answer, nor did Mir Kassim order Somru to attack again.

Shuja-ud-Daulah ordered the 5,000 *goshains* to attack, sword in hand, the south-west angle of the entrenchment, where the Bengal European Regiment was stationed:

> These fanatics rushed impetuously to the charge with wild shrieks and gestures, presenting a formidable spectacle with their painted faces, flowing hair and glittering weapons; but the English undismayed by their savage appearance received them with a close and deadly volley of musketry and grape as they closed upon the intrenchment which killed and wounded an immense number and sent the remainder howling to the rear. This attack was scarcely repelled when Inayat Khan with his Rohillas made a gallant and impetuous charge upon the same point, but with no better success.[71]

The Nawab-Vizier had one last card to play. He now ordered up his last reserves and sent in a general attack all along his part of the line, despite the continuing inactivity of most of Mir Kassim's troops. The Nawab's men made a brief lodgement in the British earthworks, actually capturing three drummers of the Bengal European Regiment,[72] but a local counter-attack by that unit soon rescued the captured musicians and the enemy was evicted from the position.

In other parts of the field, the British and Mir Jafar's troops also held their own, though not without difficulty. The fighting on the extreme right of the British line became fierce towards the end of the day after a slow and rather desultory beginning. The EIC sepoy battalions of Captain Stibbert and Captain Swinton, after some considerable fighting

69 Broome, *Bengal Army*, p.448.
70 Barbé, *René Madec*, p.30.
71 Broome, *Bengal Army*, p.448.
72 Innes, *The Bengal European Regiment*, p.169.

around a ruined mosque in front of the British line, attacked the now retreating enemy and attempted to capture a battery of guns, which was attempting to retire 'which being only bullock draught was retreating very slowly'.[73] However, they were disappointed to receive strict orders from Major Carnac to desist in their pursuit and the guns escaped to the enemy's fortified camp.

Carnac's refusal to follow up his narrow victory and pursue the Nawab-Vizier's army was a cardinal error that allowed the allies to reorganise their forces within their camp and remain in contact with the British for the rest of May 1764. During these weeks, neither side seemed willing to attack the other, though there were skirmishes in the 'no man's land' between the two armies. The British reinforcements actually arrived on 9 May. On 30 May, the Nawab-Vizier's army began its withdrawal. Carnac, again, made no real effort to follow up. For the time being, the campaign was over.

The Battle of Buxar, 23 October 1764

The troops of the three allies – the Mughal Emperor Shah Alam, Shuja-ud-Daulah, the Nawab-Vizier of Oudh, and Mir Kassim, the former Nawab of Bengal – retired to their fortified camp at Buxar on the south bank of the Ganges River, where they proceeded to fall out. As always, the root problem was money. Mir Kassim had finally run out of that essential item, and the men of Somru's *compoo* were in want of their pay. 'However two or three days after this the ungrateful Somro surrounded Mir Kassim's quarters with his Telingas, and asked the arrears of his pay. As there was no money in the treasury there came some gold coin out of the Sanctuary; and he took it in pay.'[74]

Reinhardt, it seems, had already transferred his service from Mir Kassim to the Nawab-Vizier, taking with him the guns and other equipment that had originally been supplied by Mir Kassim. The ex-Nawab ordered Somru to turn over the artillery and small arms to his steward's office, but Somru declined, saying, 'That now both the cannon and muskets, with everything else, belonged to him who had them in his power'. After this answer he quitted his post and went to encamp amongst the Vizier's troops.'[75]

Somru evidently meant to keep what he had, whichever service he happened to be in. His gift for survival had not deserted him, for the following day Mir Kassim was arrested and imprisoned by Shuja-ud-Daulah, his remaining officers were dismissed, and such as remained of his wealth was seized for the use of the Nawab-Vizier. It appeared that Walter Reinhardt had, once again, jumped just in time.

There was now a halt to active campaigning, as the monsoon had broken. It was during this time that René Madec raised and trained the '22 companies of sepoys' mentioned earlier. This would give the Nawab-Vizier at least two 'trained brigades' in his army for the upcoming campaign.

73 Broome, *Bengal Army*, p.445.
74 Khan, *Seir Mutaqherin*, vol.2, p.545.
75 Khan, *Seir Mutaqherin*, vol.2, p.545.

Meanwhile, in the English camp all was not well. Major Carnac, despite increasing his Mughal Horse to 1,200 men, had difficulty moving his army due to lack of supplies. However, Carnac's tenure of the command had run its course and he left the army on 28 June 1764, being dismissed from the service by the Council in Calcutta.

His successor to the command was Major Hector Munro of the 89th Foot (Morris' Highlanders), a King's officer, as distinct from one of the East India Company's, and therefore, by the usages of the time, automatically senior to a Company officer of the same rank. Munro had with him the cadres of three King's regiments who had been preparing to return to England: his own 89th, the 84th, and the 90th Regiments. Many of the men of these units had already transferred to the Company service, which was again common at the time, rather than return to England for probable disbandment, now that the war with the French was over. Together, these three units totalled 14 officers and 155 other ranks.[76] To these would be added the marines who had arrived in Patna in mid-May to form an *ad hoc* 'King's Battalion' for the coming campaign.

Munro had inherited the discontent in the army left by, though perhaps not entirely the fault of, Carnac. Munro tightened discipline in the EIC units, both European and Indian. He instituted new procedures and drills to bring these units up to the standard of his few King's troops. This tightening was not to the liking of some of the sepoys, and a serious mutiny broke out in the 9th Sepoy Battalion on 8 September 1764. The battalion marched off in a formed body with their arms saying that they would serve no longer. Such 'mutinies' were not uncommon in Indian armies and were often no more than 'withdrawal of labour' in pursuit of arrears of pay. Such was not, however, the tradition in the British service, and once the miscreants had been rounded up by the marines and another sepoy unit, 24 of the ringleaders were to suffer the ultimate punishment. They were to suffer death by the old Mughal method of being blown from the muzzle of a gun. Munro ordered the sentence to be carried out immediately. The condemned men met their end with courage. The grenadiers amongst the mutineers demanding that, as they held the post of honour on the right of the line in battle, they should die first. The sentence was duly carried out.

The executions put a stop to the discontent, and Munro was able to take full control of his army. 'Subordination and discipline being restored, provisions were laid in and boats and cattle being procured from all quarters... The Native battalions were equalised and completed to their complements and the rain being nearly over and the country passable for troops, Major Munro issued the welcome order to advance towards the enemy of the 6th of October.'[77]

The actual strength of Munro's force, which set out from its quarters around Patna was just under 8,000 fighting men, of whom 1,000 or so were the 'Mughal Horse'. Another 1,083 were Europeans – including King's troops, Company troops and Company artillery – and there were 22 or possibly 28 guns,[78] mostly 6-pounders but including four

76 Lawford, *Britain's Army in India*, p.326.

77 Broome, *Bengal Army,* p.462.

78 Fortescue, *British Army*, vol.2, p.96, though Williams, *The Bengal Native Infantry*, p.37 states 'two and twenty'. Williams was present as a junior officer in the Marines.

12-pounders and two howitzers.[79] Eight battalions of sepoys, totalling 5,716 officers and men, completed Munro's army. To these, as with any army operating in India at this time, must be added at least the same number of 'camp followers' and possibly many more. Bullock drivers, gun *lascars*, camp servants of all kinds, and not infrequently their families as well, would accompany the fighting men on the march. It is by no means improbable that Munro had over 20,000 people under his command.[80]

Munro's first task was to unite the main army with a detachment of two battalions of sepoys and Captain Wemys's marines under Major Champion at the town of Chopra, and also to cross over to the western bank of the Soane River, which would allow the junction to take place. Champion's detachment needed to move to the ferry at Moneah to assist Munro's main army in the crossing.

Captain Williams, who was present as a junior officer of marines, takes up the story:

> At 2 o'clock the next morning [10 October] they took up their line of march and moved along the bank of the Soane towards the ferry opposite to Moneah until daybreak, when Hicarrahs came in and reported, that Major Munro with the Grand Army were at Moneah and preparing to cross the river; that a large body of the enemy were drawn up to oppose his landing; and that we were within a short mile of them. On this the detachment immediately halted and formed in order of battle; the Marines in the center; Captain Trevannion's on the right and the Mathews on the left with the guns in the intervals. By this time the haze of the morning having cleared away, they had a distinct view of the enemy, who, on perceiving them changed their front towards the detachment. Everything being now ready Major Champion ordered three guns to be fired quick, which was the signal agreed on with Major Munro. It was immediately answered from the other side of the river, and in a few minutes after the detachment heard the Grenadiers March which at that time was music of the most pleasing kind to them. They then pushed on to attack the enemy, who after exchanging a few shot with them retired towards Arrah.[81]

This neat little operation united the two parts of Munro's force. He rested the army for two days, while deciding upon an order of battle and organising the subordinate commands. Once this was completed, Munro was able to continue his march towards Buxar. This march was not to be without mishap.

Captain Williams again:

> Every thing being prepared for marching against the enemy, the army left their ground of encampment at five o'clock in the morning of 13th October, in a single

79 Broome, *Bengal Army*, p.472.

80 Lawford, *Britain's Army in India*, p.326; but see also Broome, *Bengal Army*, pp.462–463 for slightly lower figures for the number of fighting troops. Large numbers of followers were a feature of armies in India. The fighting men could be out-numbered by followers three or more to one.

81 Williams, *The Bengal Native Infantry*, pp.35–36.

> column by files from the right, and directed their march towards Arrah. The field officer of the day, Major Champion, with two hundred of the irregular cavalry, the troop of Hussars[82] and two companies of Grenadier Sepoys, with the quarter-master sergeants and camp-colour men of the several corps formed the advanced guard. Just as the day began to dawn having passed the bridge at Arrah, a famous partisan of Sujah Dowlah's lay in ambush with a select body of horse. He suffered the front to pass; but when the center had got opposite he rushed out upon them, cutting down all before him, and throwing the whole into the utmost confusion. Little resistance was made. Every man shifting for himself by recovering the bridge or swimming across the nulla; and most of them effected it under cover of the fire of the Sepoy grenadiers. These two companies were commanded by a subaltern officer whose name the writer is sorry he cannot now recollect. He had not crossed the nulla, and, therefore, as soon as he perceived what had happened in front, he drew up his men at the foot of the bridge on the side next the army, and, as the enemy advanced threw in a close fire, which drove them back, and favoured the escape of our friends.[83]

The European 'Hussars' had been roughly handled, losing about a dozen men, and some 60 of the Mughal Horse were killed or wounded, together with four of the quarter-master sergeants of the various infantry units, whose job was to assign camping grounds for their units for the coming night.[84]

The setback obliged Munro to move with more caution, especially as the Nawab-Vizier's cavalry were hovering about looking for another opportunity to attack the column. There were several occasions when this became so threatening that guns had to unlimber and fire a few rounds to keep the impudent horse at a suitable distance. Despite this, by 22 October, Munro's army had reached the plain before the city of Buxar and could see in the distance the Nawab-Vizier's camp under the walls of the city.

Shuja-ud-Daulah, the Nawab-Vizier, still had the bulk of his army in the fortified camp next to the city of Buxar on the Ganges River. It was said to number 50,000 men, but it was most likely significantly smaller. Cavalry outnumbered the infantry, and indeed, the sheer numbers of cavalry were, as we have seen, a serious concern to Munro and would heavily influence his battle plan.

Somru was present in the camp with his trained brigade, as also was René Madec with his newly raised '22 companies':

> At his elbow were Somro and Monsher Madec with eight field pieces mounted in the English fashion upon carriages equally strong and light. They were at the head of eight regiments of Talingas that had been trained and fashioned by Mir-cassem.[85]

82 There was a single troop of European cavalry 48 strong with Munro's army.

83 Williams, *The Bengal Native Infantry*, pp.38–40.

84 Broome, *Bengal Army*, pp.469–470 provides the casualty figures and a rather more colourful version of events but was not of course present.

85 Khan, *Seir Mutaqherin*, vol.2, p.565.

These eight battalions were the only regulars present in the Nawab-Vizier's army. If Somru had five battalions, as mentioned earlier in this chapter, then Madec's 22 companies cannot have formed more than three battalions, and at the stated 60 men per company, Madec's corps must have been around 1,300 sepoys, plus those of his Europeans who remained. It is unlikely that the whole force of regulars numbered more than 5,000 men.

As for the rest, there were some of the usual irregular matchlock musketeers – sometimes referred to as *nujeebs* or *nujibs* – and heavy, almost immobile guns, but the cutting edge of the army was provided by the cavalry. The *Seir Mutaqherin* mentions several different bodies of horse. These included Mughal and Durrani cavalry, that is, Afghans who were reckoned the elite of the cavalry. There were, in addition, other cavalry and a prodigious number of guns, not all of which could be brought into battle because the Vizier,

> sunk again into a circle of entertainments, pleasures and amusements without once bestowing a thought upon the necessary quantity of balls or their quality or that of the powder.[86]

While the Nawab-Vizier was amusing himself in this fashion, Munro had ordered all the heavy baggage to be put into boats on the Ganges River, while the rest of the army encamped on the plain some distance from the Nawab-Vizier's army. Indeed, as Munro's army appeared on the plain, the Nawab-Vizier's forces had, after a short exchange of cannon fire, retired into their fortified camp, allowing Munro to encamp unmolested.

Munro's Council of War, meeting on the evening of 22 October, decided to rest the army in camp on the 23rd and then attack the enemy on the morning of the 24th. However, the Nawab-Vizier, in a perhaps uncharacteristic burst of energy, drew out his army prepared for battle on the morning of 23 October 1764. The Nawab-Vizier had achieved a small tactical surprise.

The battlefield was largely an open plain, bounded on the British right by the Ganges River and on their left by a *jheel* or morass, which they had to negotiate during the advance to contact. Munro, clearly fearing the large masses of cavalry that the opposition could bring to bear, had taken considerable pains to try to nullify the Nawab-Vizier's advantage in this regard.

Captain Williams describes Munro's careful dispositions:

> Sujah Dowlah, not agreeing in opinion with the Council of War, put his army in motion early on the morning of the 23rd, and when the commander in chief, with the field officer of the day were going out to take a view of the enemy, they discovered them in full motion to give them battle. The drums instantly beat to arms and by eight o'clock the whole were formed in the order which had been laid down.
>
> On the right was a battalion of Sepoys with two guns on its right, and two on its left;- then the Kings Battalion with two guns on its left;- then a battalion of

86 Khan, *Seir Mutaqherin*, vol.2, p.564.

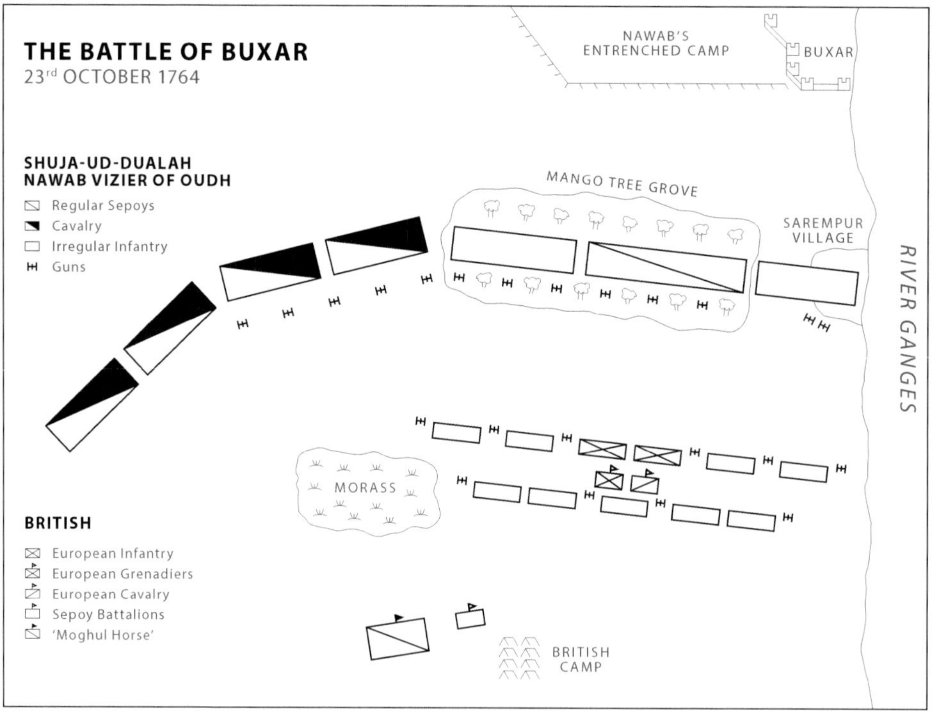

Dispositions of the two armies at the outset of the Battle of Buxar. (Gary Luxton © Helion & Co)

> Sepoys with two guns. On the left of these guns was the Bombay detachment, consisting of something more than one hundred Europeans and Topasses, that is, native Portuguese dressed as Europeans who formed the centre and rear ranks. To the left of them were two guns and upon the left of the whole a battalion of Sepoys which with two guns completed the front line.
>
> The second line was composed of three Sepoy battalions and the Company's European battalion with eight guns in the intervals. A battalion on each flank closed the square, that, on the left had two guns attached to it.[87]

Broome has four sepoy battalions in the second line and differs slightly in other details,[88] placing the 12-pounder guns in the first line and adding two companies of the Bengal European Regiment to the Bombay companies to form a larger battalion. In addition, inside the square was a small reserve, consisting of the European cavalry and the two grenadier companies of the Bengal European Regiment.[89]

The Mughal Horse, perhaps 900 strong now, were placed on the extreme British left, somewhat behind the main battle line.

87 Williams, *The Bengal Native Infantry*, pp.43–44.
88 Broome, *Bengal Army*, pp.472–473 differs in detail from Williams.
89 Broome, *Bengal Army*, p.473.

Munro had made it clear that should the enemy get behind the British, the rear line could, at need, turn about in place and become the rear face of the 'square', which was, in fact, a large rectangle several hundred yards long and about one hundred yards deep. Each of the infantry battalions was fighting, as was normal practice at that time, three ranks deep.

The precise dispositions of the Nawab-Vizier's army are somewhat harder to discern. However, the *Seir Mutaqherin* gives us some idea:

> The Mughal horse together with six or seven thousand men of cavalry and infantry commanded by Shudjah-Culi Qhan commonly called Mia-Yassa, ranged themselves behind Somro and Monsher-Medec. Beni-bahadyr, deputy governor of Aud and Allahabad, brought his troops out of the intrenchment, and took post on the banks of the Ganga, that is close to the ruined houses of the town of Bacsar. At his elbow were Somro and Monsher Madec with eight field pieces mounted in the English fashion upon carriages equally strong and light. They were at the head of eight regiments of Talingas that had been trained and fashioned by Mir-cassem. It was behind these that Mia-Yassa took his post. The Vizier himself coming out of the intrenchment with a body of troops ranged, them on the right of Mia Yassa and Beni bahadyr's; and the engagement commenced by a cannonade.[90]

Broome adds more detail to these dispositions:

> On the left, resting on the Ganges and occupying the fort and ruined town of Buxar, was the division of Beni Bahadur with several Battalions of Nujeebs under European officers, and a chosen body of cavalry, called the Sheikzadees commanded by Sheik Goolam Khadyr. In the centre were the Brigades of Somroo and Madoc, consisting of eight battalions of disciplined Sipahis with eight field pieces worked by Europeans, renegades and deserters. These were supported by a body of between 6 and 7,000 horse and foot under the command of Shoojah Khooli Khan...On either flank of the regular Brigades were powerful Batteries of the Nawab-Vizier's artillery, worked by his own Gulandaz and consisting for the most part of heavy guns, many of which were of European construction. The right wing was composed of the division of Bulwant Singh the Raja of Benares, a considerable body of Rohillas, horse and foot and a splendid corps of about 5,000 Northern Cavalry known as the Douranee Horse, many of whom were veterans who had served under Ahmad Shah Abdallee and some even under Nadir Shah. Shoojah-oo-Dowlah himself commanded the left wing; and a corps of reserve composed of his own troops chiefly Cavalry was posted in the rear.[91]

Quite how numerous this host actually was is, as usual, open to doubt. Fifty thousand seems high, but given the numbers we have, perhaps a total of somewhere between

90 Khan, *Seir Mutaqherin*, vol.2, p.564.
91 Broome, *Bengal Army*, p.474.

30,000 and 40,000 is not too far from the mark. Many, perhaps most, of this army were mercenaries. *Nujeebs* were a common type of matchlock-musket-armed, usually Muslim infantry, who by European standards were 'semi-regulars'. They were soldiers by profession but had no idea of European drill or manoeuvre, unless in this case their 'European' officers had managed to teach them. The Douranee Horse were largely Afghans. In addition, there were the Rohillas – Pathans who had migrated into India in the recent past – many of whom made their living as mercenaries, and who seem to have been in heavy demand in Indian armies at this time. The precise position of the Nawab-Vizier also seems uncertain, but he seems to have had little direct influence on the actions of his commanders once the action began.

The Nawab-Vizier's army 'outwinged' the British on their left by a considerable distance, so the Nawab's right was, 'bending a little inward so as to bring their guns to bear on the left face of our square'.[92]

The battle began with a cannonade as soon as the Nawab-Vizier's guns were in range. Initially, the British guns, being still out of range, did not reply but,

> About nine o'clock we began to advance upon the enemy, and then, for the first time, our fire opened, which we could clearly see had a fine effect. After moving about one hundred yards a jheel in front of the left wing obliged us to incline to the right in order to clear it. This took us up near an hour the enemy's cannon and rockets playing upon us the whole time; but their guns were not well served, otherwise, from the number they had in the field they must have torn us to pieces.[93]

The precise order of events is uncertain, but as soon as the British had finished the 'right incline' to clear the *jheel*, a large body of the Nawab-Vizier's cavalry, principally the Douranee Horse,

> threatened the left flank and made a daring attempt to penetrate between the two lines, Captain Hay observing this moved up promptly with the European Grenadiers and Cavalry, whilst at the same time Captains Morgan and Stables each wheeled half a Battalion, so as to close up the whole interval; whilst the Artillery on the left flank of each line were brought into the new alignment. These movements were effected with great precision; and the enemy having been unexpectedly met by a murderous fire of grape and musketry were checked in their headlong charge, recoiled and speedily retired with heavy loss.[94]

This was not quite the end of the matter in this part of the battlefield. The Douranee Horse, joined by a body of Mughal Horse, now attacked the softer target of the British camp some distance behind the rear of the square. This was protected by the *rissalahs* of Mughal Horse in British service and two companies of sepoys under a Lieutenant

92 Williams, *The Bengal Native Infantry*, p.45.
93 Williams, *The Bengal Native Infantry*, pp.45–46.
94 Broome, *Bengal Army*, p.475.

Vertue. The Mughal Horse fled after a short fight, heavily outnumbered as they were, and the Douranee Horse fell to plundering the British camp. Vertue, with his two companies, retired upon the main body: 'Lieutenant Vertue, finding himself abandoned, and unable with his small party, to resist so powerful a force, coolly retreated with his little body of Sipahis in admirable order, retiring by alternate Companies as steadily as if on parade, and though pressed by the enemy's Cavalry regained the main body though not without some loss.'[95]

At some point, the rear of the square was also fiercely attacked by the Nawab-Vizier's cavalry, probably as a result of Lieutenant Vertue's successful retirement, though this is nowhere stated. But, yet again, the steadiness and discipline of the sepoys told, and despite some severe fighting and repeated assaults by the cavalry, the Afghans and Mughals were eventually beaten off with considerable loss.

The front face of the square – actually a long rectangle – had not been idle while the action at the rear had been taking place. Not only did they have charges by yet more of the Nawab-Vizier's cavalry to face, but also considerable artillery fire from the batteries deployed on either flank of the Nawab-Vizier's centre, which, as we have seen, was composed of the eight battalions of regulars commanded by Somru and Madec. Somru was posted on the right of the regular line with his five battalions, while Madec, as the junior in this case, was on the left with three battalions: 'Whilst the regular battalions under Sumroo and Madec kept up an incessant fire of artillery and musketry.'[96]

Facing the British right stood a village, Serampur, occupied by the enemy and to the left of that a long *tope* or grove of trees which sheltered a good proportion of the Nawab-Vizier's guns and possibly the regular battalions, in the tope's southern half.

However, it was at the northern end of the *tope* and in the ruined village of Serampur where the crisis of the action would occur.

Captain Williams again:

> Major Munro rode to the right and finding it much annoyed by a battery in a tope or grove of trees, in front of the King's Battalion, he ordered Major Stibbert's battalion from the right of the line to advance and attack it in flank. The battalion accordingly moved forward in excellent order; but receiving the fire of a battalion of Nujeebs and being attacked at the same time by a body of horse on each flank, they were thrown into disorder and retired towards the line. Major Munro having gone to the left, Major Champion ordered the right wing to advance but not to give their fire until they could push bayonets.[97]

This second advance was successful, and the enemy were driven from the village and the northern half of the *tope.* The *nujeebs* may, in fact, have been dismounted cavalry, the so-called 'Shezadians' from Lucknow, commanded by Sheik Ghulam Kadir:

95 Broome, *Bengal Army*, p.475.
96 Broome, *Bengal Army*, p.476.
97 Williams, *The Bengal Native Infantry*, p.47.

> On this Sheh-ghoolam-cadyr got up with his Sheh-zadians from betwit the ruins to oppose the English Talingas; and these being now all assembled by their officers and ranged in a line, a fire of musketry ensued between the two troops. But how could the Sheh-zadians and Beni-Bahadyrs people, accustomed to fire dispersed, and at will, stand the regular and violent fire poured upon them by the English Talingas? In one or two discharges the business of Sheh-ghoolam-cadyr's and of his men was effectually done. Numbers were made to bite the dust on the spot; and the others being wounded and dispersed, fled in the greatest consternation, and left their post empty.[98]

Clearing the enemy from the village and the *tope* enabled the British to outflank the battery that had been plaguing the King's Battalion and eventually capture it as they moved south, dispersing outflanked enemy units as they did so. Somru, his genius for self-preservation working overtime, seems to have avoided the worst of what became a cataclysmic rout for the Nawab-Vizier's forces, getting off with at least some of his battalions more or less intact, though Madec's *compoo* seems to have suffered worse, as in 1765 he had barely 400 men.[99]

For the British, this was a major and decisive victory. The plunder from the Nawab-Vizier's camp was immense:

> We took in the field and in the camp, one hundred and twenty-six pieces of cannon; and a foreigner who had deserted from us at Sant, brought in, the day after the action, seven field pieces, which had been left in his charge, for which he received his pardon. Several of these deserters were found dead in the field, and two, who had been wounded and could not get off with their army, were hung up to a tree in front of the line by the provost sergeant.[100]

The British halted for three days to collect the wounded and bury the dead, but then marched towards Benares. On the march, they met with the Emperor Shah Alam, who had been a virtual prisoner of the Nawab-Vizier and now came into the British camp. In time, he would return to Delhi, but without the British help he hoped for.

As for the Nawab-Vizier, in order to ingratiate himself with the British, he offered to murder Somru and Mir Kassim. However, the British wanted to get their hands on them both. The Nawab-Vizier was therefore forced to answer the British request,

> That Sumroo being master of a good body of troops, and such as had not broke their ranks in the last defeat, but had retreated in good order, the seizing of that man's person would not be free from danger.[101]

Nevertheless, Somru thought it prudent to leave the Nawab-Vizier's service for pastures both new and as far away from the British as possible.

98 Khan, *Seir Mutaqherin*, vol.2, pp.565–566.
99 Barbé, *René Madec*, p.32.
100 Williams, *The Bengal Native Infantry*, p.51.
101 Khan, *Seir Mutaqherin*, vol.2, p.571.

4

In the Service of the Emperor

Somru's Campaigns

After the Patna Massacre and the Battle of Buxar, Reinhardt's most pressing need was to stay out of British hands. His only asset and his only protection were the battalions of his *compoo*, thus he needed to find a new employer as soon as possible.

Serving the Jat Rajas

In April 1765, a bare six months after the Battle of Buxar, Somru took service with the Jat Raja, Jawahir Singh, who had plans to expand his domain beyond the districts of Bharatpore and Dieg. In this, the Raja would at first have some success, even launching an abortive siege of Delhi in late 1764, which was abandoned in February 1765 largely due to the treachery of his Maratha mercenaries. It therefore seems likely that Jawahir saw the German mercenary as a more trustworthy alternative to the fickle Marathas. Somru would remain in Jat service for almost eight years,[1] despite the attempt of the EIC to construct an alliance with Jawahir Singh, the price of which was the dismissal of Somru from Jat service. Jawahir Singh needed trained troops more than he needed an alliance with the distant Company, so the letter of 19 August 1765[2] from the Governor in Calcutta was ignored. Somru could breathe easy, at least for the time being.

Somru's *compoo* was not the only mercenary force in Jawahir Singh's army. The Jat Raja also had the *compoo* of René Madec in his service, so the two comrades would once again be united. Both *compoos* would prove their worth at the Battle of Maonda in December 1767 against the Rajputs of Jaipur, where once again it was the trained infantry who won the day.

René Madec describes the action:

> The latter [Raja of Jaipur] piqued by the insult, followed the Jats with his army on their return. He has 16,000 cavalry. Near Jaipur the Jats had to traverse a defile.

1 Banerji, *Begam Samru*, pp.6–7.
2 K.R. Qanungo, *History of the Jats* (Calcutta: Sarkar & Sons, 1925), p.195.

> They made their baggage go ahead, in such a way as to cover them. They hoped to escape the pursuit of their enemies but were overtaken and attacked at a disadvantage. The Jats routed them by a counter march. The artillery and infantry of the assailants were too slow. The Jats took advantage of it to enter the defile, preceded by their baggage at a distance of three leagues. The Raja of Jainagar engaged in pursuing them in the gorge and overtook them in the middle. The Jats then made a half turn to offer battle.
>
> They engaged towards noon. The enemy cavalry put, at the very first, that of the Jats to rout. The latter saved themselves by falling back upon their baggage, crying out that all was lost; the peasants then plundered a great part of the baggage. But the party of Madec and that of the German Sombre, who laboured in that affair with all the bravery and prudence of a great soldier, restored the battle and defeated the Raja of Jainagar. Nearly 10,000 men fell in the two armies together among them nearly all the generals of the enemy's army.[3]

The Jats made good their escape, but had to abandon much of their artillery due to the plundering of the baggage and the consequent theft of many of the baggage animals.

Nevertheless, Somru and Madec had proved their worth to Jawahir Singh and would continue to do so in the coming years. In 1770, for example, their *compoos* would again prove their steadiness in action against Tukaji Holkar's Maratha forces, who were interfering in the Jat civil war between Nawal Singh and his younger brother Ranjit Singh. Both of the mercenaries supported the older brother Nawal Singh, whom they viewed as the legitimate heir.

Walter Reinhardt, alias 'Sombre'or 'Somru'. A flattering, late-nineteenth-century illustration. (Author's Collection)

Battle was joined with the Marathas on 5 April 1770 near the small fort of Sonkh, some 12 miles south of Dieg. A body of 2,000 Jat cavalry under Dan Sahi opened the battle by a headlong charge, but, being unsupported, was beaten off by the Maratha artillery and rocket men. Nawal Singh now seems to have completely lost his head and, dismounting from his elephant, hid behind Somru's formation before fleeing the field on horseback. The battle carried on after dusk had fallen, but with the flight of their leader the Jats lost heart and only the regular infantry of Madec's and Somru's *compoos* held together in the darkness. The Jats lost all but two of

3 From Barbé, *René Madec*, pp.49–50 as quoted by Qanungo, *History of the Jats*, pp.209–210.

their guns, these two being brought off by Somru's *compoo*. The Jats also lost some 5,000 casualties in this action and the survivors eventually made it back to Dieg.[4]

The Battle of Barsana, 30 October 1773

Nawal Singh barely had time to rebuild his army before war broke out again. This time, the main opposition was the imperial forces themselves. To be sure, the Jats had not been idle, constantly trying to defend and indeed extend their territory. But Nawal Singh was not made in the same mould as the great Suraj Mal, nor even his immediate predecessor, Jawahir Singh. Nawal Singh also had the misfortune to have to contend with Najaf Khan, a soldier in imperial service who actually knew his trade. No mere courtier or sycophant, Najaf Khan had, by dint of deft financial management and hard work, created an imperial army which was actually of some use. This force of around 20,000 contained the usual Mughal cavalry and Rohilla mercenaries, rocket men, and artillery, but it also included six trained sepoy battalions on the European model.[5] One of the major reasons for the attack on the Jats was simply that the Raja was one of the wealthiest of the supposed imperial vassals who was 'guilty' of withholding his tribute to the imperial coffers. This tribute, once collected, would enable Najaf Khan to keep this new imperial army in being.

Najaf Khan's offensive against the Jat territories began in September 1773, when he began attacking their holdings closest to Delhi. The Jat house of cards collapsed with satisfying suddenness so that, after mopping up several of their garrisons, Najaf Khan was able to confront the main Jat army under the Raja himself near the city of Barsana on 30 October 1773.

The importance of this battle in our story rests on the fact that, for the first time in northern India, both armies would contain mercenary troops trained in the European manner.

The core of the Jat force was, of course, Somru's and Madec's *compoos*, which at this time, totalled nine battalions between them, all trained in the French manner.[6] These battalions formed the right wing of the Jat army and, in total, were perhaps 5,000 strong, including their artillery. The centre was formed of Jat troops, largely cavalry, with guns to their front. The guns seemed to be chained together. The left had 5,000 Hindu Naga musketeers, useful irregulars with a reputation for toughness and religious zeal.

Najaf Khan's army was formed similarly. On his right, Najaf placed 5,000 Rohilla mercenaries, largely infantry with matchlock *jezzails*, but also capable of a fierce charge, sword in hand, and with a reputation for savagery. His centre contained all of his Mughal cavalry under his protégé, Najaf Quli Khan. The left had four battalions of sepoys, with their artillery in front commanded by Raza Beg Khan and Rahim Beg. It

4 Qanungo, *History of the Jats*, pp.230–234.
5 Sarkar, *Mughal Empire*, vol.3, p.56.
6 Qanungo, *History of the Jats*, p.264.

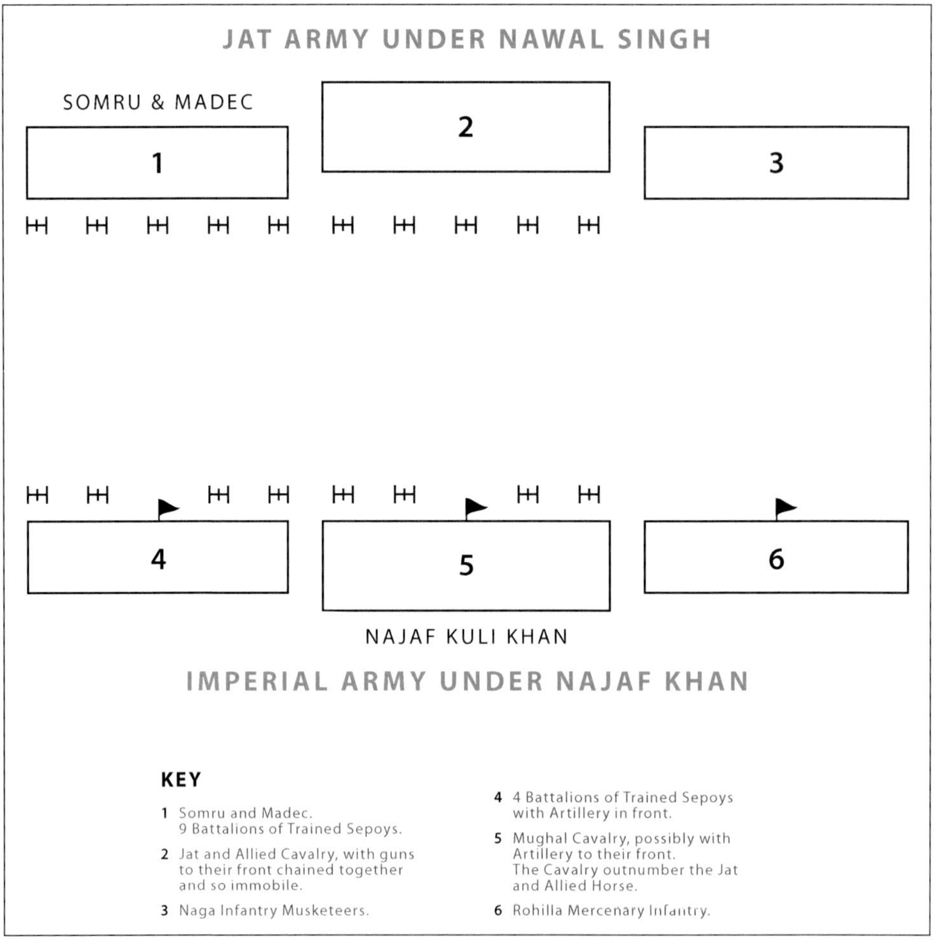

The Battle of Barsana. Initial dispositions of the two armies. (Gary Luxton © Helion & Co)

is interesting to note that the imperial 'trained brigade' does not seem to have had any European officers. This was not unusual. There would be, in later years, more *compoos* officered entirely by Indians.

The two armies were more or less evenly matched, each being around 20,000 strong. The Mughals had the advantage in cavalry, while the Jats had more regulars. However, the imperials had a commander who knew his work, while Nawal Singh had shown his nervous temperament in earlier actions.

Najaf Khan, unusually for a Mughal general, did not command from his elephant, but from horseback, so that he could encourage his men and lead help to wherever it might be needed. This seemingly minor change in 'normal' command procedure was to have useful consequences for the imperials.

As was common with Indian battles, this one began with an artillery duel. The mutual cannonade lasted for four hours. Then, with little more than an hour of daylight left,

Najaf Khan began his attack. On the imperial right, the Rohillas charged the Nagas and, after some bloody hand-to-hand fighting, put them to rout.

On the other flank, the imperial regulars were hammered by Somru's and Madec's guns as they advanced, their salvoes killing both of the sepoy's commanders.[7] Disheartened by this disaster, the imperial regulars broke and fled.

In the centre, Najaf Khan ordered a cavalry charge on the Jat centre. Nawal Singh's Jat and Rajput cavalry responded, and a bloody, swirling cavalry melee took place. The Jats captured Najaf Khan's elephant and killed the occupant, believing it to be Najaf Khan, but they were mistaken. Now, Nawal Singh's nerve once again failed him, and he fled the field in panic. Many of his cavalry then followed his example.

The seemingly victorious imperial forces, including many of their officers, now dispersed to loot the fabulously rich Jat camp. But the battle was by no means over.

Somru and Madec still stood on what had been the Jat right in compact formation. Sheltered by these orderly lines, some 500 Jat cavalry under one Jodh Raj had rallied and posed a significant threat to the now loot-hungry and disorderly imperials. Najaf Khan gathered such cavalry as were to hand (which may have been as few as 40 men)[8] and, avoiding Somru's sepoys, flung himself upon Jodh Raj's troopers. In the ensuing fight, Najaf was wounded, but Jodh Raj's men were put to flight.

Somru and Madec now remained on the field, but there was little they could do. They therefore retreated, keeping their men in formation and shooing off any inquisitive imperials with a blast of grape.

The Jat field army had ceased to exist. Much of Nawal's portable wealth had gone when his camp was looted. For Somru, it was time to look for a new employer.

In the Service of the Emperor

With the fortunes of the Jat Raja now being at something of a low ebb, it was important to Reinhardt to find new employment which would keep him away from the British. Najaf Khan, impressed by the way Somru's troops had held together at the Battle of Barsana, opened negotiations with Somru with a view to bringing his *compoo* into imperial service. This took some time, but was ultimately successful. On 20 May 1774, Somru came into imperial service.[9] His fee amounted to Rs 30,000 per month, out of which he was to pay his troops and himself. His *compoo* had suffered at the Battle of Barsana, and he was only able to bring over '5 pieces of new cannon, a considerable quantity of ammunition, about 1,900 sepoys with a few Europeans and six elephants'.[10]

Najaf Khan had wanted Somru's corps to garrison newly acquired Agra, but court intrigue meant that these now imperial troops were to be sent to Panipat to both pacify

7 Sarkar, *Mughal Empire*, vol.3, p.61.
8 Qanungo, *History of the Jats*, pp.265–266.
9 Sarkar, *Mughal Empire*, vol.3, p.64.
10 Banerji, *Begam Samru*, p.9, though Compton, *Particular Account*, p.408 states that the fee was Rs 65,000 per month.

that region and protect the frontier from the incursions of the Sikhs, whose cavalry raids were becoming more than a mere nuisance as they gained control over the Punjab and attempted to extend their territories into Hindustan. To that end, the Somru Brigade was sent to the district of Karnal, some 70 miles (112.5 km) north of Delhi. To feed and pay his troops, Somru was given the districts of Panipat and Sonnepat, from which he was to extract the resources he needed if such were possible.

A 'Romantic' Interlude

Quite when Farzana, the 'dancing girl', came into Reinhardt's life is unclear. The accepted view is that he bought her during the Jat siege of Delhi in 1764–1765.[11] The problem with that idea is simply that he was not there. As we have seen, Somru did not enter Jat service until April 1765, and the siege ended the previous February. Banerji is silent on the subject, saying only that,

> Begam Samru's uncommon beauty won the heart of that stern military adventurer so much so that he now thought more of a life of ease and pleasure than one of campaigning. The Begam made the most of this opportunity. She cleverly contrived to take away from her lord the actual exercise of all his powers. But this peaceful life he was not destined to enjoy long as death overtook him in 1778.[12]

This might imply that Somru did not acquire the girl until after the conventionally accepted date of 1765. Indeed, Herbert Compton in his *A Particular Account of the European Military Adventurers of Hindustan*, says, 'At Sardhana he fell in love with a very beautiful and very remarkable woman…'[13] This implies a somewhat later date, but Compton declines to name his source for this assertion, so the precise time of their union remains unknown.

A more modern biography has a subtly different view. After stating that Somru's *compoo* was at the Delhi siege with Jawahir Singh's forces, Julia Keay states,

> Some have claimed that Farzana herself comprised Reinhardt's share of the spoils. Wishfully portraying her as a court beauty, even a Mughal princess, they suggest that she was given to Jawahar Singh to cement the terms of his withdrawal from Delhi and that he in turn conferred her on Reinhardt. How else, they ask, could a ravishing fifteen year old have ended up in the embrace of a 'gloomy' boorish European, thirty years her senior and notable only for a string of desertions and atrocities?[14]

11 Banerji, *Begam Samru*, p.15.
12 Banerji, *Begam Samru*, p.16.
13 Compton, *Particular Account*, p.406.
14 Keay, *Farzana*, p.59.

Leaving aside the emotive and not altogether accurate content of the last line, all of the rest is quite possible, barring the 'Mughal Princess', which Farzana most certainly was not. The ancestry and early life of Farzana are likewise something of a mystery. She herself was silent upon the subject, and the biography in verse written by her secretary, Lalla Gokul Chand, in 1823 is likewise silent.[15]

The more or less accepted version of her early life, as outlined by both John Lall[16] and Julia Keay, is that she was the daughter by a second wife or concubine of a minor and impoverished nobleman, Latafat or Lutf Ali Khan. This second wife was supposedly a 'Kashmiri dancing girl called Zeldah'.[17] Latafat Khan died in 1756, when Farzana was six years old, giving the future princess a birth date of around 1750. Latafat's first wife had previously given birth to a son who, now head of the household, threw out the Kashmiri concubine and her infant daughter to fend for themselves.

We now enter the realm of 'informed speculation', for there are no direct records of Farzana's existence for the next decade. The likelihood is that the child was sold into the sex trade, quite possibly by her own mother, simply as a method of survival. This was by no means unusual in eighteenth-century India. Yet, by the time she was 15 years of age, Farzana had at least some of the 'accomplishments' of grace and charm which were deemed appropriate to 'nautch' dancers, who were far more than prostitutes:

> Common to several Indian languages and derived from the Sanskrit nautch means simply 'dance'; and just as a twenty-first century 'dancer' can be anything from a prima ballerina to a lap dancer, so an eighteenth century 'nautch girl' could be anything from a virtuoso artiste to a clumsy coquette. Yet at every level nautch girls were more than just dancers. Those at the top of their profession excelled like the Japanese geisha in such accomplishments as would appeal to the social and intellectual interests of a wealthy patron as well as those that would gratify his physical tastes.[18]

Reinhardt, immersed as he had become in Mughal culture, and no longer a young man, already had a wife, Barri Bibi, and a son – Zaffar Yab Khan – but the addition of a new, young and beautiful girl to Somru's household passed unnoticed at the time. Suffice it to say that whenever she actually joined Reinhardt's household, Farzana seems to have gained an ascendancy over the old mercenary (he was 45 in 1765) in a few short years. Whatever the precise details and timings of the transaction, Farzana became Somru's 'begum', that is to say, wife.

15 Shreeve, N. (trans.), Lala Gokul Chand, *Begam Samru: A Written Book about the History of Zeb: In Appreciation of Her Highness Farzana Zeb-un-Nissa Begum Sahib* (1823; trans. Crossbush: Convent of the Poor Clares, 1994).
16 Lall, *Fading Portrait.*
17 Keay, *Farzana*, p.14.
18 Keay, *Farzana*, p.19.

Somru's Last Campaign

The Somru Brigade did not find Karnal a congenial station. As was usual in the normally cash-strapped imperial treasury, Somru did not receive any actual money to pay his troops. As we have seen, he was assigned lands and villages from which he had to wrest the money for his *compoo*'s needs. The districts which he had been assigned to the north of Delhi had been frequently ravaged in the recent past by Marathas and Afghans during the Panipat campaign of 1760–61 and its aftermath, and then, more recently, by Sikh raids. By August 1774, Somru was writing to the Vizier (Prime Minister), Abdul Ahad Khan, complaining of the paucity of resources, but no notice was taken of his plight.[19]

In the meantime, Najaf Khan's war with the Jats continued. After a long siege, Agra – both the city and eventually the Fort – had finally fallen to the imperials. They had received significant help from the Nawab-Vizier of Oudh, Shuja-ud-Daulah, who, after coming to terms with the British, was expanding his territories wherever he might, mopping up isolated Maratha and Jat holdings. To that end, he sent a sizeable army to aid Najaf Khan, in the Emperor's name, for the siege of Agra fort. This force contained several battalions of sepoys and heavy guns under a Swiss mercenary, Major Polier. Despite Jat resistance, the fort was battered into surrender by 13 February 1774.[20]

Najaf Khan needed Reinhardt's *compoo* for the coming siege of the great Jat fortress of Dieg. This was to be Somru's last campaign. To that end, Somru's brigade was recalled from Karnal and joined the imperial army. Also present was René Madec's *compoo*, which had recently entered imperial service, as well as several thousand Mughal cavalry, plus the usual collection of irregular infantry and guns – of little use in the field, but essential in the more static environment of a siege. However, the force was barely strong enough to undertake the capture of a fortress such as Dieg, assuming it was resolutely defended.

To begin with, it was. An escalade by night was attempted in January 1776, but failed due to poor communication between the initial attacking force and its supports. Madec's *compoo*, providing the initial assault force, captured one of the fort's bastions, but could not hold it because its supports did not come up with sufficient speed, and therefore Madec's men were ejected. Once the sun rose, the Mughals, out of their trenches, faced fire from the fort's guns and a sortie from the garrison. After suffering some casualties, they panicked and began to flee. Somru came up at speed with a single battalion and two guns, the accurate fire of which drove off the Jats and enabled Somru to rescue Najaf Khan, who was found alone on the field, deserted by his own troops.[21]

The siege would drag on until 29 April 1776, when Raja Ranjit Singh would break out and flee with the remnant of his garrison. The Mughals then stormed and mercilessly sacked the defenceless fort and city.

19 Banerji, *Begam Samru*, p.10.
20 Sarkar, *Mughal Empire*, vol.3, p.65.
21 Sarkar, *Mughal Empire*, vol.3, p.73.

Somru had fought his last campaign and was rewarded with the military and civil governorship of Agra, together with a significant *jaghir* (land holding in return for military service) for the upkeep of his troops. These lands yielded an annual revenue of six lakhs of rupees (Rs 600,000): 'This Jaghir which yielded an annual revenue of six lakhs of rupees was situated in the Gangetic Doab and stretched from Aligarh to beyond Muzaffarnagar. Samru selected the village of Sardhana (12 miles north-west of Meerut) in its centre for his residence. Such was the origin of what became afterwards famous as the Principality of Sardhana.'[22]

Somru did not live long to enjoy his peaceful retirement. He died in Agra on 4 May 1778, aged 58, and was buried in the garden of his house in Agra. Three years later, the Begum Somru, now a Roman Catholic, caused his remains to be moved to the churchyard of the Portuguese Church in Agra.[23]

British historians, most notably Compton, with prim Victorian disapproval, and Bidwell and others who followed him, have given Reinhardt an evil reputation because of his direct involvement in the Patna massacre. This is overly harsh. That is not to say that he was a paragon of virtue, far from it, but Julia Keay's statement that Somru was 'notable only for a string of desertions and atrocities' (above) is to obscure the reality. He was no more 'atrocity-prone' than any other Indian or indeed mercenary commander of his time. This was a time when there were more than enough assorted atrocities to go around in the almost constant warfare of eighteenth-century India. Like most other mercenary leaders, he was loyal to his master as long as he was being paid for his services. As we have seen, he remained in Jat service for almost eight years, which directly contradicts Compton's statement that prior to entering imperial service, 'up to this period of his career Sombre had served twelve or fourteen masters.'[24]

In fact, the total seems to be five, and even this includes Gurgin Khan, the Armenian, before Somru was given his first independent command by Mir Kassim. The fourth 'master' was Shuja-ud-Daulah, the Nawab-Vizier of Oudh, in the months before the Battle of Buxar. The Nawab-Vizier and Mir Kassim were supposedly allies against the British by this time, but Mir Kassim had lost much of his value after the defeat of Udwah Nala. The Nawab-Vizier, as we have seen, took over the employment of Somru and the other trained brigades, as Mir Kassim could no longer afford their upkeep.

Whatever the precise financial arrangements, the point here is that Somru was by the standards of his time a more or less competent professional soldier who, like others of his calling, was loyal to his paymasters as long as the money lasted.

22 Banerji, *Begam Samru*, p.12.
23 Compton, *Particular Account*, p.408.
24 Compton, *Particular Account*, p.404.

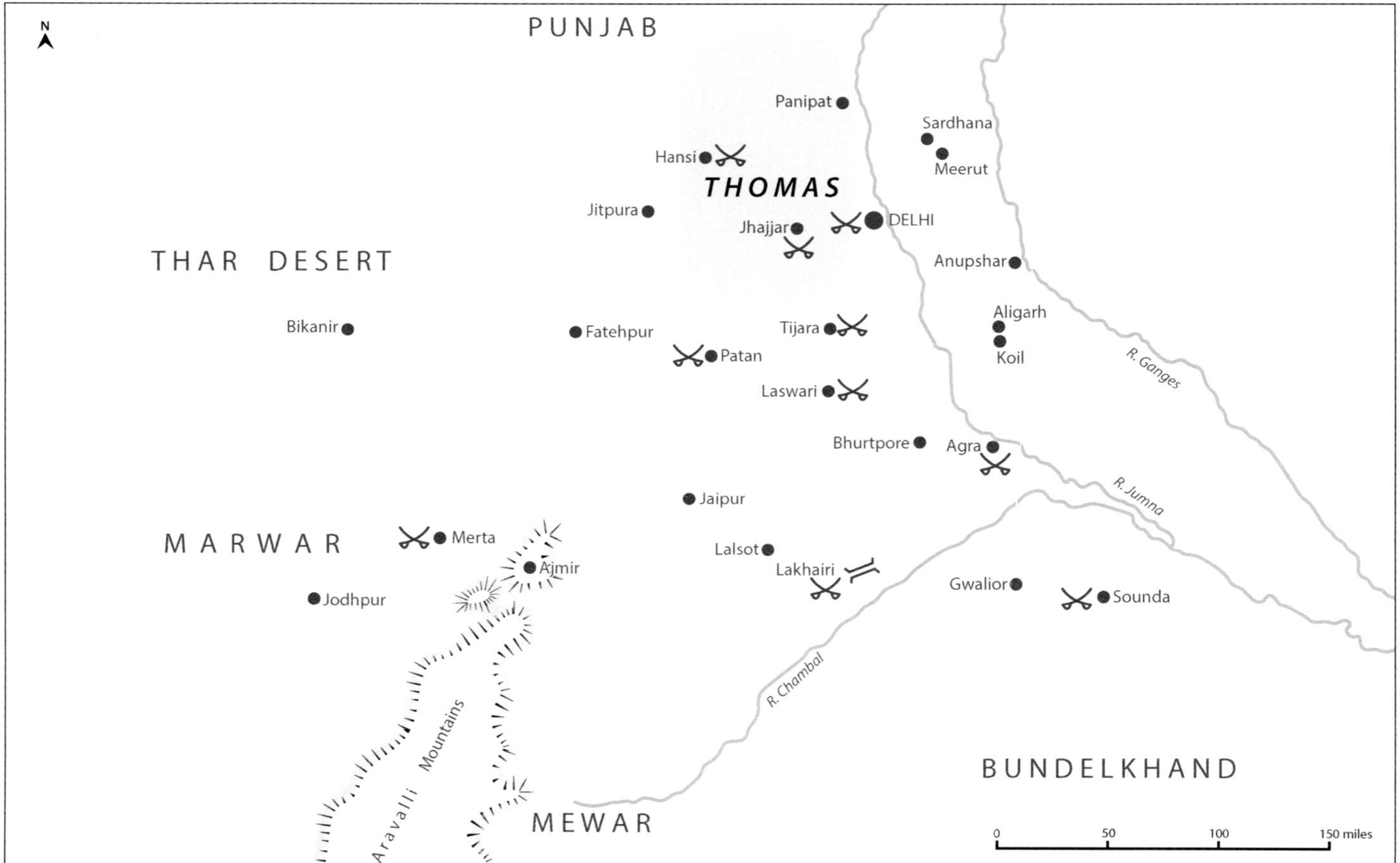

Hindustan and Rajasthan. This area saw constant campaigning in the last quarter of the eighteenth century. The shaded area shows the somewhat fluid extent of the lands that were eventually ruled by George Thomas. The map also shows Sardhana, which was the centre of Begum Somru's principality. (George Anderson © Helion & Co)

Begum Somru Takes Control

Now Somru was no more, who was to control his *compoo* and, more importantly, the *jaghir* which provided for the maintenance both of the Begum and of the Somru Brigade?

There was some confusion at first, as René Madec's surgeon relates:

> Sombre died on the sixth of this month of a neglected head-cold. The Nawab has given Sombre's titles to his son and preserved the force. It is Pauli who commands it until the younger Reynard [i.e. Somru's son] is of an age to command it himself. Sombre flatly refused to make his confession, nor would he put his affairs in any order. The only thing I could get him to do was to send for his son who came two days before his death.[25]

Somru's son by his first wife was still a minor and possibly not of sound mind. Najaf Khan had confirmed Colonel Pauli, a German mercenary who seems to have been Reinhardt's second in command, as commander of the Brigade. Yet, Farzana managed to emerge from this period with the Sardhana *jaghirs* confirmed to her, thereby gaining control over the brigade's finances. It was clear that the troops themselves did not want Somru's young son to take over.

> On the death of her husband she was requested to take command of the force by all the Europeans and Natives that composed it, as the only possible mode of keeping them together since the son was known to be altogether unfit. She consented and was regularly installed in the charge by the Emperor Shah Alam.[26]

At this time, the *compoo* – numbering possibly six battalions – was split between Delhi and Sardhana, with four battalions in Delhi and two looking after Sardhana. Four battalions seem to have been the usual size of any field force, with its accompanying artillery and possibly a *rissalah* or two of the regular cavalry. Yet Sardhana, where ultimately the troops' pay came from, needed to be garrisoned and the revenue collected.

The troops had a reputation for indiscipline, usually because Somru had kept their pay significantly in arrears, as was not uncommon in Indian armies at that time. The troops, deprived of their pay, would have no choice but to 'mutiny', which frequently meant simple refusal to do duty until they were paid at least something on account. At the siege of Dieg, for example, Najaf Khan's army was nine months in arrears.[27] Yet, despite this, the Somru Brigade were some of the best troops available to the imperial army. Najaf Khan could not afford to lose their services, whoever commanded them.

25 Keay, *Farzana*, p.90.
26 W.H. Sleeman, *Rambles and Recollections of an Indian Official* (London: Constable & Co., 1893), pp.273–274.
27 Sarkar, *Mughal Empire*, vol.3, p.74.

The Red Fort in Delhi as it appears today. This fortress was still the centre of what remained of Mughal power in the eighteenth century. (Photograph by Stanley Agar and used with his kind permission)

The Brigade's precise activities over the next few years are obscure, though it is doubtful they had time for idleness. Some of the time was definitely spent in Delhi, but, as always, the political situation lurched from drama to crisis almost continually. Najaf Khan's biggest rival at the imperial court, Abdul Ahad Khan, had made a complete mess of an expedition against those Sikh chieftains who had taken over the Sonnepat and Panipat districts and against the Sikh Raja of Patiala. Aside from some Sikh mercenaries, his army was composed of 'raw and nondescript levies'.[28] As might be expected, his mercenaries deserted him once the money ran out, and his levies, after winning one battle against Amar Singh, the Raja of Patiala, (7 October 1779), failed miserably to take his fortress, mostly because they were in a state of mutiny for arrears of pay. By 14 October, Abdul Ahad had no choice but to retreat, pursued by Sikh cavalry until he reached Panipat. What made this worse from Shah Alam's perspective was that his son, Prince Farkhunda Bakht, was with this army and was in danger of death or capture by the Sikhs. In the event, this did not happen, but panic at the imperial court caused a recall of Najaf Khan's army from its campaign to the south of Delhi suppressing rebellions and containing a new Jat offensive. It is likely that, having campaigned in this area in previous years, the Somru Brigade was in Najaf Khan's army once more, though no precise evidence has come to light.

By November 1779, Najaf Khan was once again in full control in Delhi as the Emperor's chief minister. Farzana, Colonel Pauli, and the 'field force' of the Somru

28 Sarkar, *Mughal Empire*, vol.3, p.107.

Brigade were in Delhi at this time, though they must have spent at least some of the next two years in Sardhana in order to subsist. Once again, the imperial treasury was empty and Najaf Khan, although regent, was desperately short of ready money. This was also the case for the whole machinery of government in Delhi and in Hindustan. Those nobles and rulers who had promised, usually under duress, to pay their tribute to the empire simply did not do so once the imperial army moved on to its next target. When Najaf Khan died in April 1782, yet another power struggle erupted between the four contenders, all of whom had been in the service of Najaf Khan:

> Afrasiyah Khan and Najaf Quili Khan (his two slaves) Mirza Shafi Khan (his grandnephew) and Muhammad Beg Hamadani (the Mughalia leader). The struggle for power among these four makes up the bloodred history of Delhi during the two years and a half that separate Mirza Najaf's death from the emperors willing surrender to Madhaji Scindia as his regent and commander in chief. (April 1782–November 1784).[29]

Colonel Pauli and his troops were certainly present in Delhi in 1783, as he was in the centre of affairs in the next palace revolution. Julia Keay also places Farzana in Delhi at this time: 'Seeing the Emperor's distress she detailed half her army to stay in Sardhana and moved straight back to Delhi. Here she placed Colonel Pauli and the rest of the brigade at Shah Alam's personal disposal.'[30]

Keay paints Farzana as some kind of 'imperial champion', which may or may not be true. At any event, the Begum Somru would remain in Delhi for some time, heavily involved in the deadly world of imperial politics.

Afrasiyah Khan had been appointed chief minister – Amir-al-Umara – after the death of Najaf Khan, while Mirza Shafi Khan commanded the Mughal field army and Muhammad Beg was governor of Agra. Najaf Quli Khan was also resident in Delhi as an ally of Afrasiyah Khan. September to November 1782 saw a bewildering series of coups and counter-coups in which Farzana and Colonel Pauli were deeply involved.

In August 1782, the Emperor, as always short of money, sold the office of *Mir Bakshi* –paymaster of the armies – to Mirza Shafi Khan for five lakhs of rupees (Rs 500,000), but seemingly reneged on the deal in order to have his old friend Abdul Ahad back by his side thanks to the manoeuvrings of Afrasiyah Khan. Needless to say, Mirza Shafi was furious, but did not wish to begin hostilities within the city 'out of respect for the throne'.[31] Despite this, on 21 August, a major battle within the city between Colonel Pauli's troops and some of Afrasiyah Khan's men was only averted by the Emperor forbidding any violence. A mere two days later, the Emperor was again forced to intervene to prevent the factions from commencing hostilities within the walls of Delhi.

An uneasy peace reigned for a few weeks, especially as Afrasiyah Khan had left Delhi with his troops at the Emperor's order to safeguard his own *jaghirs*, which were being

29 Sarkar, *Mughal Empire*, vol.3, p.141.
30 Keay, *Farzana*, p.121.
31 Sarkar, *Mughal Empire*, vol.3, p.150.

plundered by Muhammad Beg Hamadani, who had issued from Agra with a few thousand cavalry for just this purpose.

However, such a peace could not last. On orders from his paymaster, Mirza Shafi Khan, Colonel Pauli brought up artillery and surrounded the houses of Shafi's political rivals, Abdul Ahad Khan and Mirza Quli Khan, as well as other chiefs:

> Scarcely had Afrasiyah Khan left the city when Mirza Shuffee Khan marched in with his whole force. His success was rapid, having secured the gates and principle avenues he detached a party to surround the houses of Mujud ud Dowla, Lutafat Khan, Nujuff Cooli Khan and other chiefs attached to his rival. After a short but desperate resistance, in which several were slain these noblemen were compelled to submit.[32]

By the end of September, Mirza Shafi Khan appeared all powerful, having been confirmed in his offices by the Emperor. However, despite his attempts to reconcile the factions, secret enmities remained, including that of the Emperor himself, who wanted a reversion of those *jaghirs* that had been imperial property until given away or used by Shafi to ease his continual financial crisis.

Colonel Pauli seems to have been suborned by Lutafat Ali Khan, a eunuch in the Emperor's service, into involving the Somru brigade in the intrigue which followed. On 16 October 1782, Pauli surrounded the house where Shafi lived. However, Shafi was not there but was outside the walls of Delhi, 'that very morning exercising his troops on the sands of the Jumna'.[33]

Realising he had insufficient force at hand to fight, he prudently withdrew. This withdrawal was simply to gather his strength.

In Delhi, the Emperor invested his son, Prince Jiwan Bahkt, as Amir-al-Umara and distributed sums of money to the troops. At first, the Emperor thought he had freed himself of the restrictions imposed by the various 'over mighty subjects' who had sought to rule the empire in his name. In this, he was to be sadly mistaken.

Mirza Shafi Khan, Afrasiyah Khan, and Muhammad Beg joined forces near Muttra and worked out a division of the spoils. As they marched towards Delhi, they were joined by other partisans anxious to be on the winning side. The rebels encamped at Faridabad and sent an ambassador to seek an audience with the emperor to lay out their terms, the most important of which was the reinstatement of Mirza Shafi Khan to all of his previous offices.

In Delhi, the first reaction of the imperial council, led by the Prince, was to fight. Colonel Pauli supported the Prince in this, but the Emperor refused to give the orders, instead commanding Lutafat Khan and Colonel Pauli to enter into negotiations with the rebels. Francklin, in his history blames, 'the intrigues carrying on in the harem' for persuading the Emperor against fighting. Whatever the motives behind this craven decision, the negotiations appeared successful, but,

32 W. Francklin, Capt, *The History of the Reign of Shah-Aulum, the Present Emperor of Hindoostan* (London: Cooper and Graham, 1798), p.105.

33 Francklin, *Shah-Aulum*, p.107.

> A general reconciliation of parties being agreed to, and properly ratified by the respective signatures, Prince Mirza Jiwan Bakht accompanied by Pauli and Lutafat left the city and proceeded to the confederate armies. But scarcely had the devoted victims entered the camp, when a party of horse who had been placed in ambuscade, suddenly issuing from their concealment, attacked and dispersed the followers of the commissioners, seized and overpowered those unfortunate men, and by a bloody process struck off the head of Mr Pauli and deprived Lutafat of sight.[34]

So the Emperor was, once again, virtually a prisoner in his own palace and the Somru Brigade needed a new military commander.

The vacancy in the Somru Brigade was soon filled by Major Baours, a French officer who had been with the brigade for some time. He may have been Pauli's deputy, though this is not certain:

> Major Baours was a Frenchman and began his career in the Begum Somru's force to the command of which he succeeded in 1783 after the murder of Pauli at Delhi. When De Boigne raised his First Brigade, Baours gladly left the Begum's employ to take the command of a battalion in Sindhia's service. His career was, however, soon cut short for he was killed at the battle of Patan in 1790.[35]

Baours must have left the Begum's service around 1788 at the latest, as it was in that year that the Savoyard mercenary, Benoît de Boigne, began to raise his soon-to-be formidable 'Army of Hindustan' for the great Maratha leader Madhaji Scindia.[36]

Unlike Pauli, Baours had more sense than to involve himself directly in Mughal Court politics. The same cannot be said for his employer. The Begum seems to have become something of a favourite of the Emperor, who, in the coming years, would need all the help he could get as, once again, the rump of the Mughal Empire lurched from crisis to crisis as internal intrigue and external threats multiplied.

In the early months of 1783, the threat came from the rising power of the Sikhs.

The Sikh Attack on Delhi, March 1783

Far to the west of Delhi, in the Punjab, the Sikhs had, in the early years of the eighteenth century, finally tired of the religious persecution they received from their Mughal overlords. From mostly peaceful farmers, the Sikhs had become formidable warriors to protect their homes and religion. Their armies at this early date were not the European-trained armies that would give the British so much trouble in the mid-nineteenth

34 Francklin, *Shah-Aulum*, p.110.

35 Compton, *Particular Account*, p.338.

36 For details of de Boigne's remarkable career see Copestake, *Their Infantry and Guns will Astonish You*, p.1.

'Shah Alam on his Golden Throne', by an Indian artist. By the 1780s, it is highly unlikely that Shah Alam had a golden throne. The 'imperial magnificence' looked increasingly threadbare, as greedy and often murderous courtiers intrigued and fought over the remains of the Mughal Empire. (Public Domain)

century. Indeed, at this early date, the Sikh forces were almost entirely cavalry. Adept at the swift raid, but also capable of taking on and sometimes defeating the Mughal forces that opposed them, the Sikhs became more formidable as the eighteenth century progressed. The western frontier of Hindustan was constantly under threat from Sikh raids, which was why Somru and his troops had been sent to Karnal in 1774.

By 1783, the situation for the Mughal Empire had grown noticeably worse. There was famine in large areas of northern India due to the partial failure of the monsoon. This led to an upsurge in raiding and lawlessness,[37] which the Emperor could not alleviate due to a lack of resources.

Large Sikh raiding parties seemed to be loose within Mughal territory, pillaging almost at will. In March 1783,

> a vast Sikh horde on return from the Middle Doab threatened Delhi from the north, approaching so close to the capital as to assault the village of Barari and kill some people in Mughalpura.[38]

The Sikh version of these events is a little more complex.

This 'Sikh horde' was led by Baghel Singh and Jassa Singh Ahluwalia, and contained warriors from several different Sikh *misls* or 'Commonwealths'. These *misls* (also spelled *misals*) were the basic organisations of Sikh forces at this time.

Composed almost entirely of cavalry, each *misl*, under its *misldar* or commander, was an independent organisation, such that fighting between *misls* was not unknown. However, *misls* could and did frequently cooperate for a common aim, as they had done when harrying the retreating Afghans in the aftermath of the Battle of Panipat in 1761.

This 1783 raid was in much larger numbers than previously. Between 30 and 40 thousand men are mentioned,[39] though the lower figure is the more likely, and even that is probably inflated by the terror these warriors carried with them. Earlier raids had been with far fewer than this.

There was some consternation in Delhi. Most of the imperial forces were away on campaign. Mirza Shafi Khan was pacifying the districts around Agra, while other imperial forces were in Bhagpat. Messages were sent to these forces, but it would be some time before any kind of reaction was possible from these troops.

Baghel Singh and his army encamped at Barari Ghat, around 14 km north of Delhi,[40] sending out raiding parties to plunder the surrounding districts. There was some fighting, but the few local Mughal troops were easily defeated. On 9 March, Sikh troops entered Delhi through the Ajmeri Gate. The Emperor had no choice but to negotiate.

The chosen imperial negotiator was none other than Farzana, the Begum Somru. The Mughal Emperor had placed his trust in the one-time dancing girl.

37 Dalrymple, *The Anarchy*, p.291.
38 Sarkar, *Mughal Empire*, vol.3, p.155.
39 G.S. Mann, *The British and the Sikhs* (Warwick: Helion, 2020), p.37.
40 B. Singh, *A History of the Sikh Misals* (Croydon: CPI (UK), 2024), p.272.

Another view of the Red Fort in Delhi, showing its strength. If resolutely held, it would be a formidable place to besiege. (Photograph by Stanley Agar and used with his kind permission)

Baghel Singh and his *sardars* entered the Red Fort, the imperial palace in Delhi, on 11 March 1783. The Emperor was not present. Jassa Singh even sat on the imperial throne.[41]

Whether Begum Somru was present in Delhi at the time of the Sikh attack is not clear, but she was there by 12 March, so it is unlikely that she was in Sardhana. The bulk of the Sikh forces pulled out the same day, but Baghel Singh stayed on with 4,000 men. They restored some kind of order on the streets. Though it seems likely that any battalions of the Somru Brigade who may have been in Delhi were acting as guards in the Red Fort, this comes under the heading of 'informed speculation', as most of the imperial troops were campaigning around Agra.

Nevertheless, an agreement of sorts was put together:

> Therefore did Begam Samru send the messengers
> To Baghel Singh with elephants loaded with palanquins of gold.
> As the Mughal messengers brought Baghel Singh along with them
> Baghel Singh's forces put up their camp near Delhi.
> Thus was Begum Samru instrumental in negotiating a deal.
> Between Baghel Singh and the Delhi Ruler with solemn vows.
> Baghel Singh got a written deal signed by the King.
> That he would permit the construction of seven (ancient) Sikh shrines.[42]

41 Singh, *Sikh Misals*, p.273.
42 Chronicle of Rattan Singh Bangu as quoted in Mann, *The British and the Sikhs*, p.40.

Although the building of the shrines appears as the most important of the agreement's terms, the Sikh forces received an immediate cash payment of three lakhs of rupees (Rs 300,000), as well as 'expenses' for the building of the shrines, which according to the treaty must be completed by the end of 1783.[43]

Baghel Singh and his 4,000 men remained in Delhi until December 1783, leaving once the shrines were completed. In reality, he had little choice. His 4,000 horse could not control the city indefinitely, so he was gone by the end of 1783. The 'treaty' barely lasted until the ink was dry. Sikh plundering raids continued into Mughal territory to the north of Delhi, with supposedly up to 30,000 men in these raiding forces.[44]

Mughal efforts to stem these raids were to no avail, and much of the country north of Delhi was devastated. Zabita Khan, commanding a Mughal force which seems to have included two *paltans* of regulars and at least some 'friendly' Sikh mercenaries, was beaten in battle. This beaten force was later joined by more troops, including 'four battalions of sepoys. A thousand Mughalia horse and a thousand Sikh auxiliaries'.[45] These four battalions must have come from the Somru Brigade, as they are noted as being with the army on 23 December. Arrangements were being made between Zabita Khan and Afrasiyah Khan for Zabita to defend the upper Doab north of Delhi from further Sikh raids, but the bulk of the army was back in Delhi by the end of January 1784.[46]

The Emperor was, as usual, in a quandary. At one point, he had hoped to gain the support of the British East India Company, but when Warren Hastings was recalled in 1784, those hopes evaporated. He now turned to his last hope. Madhaji Scindia, the Maratha ruler of Ujain, was arguably the most powerful leader within the Maratha Confederacy, that squabbling collection of Hindu rulers whose territories lay across central India. In theory, the overall ruler of this confederacy was the *Peshwa*, based in the city of Poona (Pune), but in practice the main houses of the Confederation had de facto independence. After the disastrous Battle of Panipat in 1761, where much of the then Maratha leadership was wiped out, Scindia of Ujain and Holkar of Indore paid only the barest lip service to the *Peshwa*. Other smaller houses, such as Angria and Baroda, behaved in like manner, as their strength waxed or waned in the endless whirligig of Maratha politics.

Madhaji Scindia was by far the most astute of these rulers in the last quarter of the eighteenth century, and he was far too clever to take the obvious 'poisoned chalice' of the supreme office of vizier. Instead, he had the office and title of *Vakil-ul-Mutluq* (vice-regent of the Empire) conferred upon his nominal overlord, the 10-year-old *Peshwa*, while he, Madhaji Scindia, would humbly serve as the *Peshwa*'s deputy. Scindia took up the office in November 1784. Of course, everyone saw through the fiction. Scindia was now de facto ruler of the Empire.

Needless to say, the appointment of a Hindu Maratha to high office in the Mughal Empire excited considerable opposition from those Muslim nobles who thought such

43 Singh, *Sikh Misals*, p.273.
44 Singh, *Sikh Misals*, p.274.
45 Sarkar, *Mughal Empire*, vol.3, p.162.
46 Sarkar, *Mughal Empire*, vol.3, p.162.

offices were theirs alone to squabble over. Scindia's position was far from secure, though this was not at first apparent, as first Agra and then Aligarh fell to him by a combination of military action and naked bribery. Furthermore, the government in Delhi was restored to something approaching order and the imperial household granted sufficient funds for its upkeep, at least some of which was actually paid. For a time at least, something close to peace resided uneasily in Hindustan.

This was not to last. Uncharacteristically, Scindia made a political blunder by trying to deprive Mughal officers of their *jaidads* – landholdings set aside specifically for the payment of troops – to replace them with Maratha officers so that they could pay their own Maratha troops. Scindia was at this time by no means as financially secure as he would later become, and his poor financial straits caused him to overreach himself. There was also a rupture with Partab Singh, the Raja of Jaipur, who was soon in alliance with those Mughal noblemen who opposed Scindia, such as Muhammad Beg Hamadani and his nephew Ismael Beg.

These machinations resulted in the Battle of Lalsot or Tunga, fought on 28 July 1787, where, despite the steadiness of two European-led *compoos* under the mercenaries de Boigne and Lestineau and the death of Muhammad Beg Hamadani, Scindia's Marathas were narrowly defeated.[47]

The Somru Brigade was not directly involved in this campaign, even though Scindia had confirmed and even added to Farzana's *jaghirs* for her continued support of the Emperor. Some of the brigade were stationed at Panipat to secure the frontier against the Sikh raids, and apparently Farzana was with them, according to Francklin.[48]

However, the reversal of Maratha fortunes as a result of the Battle of Tunga created a power vacuum in Delhi, into which the singularly unpleasant Ghulam Kadir inserted himself. This Rohilla chieftain had succeeded his father, Zabita Khan, as lord of Seharunpore and had determined that those offices held as part of the Delhi government by his predecessor were his by right. He is described by Francklin as 'proud, cruel and ferocious',[49] which – judging by his later actions – was possibly far too kind a verdict.

He now determined to enter Delhi and to claim his self-asserted rights to the government. He expected to have aid from fellow plotters within the imperial palace, most notably the Emperor's *nazir*, or Superintendent of the Household, one Munsur Ali Khan, who seems to have been Ghulam Kadir's creature. Kadir approached Delhi with a Rohilla army. A mismanaged attempt by the garrison to engage the Rohillas in battle outside of the city only resulted in the defeat of the imperial forces. At this, most of the remaining Maratha officials fled, and Ghulam Kadir entered the city and the imperial palace in the Red Fort, and into the imperial presence. Shah Alam could do little to stop him, but Kadir still lacked influence at court, and to that end, he proposed an alliance between himself and the Begum Somru. But, as Franklin pithily explains:

47 Copestake, *Their Infantry and Guns*, pp.48–52.
48 Francklin, *Shah-Aulum*, p.151.
49 Francklin, *Shah-Aulum*, p.139.

Another view of the Red Fort, showing the strength of the walls. It would take treachery within the emperor's court for Ghulam Kadir to take the Red Fort. (Photograph by Stanley Agar and used with his kind permission)

> The prospect was tempting; but the Begum, well acquainted with the characteristic perfidy of the Rohilla and resolved to defend her sovereign; rejected all his solicitations; and to give proof of her determination to maintain the king's authority, she with her whole force repaired to the palace and declared her intention of sacrificing her life in his majesty's cause.[50]

Ghulam Kadir was with his army outside the city, on the other side of the Jumna River, and was so incensed by Farzana's actions that he began to bombard the Red Fort. The Fort's guns on the ramparts replied, aided by the guns of the Somru Brigade – 'a battery which had been erected with great expedition by Begum Somroo'.[51]

The arrival of a Mughal army close to Delhi, under Prince Mirza Bakht, put an end to the fighting, and caused Kadir to attempt negotiation instead. This was aided by the treachery of Munsur Ali Khan, who gave prior notice to Kadir of the approach of the imperial army. A sort of peace was patched up, whereby Kadir promised to return the *jaghirs* he had usurped and gave a fulsome apology for the insult of firing upon the imperial palace. It was unlikely that he would keep his word, but it gave him time to retire from Delhi and return with his army to Seharunpore.

50 Francklin, *Shah-Aulum*, p.152.
51 Francklin, *Shah-Aulum*, p.152.

This event did not grant Shah Alam more than a short breathing space, for despite the manful efforts of his son, the prince, the financial situation was once again dire. The troops clamoured for their arrears of pay, such that the Emperor was more or less forced to leave Delhi with such troops as he had – including those of the Begum Somru, who accompanied the Emperor herself – on a campaign to collect revenue.

Included in this army was a new European recruit to the Somru Brigade who had arrived in Delhi from the south of the subcontinent sometime in 1787 – a tall Irishman who had been a sailor in the Royal Navy, George Thomas.

5

Enter An Irish Sailor

George Thomas and his Early Career with the Somru Brigade

George Thomas arrived in India in 1781–82, supposedly as a quartermaster or perhaps a gunner,[1] a common sailor, or even a cabin boy in one of Admiral Hughes's ships,[2] deserting when Hughes's squadron touched at Madras. Britain was at war once again with France, and the East India Company was at war with Haidar Ali of Mysore, a soldier of skill and daring. Furthermore, Hughes's fleet would also have to contend with one of France's greatest admirals, Suffren. Desertion from the Royal Navy was no easy task, so quite how Thomas deserted at Madras – which was an open roadstead rather than a proper port with wharfs and docking facilities – if indeed he did, is unclear. His own memoir, told to Captain William Francklin in 1802 or thereabouts, is virtually silent on the subject.

Drawing a picture of the early years of this astonishing adventurer is no easy task, and some of what follows is conjecture based upon a few hints scattered about the available sources.

Thomas was born around 1756 in Roscrea, County Tipperary, in what is now the Irish Republic, but was then, of course, under British control. That is almost all we know, with any degree of certainty, of Thomas in Ireland. Maurice Hennessy constructs an early life for Thomas as an oppressed Irish peasant who runs away,[3] first to work in Youghal docks (where the name George Thomas appears as a worker in the account books),[4] then to sea, to escape the drudgery of a peasant farmer. This is certainly possible, but since he does not reveal his sources for this assertion other than an airy wave to 'local tradition' it may be mostly guesswork. Other possibilities, such as that put forward by Keene,[5] may be equally likely. However, while Thomas is not a common Irish name, his

1 C. Grey, *European Adventurers of Northern India 1785–1849* (Lahore: Punjab Government, 1929; repr. New Delhi: Asian Educational Services, 1993), p.36.
2 'An Authentic Account of GEORGE THOMAS, an Irish Adventurer in India, a most extraordinary and Enterprising Character. Just received from a Correspondent at Lucknow', in *The Asiatic Annual Register* (London, 1802), p.55.
3 M. Hennessy, *The Raja from Tipperary* (New York: St. Martin's Press, 1971).
4 Hennessy, *The Raja*, p.8.
5 H.G. Keene, *Hindustan under Free Lances* (London: Brown, Langham & Co., 1907), p.75.

family does appear to have been Roman Catholic,[6] so having him descended from one of Cromwell's Protestant 'colonists' does not seem probable.

However, whatever George Thomas's ancestry actually was, it did not stop him from appearing in India, possibly as a deserter from Admiral Hughes's fleet in 1782, or even as a 'cabin boy' on a merchant ship, as mentioned, without naming a source, by Compton.[7]

As his biographer, Captain William Francklin, put it in the opening chapter of Thomas's memoirs: 'From the best information we could procure it appears that Mr. George Thomas first came to India in a British ship of war, in 1781–2. His situation in the fleet was humble, having served as a quarter master, or, as is affirmed by some, in the capacity of a common sailor.'[8]

Captain Francklin knew Thomas in his later years, and Thomas would dictate much of his memoirs to Francklin in the months before his death. The memoir is the major original source for Thomas's career and, despite the good Captain's often pedestrian style, still repays careful study. However, Thomas's own account does not begin until 1787 when he appears in Delhi in the service of the Begum Somru. The intervening five or six years are something of a mystery.

Francklin fills the gap with a single sentence: 'His first service was among the Polygars to the southward where he resided a few years – but at length, setting out overland he spiritedly traversed the central part of the Peninsula and about the year 1787 arrived at Delhi.'[9]

What happened during the 'missing years' can only be speculated upon, though Hennessy does provide the odd clue based upon the information he had from Lieutenant Colonel John Eadie, who had conversations with Thomas's surviving descendants in India in the 1920s.[10] His initial service with that assorted collection of petty Rajas in the Carnatic known as Poligars must have been something of a hard school. The various chiefs of the border areas between British territory and that of the Nizam of Hyderabad, known as Kanara, were a somewhat lawless bunch, quite capable of playing off the British and the Mughals against each other and engaging in almost constant petty warfare amongst themselves. They also conducted cattle and even slave raiding on the more 'settled' districts, though anyone deemed wealthy enough was held for ransom rather than servitude. The British sometimes paid them off and sometimes chastised them, but never really subdued them until the following century. Thomas, therefore, appears to have been no more than a bandit at this time.

After some time, Thomas moved on – we have no idea why or even how long with any degree of certainty – into the service of the Nizam of Hyderabad. Hennessy implies that he became a gunner, and this is by no means impossible. The 'blueprint' for the 'trained brigades' at this time gave each trained artillery crew a 'European'

6 Hennessy, *The Raja*, p.7.

7 Compton, *Particular Account*, p.109.

8 William Francklin, *The Military Memoirs of Mr. George Thomas, who, by Extraordinary talents and Enterprise Rose from An Obscure Situation to the Rank of General in the Service of the Native Powers in the North West of India* (Calcutta: Hurkaru Press, 1803), p.2.

9 Francklin, *Military Memoirs*, p.2.

10 Hennessy, *The Raja*, pp.xiv–xv.

gunner for each artillery piece in the *compoo*. Thomas's time in the Royal Navy would have given him at least a basic familiarity with artillery, and perhaps much more, but other than Grey's reference, any concrete details are lacking. There is not even agreement on how long he spent in the service of the Nizam. Grey says six months.[11] Compton gives this a single sentence: 'he took service as a private soldier in the army of Nizam Ali Khan.'[12] Thomas's own biographer, Francklin, never mentions it. Hennessy seems to conflate Thomas's service with the Poligars and the Nizam while also giving Thomas a band of *Pindaris* to command. *Pindaris*, in this context, were essentially mounted bandits, preying on villages and any likely target, such as travellers, that their eye might light upon. Again, this is by no means impossible and is even given some little indirect support by no less a contemporary source than Captain, later Major, Lewis Ferdinand Smith, who knew Thomas personally later in his meteoric career: 'Thomas commenced his ambitious career in 1794 after he left the Begum Sombre's service by collecting a few men near Delhi, with whom he stormed a large village.'[13]

Although Smith dates this action as 1794, the idea that Thomas was capable of such a raid and had the experience to carry it out successfully, lends some little colour to Hennessy's narrative, which he once again supports by reference to the mysterious Colonel Eadie giving Thomas a band of desperadoes which Hennessy refers to as 'Irish *Pindaris*' for his journey north to Delhi.[14]

Whatever the precise details of Thomas's early career, and no matter how disreputable they may have been, he arrived in Delhi in 1787 and 'received a commission in the service of the Begum Sumroo'.[15] As always, that enterprising lady needed European officers and gunners for her *compoo*, and Thomas remained in her service for almost five years, becoming in Francklin's words, 'In various successive actions against the Sikhs and others of the Begum's enemies, Mr. Thomas, by his courage and perseverance rendered her Authority respectable. By these successes he obtained a considerable influence over the mind of his mistress, and was for some time, her chief advisor and counsellor.'[16]

Compton puts it both rather more gently, but with more than a little Victorian archness:

> The only body of regular troops in Hindustan was that belonging to the Begum Somru, to whom Thomas offered his services. She held the fief of Sardhana, a district lying about forty-five miles north of Delhi, where her troops were cantoned. Thomas's application was entertained and he was appointed to a subordinate command in the Begum's army. Before long this handsome Irishman attracted his mistress's attention. He was a tall soldierly fellow endowed with a pleasing address

11 Grey, *European Adventurers*, p.37.
12 Compton, *Particular Account*, p.110.
13 Smith, *Regular Corps*, p.20.
14 Hennessy, *The Raja*, p.37.
15 Francklin, *Military Memoirs*, p.2.
16 Francklin, *Military Memoirs*, pp.2–3.

> for one of his station and gifted with the honeyed speech of his countrymen, and, except when his temper was aroused, gentle in his manners, though not without that dash and spirit which always commends itself to womankind.[17]

Despite Compton's coyness, the inference is clear – Farzana and George became lovers. There is no clear evidence, of course, but it is entirely possible and would be given some additional weight by later events as they unfolded. Yet, there is considerable doubt if Thomas ever actually commanded the Somru Brigade as a whole. Sleeman, who lists all of the brigade's commanders up until Le Vaisseau,[18] does not mention Thomas in this context, nor does Thomas himself mention or imply that he ever commanded the brigade. Indeed, his first 'commission' may have been simply as the 'European gunner' in one of the Somru Brigade's artillery units, the usual custom being to have a European 'gun captain' in an otherwise Indian gun crew. Thomas never mentions any rank he may have held in the Somru Brigade, though later on in his service, as we shall see, as governor of Tappal he must have commanded at least a battalion and possibly more, but that was still to come.

A Time of Constant Warfare

As we have seen in the previous chapter, these years were perilous ones for the rump of the Mughal Empire, as the various factions sought either to control the Emperor or carve out an independent state for themselves. The rising power of the Sikhs menaced the north-western borders of the surviving imperial territory of Hindustan. The Marathas sought to control the Emperor, and thus the Empire, and the various Mughal nobles fought for power and wealth amid the wreckage of that once mighty empire. Warfare and campaigning were continuous. This would range from 'simple' revenue collection – for in these perilous times the taxman, of whichever kind, had to levy the taxes sword in hand – to full-dress campaigns such as those against the Jats. The Begum's troops were in the thick of this, but there were never enough of them. The 'field force' only rarely seems to have exceeded four battalions and perhaps 20 guns. The remainder, one or two battalions plus the cavalry regiment and a varying number of irregular *seebundies*,[19] were used to garrison Sardhana and keep the Begum's territories protected from harm.

Thomas and the Begum herself were at this time in Delhi, with probably three battalions. In 1787, there was yet another crisis for the Empire, and the Emperor was, as usual, in dire financial straits.

In order to repair his finances, Shah Alam was making one of his rare journeys outside the city of Delhi, receiving the submission of local rulers who had, perceiving the weakness of the Delhi government, refused their usual tribute for several years. Most submitted rapidly at the appearance of the imperial army, but the strong fort

17 Compton, *Particular Account*, p.110.
18 Sleeman, *Rambles and Recollections*, p.603.
19 *Seebundies*: irregular troops most often used as revenue collectors.

Another photograph of the Red Fort as it appears today. It is doubtful that George Thomas was as overawed by the magnificence of the structure as many of today's tourists. (Photograph by Stanley Agar and used with his kind permission)

of Gokulgarh, held by Najaf Kuli Khan, once an imperial minister of state, refused to submit. Instead, the khan tried to negotiate his way back to power. This included offering a payment of six lakhs of rupees (Rs 600,000) to the Emperor in return for the restoration of Najaf Kuli Khan to power in Delhi. The members of the imperial Council saw no reason why they should let their rival back into power and persuaded the Emperor against this offer. The decision was therefore taken to besiege the fort of Gokulgarh.

Captain Francklin, in his contemporary *History of the Reign of Shah Alam*, takes up the story:

> The royal army at this time composed of several battalions of Nujibs,[20] the body-guard called the red battalion; a very considerable body of Mughal horse; and three disciplined battalions of Sepoys, which had belonged to the late Sumroo and were then commanded by his Begum in person and furnished with a respectable artillery served by European cannoneers. The Headquarters of Najaf Quli Khan were in a village about one mile distant from the fort. The remainder of his force under

20 *Nujibs, nejeebs*: matchlock-armed infantry.

the command of Munsur Khan were stationed in Gokulgarh. The rebel entrenchments being strongly fortified his majesty directed Raja Himmat Bahadur and Shah Mir Khan, with a chosen detachment to erect batteries against the village. And with the remainder of his army, he, in person, invested the fort of Gokulgarh. The batteries of Himmat Bahadur soon commenced a vigorous fire on Najaf Quli Khan's entrenched post.

The Officers who served in the camp of Himmat Bahadur, disgusted at their absence from their comrades in the grand army, and harassed by incessant duty in the trenches, forgot the danger of their situation and abandoned themselves to the most licentious excess; nor could all the admonition or threats of their commander prevail on them to desist; they passed the whole night in riot and debauchery, and the soldiers, availing themselves of the pernicious example indulged themselves in similar excess. Najaf Quli Khan who was equally brave as vigilant, informed by his spies of what was transacting, resolved to profit by the enemy's neglect and folly; having selected a strong detachment of cavalry, he put himself at their head, and marching in silence out of his entrenchment he fell with great violence upon the royal troops as they lay buried in sleep, and under the influence of their late debauch. A dreadful and indiscriminate slaughter now took place, the lines were instantly carried, and a very large booty acquired by the soldiers of Najaf Quli Khan. The terror excited by this extraordinary attack was so great, that the news being communicated to the main body of the king's army, they were thrown into disorder, and began to prepare for flight; nor did the mischief end there, for to increase the dismay, just at the moment the lines were carried, Munsur Khan, who commanded in Gokulgarh, by a preconcerted agreement with Najaf Quli Khan, issued out of the town with a strong detachment and four pieces of cannon. Having by a circuitous route reached the rear of the royal army, he commenced a very heavy fire from his artillery; the confusion in camp now increased tenfold; everything was uproar, disorder and dismay. The king himself was, by this manoeuvre exposed to the greatest personal danger, and the royal tents, being within range of the shot, many persons about his majesty were killed and wounded. In this distracted state the king was advised to remove with the royal family, (there being at this time six princes in the camp) to the Herawul or advanced guard of the army, which was without the range of the enemy's cannon. To that spot on the first alarm Shah Mir Khan had repaired, and was endeavouring by his presence and example to animate and rally the flying troops. The king's tents were accordingly struck and Shah Alam, accompanied by his family proceeded to the advance guard. But the misfortune was now happily remedied by the magnanimity and gallantry of Begum Somru. That spirited woman was encamped to the right of the line; her force remained entire, unaffected by the general panic, and stood ready in dressed ranks. On perceiving the extreme confusion that reigned throughout the line, she bravely resolved, by a personal effort, to prevent the king's disgrace she sent a respectful message to his majesty, desiring him to repair to her quarters, and assured him of her determined resolution to punish the rebel, or perish in the attempt...

> The gallant lady, then getting into her palanquin. Placed herself at the head of 100 of her own sepoys, accompanied by a six pounder commanded by an European officer. With this detachment she proceeded to the spot occupied by Munsur Khan, and advancing upon the rebel with much spirit, she commanded her palanquin to be set down, and ordered her artillery to charge with grape shot; a well-directed fire from the gun assisted by volleys of small arms from the sepoys, soon had the desired effect. Munsur Khan astonished at this sudden and unexpected check began to give ground and having lost numbers of his men, he retreated with precipitation under the walls of the fort. The king's troops having now time to breathe, were rallied, under the direction of Himmat Bahadur and Shah Mir Khan; most of them having rejoined their standards, attacked the enemy, in their turn with great spirit, when after a short but desperate conflict Najaf Quli Khan was compelled to retire.[21]

The 'European officer', unnamed in Francklin's narrative, was George Thomas, as Francklin later explained:

> Among other brilliant acts performed by Mr. Thomas during his service with the Begum was the circumstance related in the History of Shah Alam. The compiler of these memoirs did not know, at the time, that Mr. Thomas was the Officer who commanded the party. But that Gentleman, during his Residence at Benares communicated a detail of the affair, with a slight variation, in a few particulars, happened as is stated in the printed Work.[22]

The actions of the Begum Somru and George Thomas had turned the tide of battle and, indeed, had quite possibly saved the Mughal Emperor's life. Not only that, but dispirited by this defeat, Najaf Kuli Khan soon afterwards came to terms with the Emperor, aided by the 'good offices' of the Begum Somru.[23]

The Emperor was grateful for his deliverance. He rewarded the Begum: 'clothed her in a magnificent vest, and, in addition to her former titles honoured her with the appellation of 'his most beloved daughter'.[24]

Farzana, the dancing girl, was now a member of the imperial family. She was also granted more lands, the *purganah* (district) of Badshahpur, which was granted to her 'in perpetuity', and the district of Tappal on the eastern bank of the Jumna as a *jaghir*, for which she would need a military governor she could trust.[25]

As for Thomas, this action seems to have begun his rise in the Begum's service. Precise details are sparse, to say the least, but at some time he was made governor of Tappal, the Begum's new *jaghir*, but this may not have been immediate.

21 Francklin, *Shah-Aulum*, pp.165–168.
22 Francklin, Footnote in *Military Memoirs*, p.3.
23 Francklin, *Shah-Aulum*, p.169.
24 Francklin, *Shah-Aulum*, p.169.
25 Keay, *Farzana*, p.159.

Indeed, the Somru Brigade is absent from the record of Delhi events for some time, and it seems likely that the troops had either returned to Sardhana with their mistress or perhaps back to Panipat to guard the frontier against the Sikhs. In any event, it seems unlikely that the *compoo* could have been in Delhi when Ghulam Kadir returned and attempted to seize the imperial throne by force in July 1788. The Emperor had already sent orders for Madhaji Scindia to return to Delhi, but for reasons of his own Scindia dallied in the execution of his supposed overlord's command and would not be in time to stop Kadir's barbarities. Scindia did, however, send a body of 2,000 horse under Ravloji Scindia, one of his kinsmen, but as was usual, treachery within the imperial household was rife, even to the extent of sending wagonloads of powder and shot to Kadir's army from the magazines within the Red Fort:[26]

> At first Shah Alam took up a strong attitude of opposition to the Ruhela and ordered the city to be held against him. But he had no longer the efficient corps of the Begum Samru at his back. His only generals were Himmat Bahadur Gosain and Badal Beg the Mughalia leader. The exactions of Gosain had roused the entire Delhi population against him and his troops were also weakened by starvation. Badal Beg and the entire Muslim force at Delhi were corrupted by Ghulam Qadir through his friends at court.[27]

Faced by this, the Maratha force withdrew, and Kadir's army took possession of the city by 18 July 1788.

Kadir was now in possession of the city and of the Red Fort. During the next two months, he would loot the palace, sexually assault the imperial princesses and deliberately humiliate the imperial princes by making them dance before him.[28] He would also personally blind the Emperor with his own hands and set up puppet Emperors to do his bidding. His Mughal 'allies', disgusted by his conduct, would desert him. Ismael Beg even formed a very temporary alliance with Scindia as the lesser of two evils, until finally a large Maratha army under Rana Khan, one of Scindia's best commanders, would reconquer Delhi and break the hold of Ghulam Kadir.

So where was the Somru Brigade?

Julia Keay has Farzana and Thomas going to the new *jaghir* of Tappal, which is certainly possible, as that new territory would have to be pacified and brought under control by its new mistress.[29] Their stay in Tappal is not otherwise recorded. If there, they could not have stayed too long, as they were back in the environs of Delhi by late September 1788 with Rana Khan's army,[30] driving the Rohillas first into the city of Delhi and then into the Red Fort itself by 2 October.

26 Sarkar, *Mughal Empire*, vol.3, p.262.
27 Sarkar, *Mughal Empire*, vol.3, p.263.
28 M. Edwardes, *King of the World: The Life of the Last Great Moghul Emperor* (London: Secker & Warburg, 1970), p.204.
29 Keay, *Farzana*, pp.162–163.
30 Sarkar, *Mughal Empire*, vol.3, p.275.

This army was something of a polyglot affair, containing as it did, large bodies of the usual Maratha cavalry, very adept at raiding, but not always as reliable in a stand-up fight. Also present were the original two battalions of the soon-to-be much larger mercenary *compoo* of the Savoyard mercenary Benoît de Boigne.[31] This was probably the first time these two forces – de Boigne's and Begum Somru's – had met, but it would be by no means be the last. Other troops in the army included Ismael Beg's Mughals and another mercenary *compoo* of three battalions under the French mercenary Lestineau, who had Pierre Cuillier Perron and Louis Borquien as junior officers.[32] Both of these French officers would later play major parts in Thomas's story. We cannot know, but one is forced to wonder if Thomas and Perron first encountered each other during this campaign, thus beginning what would, at least in Thomas's case, become a deep distrust of Perron to add to his dislike of French officers in general.

Kadir was now in serious trouble, yet he managed to transfer much of his booty out of the city and over the Jumna River, though the convoy was seemingly looted by a Sikh raiding party aided by the Marathas,[33] whose light cavalry were scouring the area. Kadir abandoned Delhi in order to protect his *jaghirs* on the eastern side of the Jumna from these raiders. He still visited the Red Fort to extort the last dregs of any valuables that he could extract from the imperial family, but on 10 October 1788 a shattering explosion occurred in the powder magazine of the fort due to negligence. This calamity forced Kadir to finally abandon the place, taking several members of the imperial family with him as hostages.

Rana Khan entered the fort on the following day and immediately released the blind and starving Shah Alam from the prison where Kadir had held him for the previous two and a half months. The Marathas restored at least a semblance of the imperial dignity as Shah Alam regained his throne.

De Boigne's battalions were left to garrison Delhi, along with some Maratha horse, but by the beginning of November 1788, the pursuit of Ghulam Kadir had begun in earnest. The Somru Brigade, including George Thomas, was with Rana Khan's army. This must have been Thomas's first full campaign with considerable forces – perhaps a steep learning curve, which Thomas seems to have negotiated rather well, to judge by his later military exploits.

The mopping up of Kadir's possessions also continued apace. On 20 November, his fortress at Aligarh fell to the Marathas. This was a severe blow to Kadir, as Aligarh was his main magazine. His main problem now became one of supply. Bands of Maratha horse were cutting off the food supplies to his remaining troops. He could still beat these raiders in a stand-up fight,[34] but could not supply his army.

Finally, he was cornered in his fortress at Meerut, where at first he stood a siege, but again lack of supplies forced his hand. His garrison was starving, so on the night of 17 December 1788, he broke out with 500 horse. The party encountered a Maratha patrol

31 Duff, *History of the Mahrattas*, vol.1, p.147.
32 Copestake, *Their Infantry and Guns*, p.77.
33 Sarkar, *Mughal Empire*, vol.3, p.275.
34 Sarkar, *Mughal Empire*, vol.3, p.277.

under Jiva Dada, who pursued. Kadir was separated from his escort and fell from his horse when the poor beast put its hoof into a hole in the dark and broke a leg. Kadir found shelter with a Brahmin, who gave away his presence to the Marathas. He was captured on 19 December 1788.[35]

Taken back to Delhi, his fate was a grisly one,

> Ghulam's ears were cut off and hung around his neck. With his face blackened he was paraded around the city in a bullock cart. Next day his nose and lips were cut off and again he was shown to the city. The following day his eyeballs were torn out and yet again he was placed in a cart and trundled slowly through the streets. His eyes were followed by his hands and then his feet. Finally his head was cut off and his corpse was hung upside down from a tree.[36]

The eyes, nose and lips were sent to the restored emperor, as proof that justice had been done upon this 'scourge of God'. His body disappeared from the tree where it had been hung after four days, taken, so it was said, by his true master, the devil.[37]

Madhaji Scindia was now the real ruler of Hindustan. He and his mercenary army would institute a period of relative peace, which would last for over a decade. De Boigne would eventually become the de facto ruler of Hindustan under the auspices of the House of Scindia. His mercenaries replaced the Somru Brigade as the emperor's guards and security. The old, blind emperor would know more peace than he had known for years.

As for the Somru Brigade, the 'field force' returned from the campaign and siege of Meerut either at the very end of 1788 or early in 1789. There was some little doubt over the continuation of Begum Somru's *jaghirs*, but this was soon dispelled when the Emperor confirmed all of her possessions and bestowed upon her another hollow but perhaps pleasing title, *Umdat-al-Arakin*, Pillar of the State.[38]

Thomas was, of course, with the 'field force' at this time, which Dalrymple puts at a single battalion commanded by Thomas,[39] which is rather unlikely, as both infantry and guns would be required for the siege of Meerut. Also, Thomas, with less than two years' service with the brigade, was probably too junior for such a command, despite his talents. There is no certainty here, but it is more probable that either Baours, assuming he was still with the brigade, or Evans, who succeeded Baours in command of the brigade, commanded the 'field force' for this campaign. Even if we assume that the brigade cavalry and one or two battalions acted as Farzana's escort in Delhi, and this is speculation, that would still leave two or three battalions plus an artillery train as the field force for the pursuit of Kadir, and more particularly the siege of Meerut. Surely this was too large a command for an officer as junior as Thomas when others were present.

35 Sarkar, *Mughal Empire*, vol.3, p.279.
36 Edwardes, *King of the World*, p.209.
37 Edwardes, *King of the World*, p.210.
38 Keay, *Farzana*, p.196.
39 Dalrymple, *The Anarchy*, p.301.

Whatever the actuality, once the campaign was over, we lose sight of Thomas and Farzana for some time. We are not, however, entirely ignorant of the command problems within the Somru Brigade. Baours left sometime in 1788 or 1789 to be succeeded by Evans, who was possibly English. He does not seem to have lasted very long and he would move to become a captain in de Boigne's *compoo*.[40] Evans was succeeded by the Chevalier Dudrenec, another French officer who would have a long and eventful mercenary career, which he seems to have begun in the *compoo* of René Madec around 1780.[41] Like his predecessors, he soon, 'gave it up in disgust at the beastly habits of the European subalterns and the overbearing insolence to which they and the want of regular pay gave rise among the soldiers.'[42]

The probability is that Thomas went off to Tappal sometime in 1789 to take up the administration, but also sometime during the next few years, he married one of the Begum's adopted daughters.[43] Thomas would father several children, including two sons, one of whom would serve in Skinner's Horse and another in the Begum's service in 1803.[44] It is also likely that he picked up the sobriquet 'Jehazi Sahib', by which his Indian troops knew him, at this time, though we cannot know for certain when this name, meaning roughly 'Sailor Sir', became attached to him. In his biography of Thomas, Captain Francklin always refers to him as Mr Thomas.

Whatever the precise timings, Thomas seems to have had at least some success in his new role. Aside from collecting revenue, his main task was to protect the town and territory of Tappal from the raids of the Sikhs, who were, as usual, attacking Hindustan at every opportunity. He also needed to pay the Begum her share of what was, in essence, 'protection money', some of which she may or may not have paid on to the imperial treasury. In order to pay his 'dues', Thomas needed to protect the territory he was governor of. To do this, he needed troops. We have no precise idea of how strong his garrison was, but it cannot have been less than a battalion, with at least some cavalry and guns, and he may have been able to increase his military strength with local recruits. Of course, he would have to pay these men with the revenues raised from the territory he controlled, taking his own pay from the same source.

On this period, Thomas's own account sheds no light whatsoever, as the details only begin once he leaves the Begum's service.

Compton is really no more forthcoming when he says,

> Not long after this the Begum was entrusted with the defence of the northern Mughal districts against the incursions of the Sikhs and a valuable *jaidad* [land grant to pay troops] assigned her as payment for this special service, to the management of which she appointed Thomas, who took up his quarters in a fort called

40 Compton, *Particular Account*, p.351.
41 Compton, *Particular Account*, pp.347–351 for an outline of his varied career.
42 Sleeman, *Rambles and Recollections*, p.603.
43 Edwardes, *King of the World*, p.241; *The Asiatic Annual Register* for the Year 1802, 'Characters', p.55.
44 Sleeman, *Rambles and Recollections*, p.604.

> Tappal the principle place in it. It was a wonderful piece of promotion for it elevated him to the position of Military Governor and Civil Administrator of an extensive territory.[45]

It also kept him away from Sardhana for long periods, especially as Thomas and Farzana were probably no longer lovers. With the Marathas now firmly in charge in Delhi, Farzana seems to have lost much of her influence over the emperor, and consequently her importance at the imperial court. Her troops were still of use, often protecting the north-west borders of Hindustan against the Sikh raids, and in this endeavour Thomas was a vital component.

Compton has it thus,

> He doubled the revenues of the *jaidad* before long and established the Begum's authority in a district which has never previously acknowledged any authority but the drawn sword. In the intervals of collecting rents and dispensing justice Thomas was frequently called away northwards to repel the periodical incursions of the Sikhs, a task in which he distinguished himself no less by his personal prowess than by his uniform success.[46]

Such a mammoth task could not be achieved overnight, and we could wish for more details. Thomas seems to have held the Tappal district for around two or three years, from sometime in 1789 until September 1791,[47] spending time both there and in Sardhana where his family lived.

His fall from Farzana's favour was to be rapid:

> The expenses of his mistress exceeded her income. He felt himself sufficiently established to attempt a reform. She had Frenchmen in her service whom she supported at a great expense and who were entirely useless to her. These Thomas intended to have reduced. The Sikhs at this time committing depredations upon the Begum's country, Thomas went to retaliate, which he has often before done with great advantage. During his absence the Frenchmen found means to make his mistress believe that his plan was to take her country from her, and that for that reason he had wished for their dismissal.
>
> She took the first opportunity of showing Thomas the change of sentiments towards him by insulting his wife while he was absent. He immediately returned; protected his wife and left her (the begum's) service.[48]

There was actually a bit more to it than that. The latest commander of the Somru Brigade was Le Vaisseau, who considered himself a cut above the normal run of

45 Compton, *Particular Account*, p.111.
46 Compton, *Particular Account*, p.111.
47 Sarkar, *Mughal Empire*, vol.4, p.194.
48 *The Asiatic Annual Register* for the Year 1802, 'Characters', pp.55–56.

European officers of the brigade. He was 'a person of talent, good birth, and pride of character'.[49] His expertise was in artillery and gun founding. The Begum seems to have fallen for this gentleman, and he replaced Thomas in her affections. Le Vaisseau seems to have convinced the Begum that Thomas's aim was to deprive the Begum of her lands and set himself up as an independent ruler in her stead. This was why Thomas wished to dismiss many of the French officers, and despite the strictures of later English secondary sources, not all of the officers, French or otherwise, were incompetent.

Bidwell overstates the case when he opines, 'The crew of officers she had inherited from her husband had no intention of ever fighting, or being dismissed, or of allowing the number of their useless mouths to be reduced or of being disciplined.'[50]

As we have seen, by the 1790s, the Somru Brigade had a record going back over 30 years and, while this record was far from unblemished, officers such as Baours, Saleur and Bernier had led the units of the brigade into many an action. This blanket disparagement of the brigade simply does not hold water.

However, that does not mean that there was no plotting against the newcomer Thomas, who had risen somewhat fast for some of the old hands.

After rescuing his family from Sardhana, Thomas returned to Tappal and declared his 'independence'. This Farzana simply could not allow. Thomas's impertinence had to be crushed, so the bulk of her available forces were sent to bring Thomas to heel. Thomas was forced into surrender in September 1791.[51] Unusually, he and his family were allowed liberty to retire to British territory with their personal possessions. This seems to have been due to the intercession of the Maratha agent in Delhi, Shah Nazamuddin,[52] who perhaps wished to show where the real power lay now to the 'Pillar of the State'. Thomas retired to Anupshahur, which was the most northerly British cantonment, there to consider his future and look for work.

49 Compton, *Particular Account*, p.369.
50 S. Bidwell, *Swords for Hire: European Mercenaries in Eighteenth-Century India* (London: John Murray, 1971), p.89.
51 Sarkar, *Mughal Empire*, vol.4, p.194.
52 Sarkar, *Mughal Empire*, vol.4, p.194.

6

A Mercenary Adventurer

George Thomas in the Service of Appa Khande Rao

When Thomas left the Begum Somru's service in late 1791 after about six years with the Somru Brigade, he had little money, despite the chance to amass a small fortune as governor of Tappal. It was now that, once again, he reverted to simple banditry:

> Having expended his small capital in arming a band of desperate followers, he stormed and captured a large village near Delhi from which he plundered a considerable sum of money. With the sinews of war thus obtained he increased his force to 250 mounted men and marched them to Anupshahr, the frontier British station, there to await events. After putting his followers through a course of training until they presented a semblance of discipline he offered the services of his party to Ali Bahadur one of the leading Maratha princes who had established an independent rule in Bandelkhand.[1]

In the event, Ali Bahadur did not take up Thomas's offer, but he did not have to wait too long, for another Maratha chief, Appa Khande Rao (usually known as Rao Sahib), to make Thomas a proposal which the Irishman would be happy to accept. Nevertheless, the training of his followers and the assorted negotiations with Rao Sahib took some time, so it was not until early 1793 that Thomas was able to take up Rao Sahib's offer:

> In the beginning of the year 1793 being at Anopshire received letters from Appakandarow, a Mahratta Chief, conveying offers of service and promises of a comfortable position.[2]

Once the negotiations were completed, Thomas now had a chance at his first independent command.

1 Compton, *Particular Account*, p.113.
2 Francklin, *Military Memoirs*, p.4.

'A Cavalry Soldier of the Mughal Empire'. This mid-nineteenth-century illustration gives a reasonable impression of the less-well-equipped or light cavalry common in Hindustan. The lance would often be replaced by a matchlock musket, and a shield could be carried, often strapped to the rider's back. Thomas's cavalry would be mostly of this type, though, being Rohillas or Pathans, they would be more ready to charge sword in hand than many others. (Author's Collection)

George Thomas Takes the Field

Appa Khande Rao had some experience with foreign mercenaries, as he had been de Boigne's first commander in 1786–87, though that association did not last past de Boigne's first campaign. Nevertheless, Appa had a use for a fighting mercenary, and Thomas needed the work. By the time the negotiations were over, it was October 1793.[3] Thomas would remain in Appa's service until the latter's death in 1797. The relationship was often tempestuous, usually brought on by Appa's refusal to part with any actual money to pay Thomas and his troops. As usual in these times, the often impecunious chieftain would grant lands as *jaghirs*, or the more specific *jaidad*, for the mercenary commander to pay his troops with the revenues from those lands. This was, after all, how Reinhardt had acquired Sardhana, upon the revenues from which the Somru Brigade and the Begum now subsisted. There was, in theory, nothing wrong with this system, provided both parties stuck to the agreement, and that the lands assigned were capable of producing the sums required. Of course, in the often disordered state of much of the Mughal Empire, this was rarely the case.

In fact, although Appa was supposedly one of Scindia's *sardars*, he was actually trying to carve out an independent state for himself, paying lip service to his 'overlord' when

3 Sarkar, *Mughal Empire*, vol.4, p.194.

he had no other choice or perhaps lending aid when it furthered his own ends. In this, he was really no different from many other Maratha chiefs – the only difference being the scale of their success or failure.

Francklin describes the beginning of Thomas's involvement with Appa:

> Mr Thomas was now directed by Appakandarow to raise a battalion consisting of 1000 men and 100 cavalry. For the maintenance of this force he assigned to him the pergannas of Thajara, Thopookara and Ferozeepore. They are all in the Mewatty district, situated to the south-west of Delhi. Those districts had some years preceding, been in a state of rebellion, nor was Appakandarow able to reduce them to submission. The inhabitants, when a large force was sent against them, usually took shelter in the mountains: but when the force was inferior in numbers, by uniting they proved victorious. With cavalry, likewise, they committed depredations in every direction. These excesses naturally rendered the Mahratta Chief anxious of transferring to any person who would exert himself to prevent their plundering the industrious peasants.[4]

It looked very much as if Thomas would have a difficult and dangerous commission from Appa, for which he received no money up front, only 'two guns, some ammunition and a few bullocks'.[5] The cattle, of course, were to move the guns.

Thomas now needed to raise, arm, and organise his command before setting out to take control of his new territories. However, Maratha politics intervened. Upon the news of the death of Madhaji Scindia reaching Appa, that chief went to Delhi with Thomas in his following to forestall any possible rebellion there. This gave Thomas the opportunity to recruit his force to 700 men.[6]

Finally, setting out for Tejara in late 1793 or early 1794, Thomas immediately faced the problem of lack of funds to pay his troops. He was 'forced' therefore to 'levy contributions' from villages and towns on his route of march. In order to bring his mutinous troops back into a semblance of discipline, 'high words' were exchanged between Thomas and Appa. The end result was that Thomas extracted Rs 14,000 from his employer, plus the promise of further money. 'The latter however was never fulfilled.'[7]

His plundering expeditions even included looting villages belonging to Begum Somru,

> ...who he now considered his bitter enemy, laying under contribution, that part of her country which came within his route.
>
> Arriving at Goorah, a large and populous village, he imposed heavy contributions. These amounted to a considerable sum. He found here also an ample supply of bullocks and forage.[8]

4 Francklin, *Military Memoirs*, p.5.
5 Francklin, *Military Memoirs*, p.6.
6 Francklin, *Military Memoirs*, p.14.
7 Francklin, *Military Memoirs*, p.14.
8 Francklin, *Military Memoirs*, p.15.

Thomas was really only using the same methods to supply his troops that many another Maratha or Mughal *sardar* had used, and would continue to use, in the almost continuous campaigning then taking place in northern India. Inability to pay your own troops led to desertions and 'withdrawal of labour', Thomas had yet to establish a reputation as a trusted paymaster, so at this early stage in his career as an independent commander, keeping his troops paid was something of a priority.

However, as he entered the Mewatti country, it looked as if Thomas's career would be cut short before it was barely begun.

As he encamped his force for the night, some local thieves stole one of his horses. In the morning, Thomas sent out a party to follow the trail of the thieves and recover the horse. This party was ambushed and forced back to Thomas's camp. Thomas sent out his cavalry to cover the retirement and give time for his infantry to form up. He then marched his troops out of the camp in three bodies left, centre, and right. Thomas himself was with the centre, which quickly joined with the cavalry and attacked and destroyed the offending village. The Mewatties had not been idle though, and had increased their numbers significantly, now outnumbering Thomas's men. They attacked, first pushing back and then routing the two flank divisions, before turning their attention to the centre, where Thomas himself was. The centre division now also collapsed, leaving Thomas with 'only a dozen infantry and a few cavalry'.[9] With these few, Thomas formed a hasty rearguard, which managed to extricate a previously abandoned 9-pounder gun from where it had become stuck in a *nullah* during the advance. A few blasts of grape and canister from this piece were enough to discourage the Mewatties and send them off into the nearby ravines.

It had been, to borrow a quotation from a more famous battle, 'a close-run thing', but the action had useful consequences:

> The immediate consequence was an overture, on the part of their chief of terms, which shortly led to an amicable adjustment. They agreed to pay Mr Thomas a year's rent and to restore to him the property that had been stolen. The performance of these articles was guaranteed by securities.
>
> The punishment of this village, the strongest in the whole district, was highly favourable to Mr Thomas's interest; the more so as in a preceding campaign, the whole force of the Begum Sumroo had been in vain exerted to reduce it. Mr Thomas next prepared to march against the remaining districts which were still in rebellion; and having recruited his force for the purpose he was ordered by Appakandarow to assist the collector of the district of Kishnagar.
>
> Convinced by experience that vigorous measures could alone ensure success Mr Thomas marched towards the refractory villages, of which having gained possession, they were quickly consumed by fire.
>
> An example so severe, deterred others from pursuing a similar conduct. Of these the most considerable was the town of Jyjur, which however submitting on the approach of the troops, opposition was at an end and Mr Thomas returned to Tejara.[10]

9 Francklin, *Military Memoirs*, p.16.
10 Francklin, *Military Memoirs*, pp.17–18.

We could wish to know more details here, especially of the Somru Brigade's failure, but the above gives a good example of Thomas's style of warfare. The sudden attack on refractory villages with dire consequences, combined with a readiness to come to terms with those who did not resist, became the basis of Thomas's method of 'levying contributions'. This would be something of a hallmark of 'Mr Thomas's party' throughout his career.

He also fought and defeated Bakhta of Rewari, and forced Ganga Vishnu Ahir to surrender the fort of Belji. Both of these chieftains were in rebellion against Appa Khande Rao, their nominal overlord.[11] Slowly, Thomas 'pacified' lands that had been assigned to him, capturing Jhajjar, which Appa added to Thomas's *jaghirs*, along with other lands such that their total worth was, in theory, a *lakh* and a half of rupees (Rs 150,000) per year, assuming Thomas could actually collect such a sum.

As for Thomas's troops, it is doubtful that at this early stage they were much better equipped than the irregulars he fought. Flintlock muskets had certainly become more available on the open market. There were arms factories around Agra and Gwalior, providing weapons for de Boigne's regulars.[12] Doubtless, there was some overspill, but aside from a short time in Delhi, one wonders if Thomas had been given the time or money to properly arm his forces. Indeed, by the end of this first campaign, Thomas's force was reduced to a mere 300 men, largely from desertions due to lack of pay.[13]

At the end of this campaign, Thomas and his remnant returned to Tejara to recruit his forces. This first campaign with an independent command had been a steep learning curve for Thomas, but despite his difficulties he had succeeded well enough to continue in his current employment.

Mutinies, Rebellions, and a Gallant Rescue

Thomas was not allowed much leisure in Tejara, as Appa was in deep trouble. As usual, the trouble was brought about by Appa's refusal to actually pay his troops, and these much put-upon men had therefore 'withdrawn their labour' and were besieging their chief in the fort of Kot Putli, some 40 miles (64 km) from Tejara. It appears that there was something more to this than a mere mutiny for arrears of pay:

> Scarcely had he reached Tejara than he received an urgent message from Appa, calling him to advance with all speed to Kot Putli, a fort about 40 miles distant where the chief was detained by his mutinous troops who had been tampered with by Gopal Rao Bhao, Dulat Rao Scindia's viceroy in Hindustan. Appa was fearful of being delivered up to his enemies and implored Thomas to rescue him without fail.[14]

11 Sarkar, *Mughal Empire*, vol.4, footnote p.194.
12 Copestake, *Their Infantry and Guns*, p.69.
13 Francklin, *Military Memoirs*, p.19.
14 Compton, *Particular Account*, p.118.

Never a man to procrastinate when action was required, Thomas set off from Tejara with such troops as he could gather, and covered the 40 miles in under two days in the pouring rain over almost non-existent roads, encamping under the walls of the fort and establishing communication with Appa, whilst the mutineers were seemingly sheltering from the downpour. The situation was still dangerous, as the mutineers outnumbered Thomas's men and those still loyal to Appa. Thomas therefore proposed to break out and march to Kanaund, while also sending letters to Daulat Rao Scindia to apprise him of the situation and doubtless to blacken his enemies where he could. Such was the normal course of Maratha politics in those days.

Preparations for the breakout were made with the utmost secrecy, and the operation went ahead, with Appa and his family surrounded by Thomas's men as they began their march:

> Mr Thomas without further delay, joined that chief, they had not proceeded far when the van of the enemy made their appearance. Mr Thomas, as the only means of inspiring confidence, recommended to Appakandarao to mount an elephant and show himself to the troops. The measure was instantly adopted and attended with the happiest effect, for the enemy, perceiving this resolute conduct thought it most prudent to retire, and Mr Thomas, without further opposition, conducted his chief to safety in Kanoond.[15]

Appa was suitably grateful for his deliverance, adopting Thomas as his 'son' and giving him Rs 3,000 to purchase an elephant and a palanquin suitable to this new 'dignity'. Most importantly, he ordered Thomas to increase his *compoo* by another 200 infantry and the same number of cavalry and, best of all, granted him title 'in perpetuity' to several of the districts in Mewat, which he had so far conquered, including Jhajjar, a town about 50 miles west of Delhi, which, from now on, he would hold almost until the end of his career.

Thomas now spent some time organising and administering his recent conquests, but any respite was again short-lived, for, as seemed normal, rebellion was in the air. This time, the 'miscreant' was one Gunga Bishen, a major *zemindar*, or landlord, of the Ahir tribe, who, according to Francklin, could 'bring into the field a body of 14 thousand men'.[16] In the event, they brought nothing like this total out. As usual with these constant rebellions, the major cause was financial. Bishen sought better terms from Appa, but to this end he had gone somewhat too far, entering into a correspondence with Gopal Rao Bhow, already an avowed enemy of Appa's, claiming that Appa was defrauding Scindia by undervaluing the territory and therefore not paying the correct amount to his 'overlord'. Such 'treason' needed to be nipped in the bud, but Bishen had fled to his fort of Belji in Mewat:

15 Francklin, *Military Memoirs*, p.21.
16 Francklin, *Military Memoirs*, footnote p.22.

> The orders for the march had been kept a profound secret in Mr Thomas's camp. Arriving before the place, by a successful stratagem Mr Thomas took Gunga Bishen prisoner whom he sent to Appa. The fort was still maintained by his nephew, and a garrison of 1000 men. They had abundance of provisions, ammunition and stores of all kinds, the only inconvenience sustained by the inhabitants was a scarcity of water. This article was not to be procured within two miles of the place. Mr Thomas in the hope of compelling them to surrender, commenced a blockade and the better to ensure success he constructed a chain of redoubts round the fort.[17]

The siege proceeded slowly, and Thomas decided upon mining, as he lacked heavy guns to batter the walls. Consequently, undermining the walls by digging under them, then placing a powder charge in the resultant chamber, was his only recourse, other than starving the garrison out. It seems unlikely that Thomas had either the patience or the resources for a long siege, so mining was his only remaining option.

However, the garrison was not idle. One night, they mounted a sortie which surprised, drove out, and put to flight the garrison of one of Thomas's redoubts. Thomas, awakened by the noise, rushed unarmed to the spot, to be immediately attacked by a party of the enemy who fired matchlocks and threw spears at him, without result. Had it not been for his servant following with Thomas's sabre, matters might have gone ill for the Irishman:

> Perceiving a stand of colours which his own men had left behind, he stooped to pick them up which the enemy observing, concluded by the motion of his body that he had been wounded; they rushed on him in numbers and wounded him in several places. This compelled him to relinquish the colours and attack the enemy whom he soon obliged to retreat; Mr Thomas then ascended an eminence in order to discover if possible the direction his own troops had taken in their pusillanimous flight, but in vain. Faint from the wounds he had received in the late encounter, he now retreated within his trenches and got them dressed.[18]

Francklin's rather pedestrian writing describes what must have been a vicious, killing brawl, nevertheless Thomas had survived the encounter and the siege was concluded when the mines were detonated. The explosions caused the garrison to come to terms. However, Thomas's men were, once again, short of provisions and the weather inclement, so he was forced to sell his own horses to raise sufficient cash to buy blankets for his men.

Thomas and his reduced forces then returned to Jhajjar for a well-earned rest. Money was extracted from the local landowners sufficient to pay the troops at least some of their arrears.

Appa's continual financial problems now came home to roost. Gopal Rao, Appa's enemy, was replaced as 'Deputy' *subahdar* of Hindustan by Lakwa Dada, a Maratha

17 Francklin, *Military Memoirs*, p.23.
18 Francklin, *Military Memoirs*, p.24.

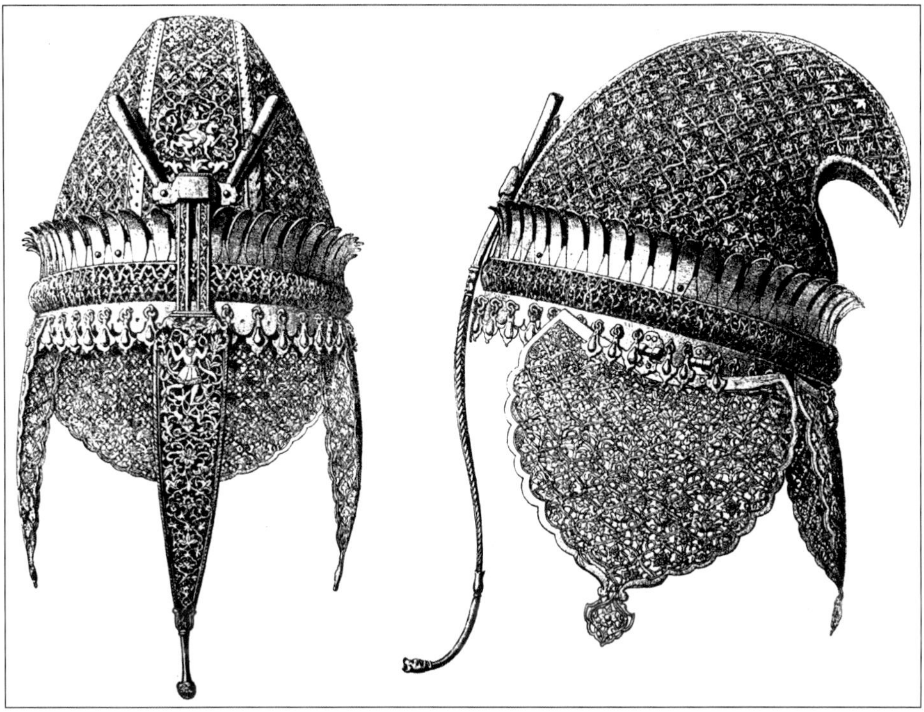

A Maratha helmet. This drawing shows a type of helmet peculiar to the Marathas. A highly decorated example such as this would be worn by a chieftain or *sardar* of considerable standing. While the paid cavalry or *kala-paga* of the larger Maratha houses would wear armour, the bulk of the cavalry would wear little or none. (Public Domain)

commander of considerable talent. Francklin calls him Lieutenant General,[19] since in theory he was sub- ordinate to Benoît de Boigne, commander of the Army of Hindustan, that great mercenary army which enabled Madhaji Scindia and now his successor, Daulat Rao Scindia, to rule the rump of the Mughal Empire in the name of the old, blind Emperor Shah Alam II.

Lakwa therefore represented Appa's supposed overlord, Daulat Rao, who in turn 'represented' the supposed head of the Maratha Confederacy, the *Peshwa*, who reigned in far-off Poona, and whom no one in Hindustan cared much about, unless it was in their interest to do so. Nevertheless, Lakwa was making a tour of the western districts of the province, when it came to light that Appa owed a significant sum in unpaid tribute.

Appa went to Lakwa's camp to negotiate better terms in the usual manner, but declaring himself unable to pay the sum demanded, he was detained in Lakwa's camp until the monies were forthcoming. Appa was forced to make over some of his *jaghirs* in mortgage and, furthermore, the troops used to collect the sums, belonging to the mortgage holder, Bapu Farnavis, were to be paid for by Appa himself.

19 Francklin, *Military Memoirs*, p.25.

Since three of the mortgaged *jaghirs* were those previously assigned to Thomas to pay his troops, Thomas was somewhat concerned. Furthermore, once it became known that Appa was a prisoner, many of the landholders in his *jaghirs* immediately rose in rebellion, refusing to pay their rents. As Appa's 'enforcer', Thomas took his 800 surviving men on a tour of Appa's remaining lands, bringing these rebellious landholders back into line.

His methods could be brutal, as we have already seen. Night assaults are mentioned, and at least one massacre of the defenders of a town and fort. None of this was really unusual by the standards of that time and place. Fighting could be severe, as at the storming of Bairi, the *Killadar* or governor of which had hired 300 Jat and Rajput mercenaries to help defend the place. Thomas tried to storm it but was beaten back with loss:

> ...one of my *Sardars* was wounded, and from the confusion that occurred left behind in the hands of the enemy; the danger was every moment increasing, the town was on fire in several parts and our retreat nearly cut off by the flames that surrounded us.
>
> In this situation we had the additional mortification to perceive the merciless enemy seize on the wounded officer, and with savage barbarity precipitate him into the fire. Equally animated, as enraged, by this spectacle, my troops now rushed forward to the attack, with an ardour that was irresistible. Having gained entire possession of the fort, the soldiers, with clamorous expressions of revenge insisted on the death of every one of the garrison that remained and I was not inclined to refuse. But it cost us dear, the enemy to a man made a brave resistance. This contest was continued so long as to afford time to those who had retreated, to return; by this means we were again engaged, and at one time almost overpowered; but receiving a reinforcement of our own party, the enemy by slow degrees, began again to retreat; which they effected. I pursued with the cavalry, the enemy once more made a stand in the jungles, adjoining the town; when after a second desperate conflict, they gave way on all sides and most of them were cut to pieces.[20]

Such desperate hand to hand fighting seems to have been almost a common occurrence in Thomas's career.

At this juncture, Thomas and Appa often seemed to lurch from crisis to crisis without respite. Now Appa maintained that he was being forced to dismiss Thomas's troops by Lakwa Dada, who apparently deemed Thomas 'a dangerous person'.[21] Thomas refused to do this until the troops had been paid their arrears, even meeting Lakwa, who maintained that this was untrue, and offering Thomas a contract for 2,000 men.

Thomas refused this offer, possibly because he felt some loyalty to Appa, but equally possibly because 'better the devil he knew' than fishing deeper in the choppy waters of Maratha politics.

20 Francklin, *Military Memoirs*, pp.27–28.
21 Francklin, *Military Memoirs*, p.28.

Sepoy, 'Somru Brigade'. This man represents the backbone of the Somru Brigade, the infantry battalions trained in the French manner by Somru and his European officers. He carries a European-style flintlock musket and bayonet. The white crossbelt supports a European-style cartridge pouch, the black belt an Indian tulwar and his bayonet when it is not fixed to his musket. His uniform is entirely Indian in style, and similar uniforms were also worn by other mercenary *compoos* including the 'Lal Paltan' or 'Red Battalion' in imperial service, whose long coats were of course red in colour as distinct from the Somru Brigade's blue. (Colour artwork by Giorgio Albertini © Helion & Company 2026)

Artilleryman or *Golandauz*, 'Somru Brigade' This plate shows a trained gunner or *golandauz* who would man the Somru Brigades artillery pieces. He has tucked the bottom of his green coat into his sash for ease of movement when working the guns. He has also tied his turban onto his head for much the same reason. He might discard his uniform altogether and serve the guns almost naked if the conditions allowed. Serving smoothbore artillery in Indian heat was hard physical work, even before we consider the dangers of the battlefield and such *golandauz* were paid a higher wage than the ordinary sepoy. (Colour artwork by Giorgio Albertini © Helion & Company 2026)

'Somru Brigade'. This cavalry trooper is a member of the Somru Brigade's cavalry regiment. This unit does not seem to have been primarily 'battle' cavalry but seemingly filled internal security roles in Sardhana for much of the time. It is also possible that one or more *rissalahs* (a term similar to the European 'troop' for a body of cavalry about 80–100 strong) were escorts to the Begum on her travels. He is armed with a matchlock musket and tulwar. He may also have had a pair of pistols in holsters on his mount in the European manner, though this is not certain. Horse furniture is red-brown, and the saddlecloth is yellow with red rectangles along the outer edges and square yellow corners. (Colour artwork by Giorgio Albertini © Helion & Company 2026)

Rohilla Mercenary. Rohilla warriors were in constant demand in eighteenth-century Indian armies. Rohillas were Pathans from the northwest of India or Afghanistan who had settled in Hindustan in the previous century. The unspeakable Ghulam Kadir was a Rohilla. This plate represents an ordinary infantry soldier or *jezzailichi*, named for his long matchlock musket or *jezzail*. This weapon, although slower to load than a musket, had a longer range. This warrior's secondary weapon is a tulwar, used with his round shield to deliver ferocious 'sword in hand' charges against enemies who had been disordered by the fire of the *jezzail*. All of the major Indian rulers used Rohilla mercenaries, often as fortress garrisons. There were also Rohilla cavalry and, indeed Rohilla armies in which this man would be the most common type. Richer men would have more coloured clothing. Officers and cavalry might wear Mughal-style armour. George Thomas usually had a few hundred Rohilla mercenaries in his forces, and most of his cavalry seem to have been Rohillas or Pathans. (Colour artwork by Giorgio Albertini © Helion & Company 2026)

Sikh 'Ghorcharra' cavalryman. George Thomas spent much of his career fighting the Sikhs, and this man represents the cavalry, who were the most constant thorn in his flesh. Their dress was entirely personal and non-uniform, and their primary weapon was the matchlock musket, backed up by two tulwars. He might also have had a round shield slung upon his back. If he was wealthy enough – or lucky enough to loot – he might wear armour in the Mughal style. (Colour artwork by Giorgio Albertini © Helion & Company 2026)

Maratha Light cavalryman. While a small proportion of the often large numbers of Maratha cavalry might wear armour to a greater or lesser extent and be competent 'battle' cavalry, most were comparatively poorly equipped with lance and shield or perhaps a matchlock musket, with in all cases a sword or tulwar as a secondary weapon. Light cavalry such as these, on their hardy ponies, were expert scouts, raiders and indeed looters, but sometimes a liability in battle. The lowest class of Maratha cavalry, the *Pindaris*, received no pay but served only for what they could loot. This man might well be a *Pindari*. (Colour artwork by Giorgio Albertini © Helion & Company 2026)

Thomas's next expedition was, as usual, to collect unpaid tribute, but this time his men were part of a combined force, which also contained several battalions of the Second Brigade of the Army of Hindustan, under the command of Major Gardiner. This must have been in late 1794 or early 1795, as Lewis Ferdinand Smith has Gardiner in command of this brigade in 1794, with Robert Sutherland taking over sometime in 1795.[22]

This seems to have been Thomas's first contact with the Army of Hindustan as an independent commander himself. The last time he encountered the troops which were the foundation of this army, he was still a subordinate officer in the Somru Brigade, when he campaigned against Ghulam Kadir in late 1788.[23]

Gardiner seems to have favoured a more formal and deliberate approach to siege operations than Thomas's usual 'neck or nothing' assault tactics. To that end, he called a council of war to discuss the situation and decide upon a course of action. The enemy garrison of this fort, which Francklin does not name, was very active and had taken possession of several ravines adjacent to the fort and were harassing the besiegers. No progress could be made against them until a redoubt they also occupied was taken. Taking this redoubt would allow the siege to move forward by enabling the besiegers to open the second parallel – thus moving their siege works and heavy guns closer to the fort so that first the walls could be breached by the guns, and the storming parties could eventually make the assault. The council, however, would make no decision, so Thomas decided to act: 'On the ensuing day, Mr Thomas of his own accord, took an opportunity, when the enemy were off their guard, to storm the redoubt, repeated attempts were made to regain possession but he bravely maintained himself in it, till a reinforcement arriving, they gave up the contest.'[24]

Thanks to Thomas, the besiegers were able to advance the second parallel, and rather than face a storm, the *khilladar* opened negotiations, eventually agreeing to pay a ransom of two lakhs of rupees (Rs 200,000), of which Thomas received his due share, enabling him to pay his men. He then returned to his *jaghirs* to rest his men and recruit his strength.

Thomas seems to have been able to recruit sufficiently to form a 'regiment' of two battalions, possibly in late 1794 or early 1795,[25] as soon after his army is noted as 2,000 infantry, 10 pieces of artillery, 500 irregulars, and 200 cavalry.[26]

The simmering distrust between Thomas and the Begum Somru seemed likely to become open war. Thomas, as written by Francklin, ascribes this entirely to the intrigues of some of the French officers of the Somru Brigade,[27] but there was more at work here than simple avarice and jealousy. The current commander of the brigade was the French officer, Le Vaisseau – or Levassoo as the name is spelled in Thomas's memoirs. He was a

22 Smith, *Regular Corps*, p.52.
23 See Chapter 5.
24 Francklin, *Military Memoirs*, p.30.
25 Francklin, *Military Memoirs*, p.31.
26 Francklin, *Military Memoirs*, p.32.
27 Francklin, *Military Memoirs*, p.32.

man of some talent and of a finer education and breeding than the usual run of officers in the Begum's army. So much did he dislike the behaviour of the junior officers, that he refused to sit at table with them.[28] He seems to have exerted considerable influence over Farzana, while managing to alienate many of the junior officers of the brigade, and may indeed have been the prime mover in persuading the Begum to attack Thomas.

Indeed, the Begum – or perhaps rather Le Vaisseau – went so far as to, 'She accordingly ordered her army to Tharu, a place about twenty- five miles south-east of Jhajjar. The force consisted of four battalions of infantry 400 cavalry and 20 guns and it was publically given out that the object of the expedition was a war of revenge against her former officer.'[29]

Le Vaisseau and the Begum were married on 1 May 1793.[30] The marriage was conducted by Father Gregorio, a Carmelite monk, and witnessed by two officers of the brigade, Bernier and Saleur, who evidently Le Vaisseau thought better of than he did the bulk of his officers. Bernier would later command a battalion in the Third Brigade of the Army of Hindustan,[31] and would fall fighting Thomas in 1801.[32] Saleur would command the Somru Brigade later in his career.

This marriage may have been one of the reasons Thomas left Farzana's service. Certainly, Thomas vents considerable spleen in his memoir when Le Vaisseau is mentioned, 'On every occasion he was the declared and inveterate enemy of Mr Thomas; and had by his influence, wrought in the Begum her present determination.'[33]

In the event, the war did not happen, simply because many of her officers did not want to fight Thomas or indeed anyone else. Sleeman[34] has Le Vaisseau writing to the nearest British garrison at Anupshahur on the Ganges River, commanded by one Colonel McGowan, asking to be allowed to enter British territory with his wife and property en route to Farrukhabad, as they wished to retire and reside peacefully in that place. There was considerable negotiation, mostly around who would succeed to the command of the Somru Brigade – and, of course, its *jaghirs*. The Maratha government in Delhi was aware of these negotiations, as it was a Maratha officer who would succeed to the brigade and its income, and also who was to pay Farzana for the weapons and equipment of the troops which she had supplied. Scindia would obviously want one of his officers to have the command. These negotiations took place during April and May 1795, and, had they been successful, Farzana and Le Vaisseau would have been allowed to live privately in the French settlement of Chandernagore.[35]

However, events overtook Farzana and her French husband, as those of her troops still in Delhi – probably two battalions, as Thomas expected to face four battalions with

28 Sleeman, *Rambles and Recollections*, p.605.
29 Compton, *Particular Account*, p.125.
30 Keay, *Farzana*, p.214.
31 Compton, *Particular Account*, p.339.
32 Copestake, *Their Infantry and Guns*, p.208.
33 Francklin, *Military Memoirs*, p.31.
34 Sleeman, *Rambles and Recollections*, pp.605–6.
35 Sleeman, *Rambles and Recollections*, p.606.

20 guns and 400 cavalry[36] – decided that they preferred Reinhardt's son by his first wife, Zaffar Yab Khan, as their new leader,[37] and began a march from Delhi to Sardhana to depose the Begum and install Zaffar. At this, the Begum and Le Vaisseau determined upon flight with only a small number of personal servants, both declaring to each other that they would commit suicide rather than fall into the hands of the rebels. The couple was captured by the rebels a few miles from Sardhana, and the Begum supposedly stabbed herself rather than fall into their hands. Le Vaisseau, hearing the screams of Farzana's servants, 'and looking in, Le Vaisseau saw the white cloth covering the Begum's breast stained with blood'.[38] At this, thinking Farzana dead, the Frenchman pulled a pistol from his saddle holster and blew his brains out.

The rebels left his lifeless corpse in the road for three days, later dumping it into a ditch.

Farzana was taken back to Sardhana a prisoner, where she was, 'kept under a gun for seven days, deprived of all kinds of food, save what she got by stealth from her female servants, and subjected to all manner of insulting language.'[39]

Thomas seems to have been well aware of what was afoot in Sardhana, as he still had friends in the Somru Brigade, in particular, an officer known only as Liegeois, as he was apparently from Liege. Indeed, Liegeois, so Thomas avers, tried to dissuade the Begum from the 'proposed hostilities' against Thomas and was degraded for his temerity by Le Vaisseau, which so incensed the troops that they began the mutiny which ended with the elevation of Zaffar Yab Khan to his step-mother's *jaghirs*, Le Vaisseau dead and Farzana chained under a gun.[40]

By no means were all of the brigade's officers involved in the plot. Sleeman blames Thomas as the instigator, 'At last the officers were advised by George Thomas who had instigated them to this violence out of pique against the Begum for her preference of the Frenchman to set aside their puppet and reseat the Begum in the command as the only chance of keeping the territory of Sardhana.'[41]

While it is hard to see Thomas as so petty – after all, he was now in command of troops of his own with *jaghirs* of his own to administer – he would have been foolish not to keep a conduit for information open between himself and some of his old friends in the Somru Brigade. That he may have tried to suborn and unsettle a potential enemy who was threatening to attack him, is, of course, not impossible by any means, but 'pique' was not Jehazi Sahib's style.

Had Thomas indeed 'instigated' the mutiny out of pique, it would hardly be in character for him to act as he now did. Some considerable time after the mutiny and the replacement of Farzana by her stepson, Thomas received a letter from the Begum – this must have been in 1796, as Thomas had been campaigning once again in Mewat, collecting revenue, and had been with both Lakwa Dada and Appa Khande Rao for

36 Francklin, *Military Memoirs*, p.32.
37 Sleeman, *Rambles and Recollections*, p.606.
38 Sleeman, *Rambles and Recollections*, p.607.
39 Sleeman, *Rambles and Recollections*, p.607.
40 Francklin, *Military Memoirs*, p.32. Thomas places all blame for the mutiny and subsequent events at the door of Le Vaisseau.
41 Sleeman, *Rambles and Recollections*, p.608.

some months. Indeed, Sarkar places the first mutiny and the placing of Zaffar Yab Khan in the Begum's place as October 1795 and Thomas's 'noble revenge' as 9 July 1796,[42] so something like nine months had passed before Thomas took action.

Whatever the precise timings, this letter was addressed to Thomas:

> in a manner most abject and desponding, she addressed Mr Thomas, she stated her apprehension of being poisoned or otherwise put to death; affirmed that her only dependence was on him, implored him to come to her assistance, and finally, offered to pay any sum of money the Marathas would require, on condition they would reinstate her in her jaghir.[43]

Evidently, Farzana was no longer chained under a gun, though she was still a prisoner of some sort.

As ever, once action was required, Thomas moved with alacrity:

> On receipt of this letter, Mr Thomas, by an offer of 120,000 rupees prevailed upon Bapoo Scindia to make a movement towards Sardhana. Convinced from his former experience that unless he could gain over a part of the troops under Zaffar Yab Khan to the Begum's interest, not only his exertions would be fruitless, but he himself would be exposed to the greatest personal danger. He therefore set on foot a negotiation for this purpose.[44]

This 'negotiation' involved bringing over the officers of the *compoo* to the advantages of loyalty to their mistress. To that end, Thomas, according to Sleeman,[45] gave out the statement that, 'If, said he, the Begum should die under the torture of mind and body to which you are subjecting her the minister will very soon resume the lands assigned for your payment, and disband a force so disorderly, and so little likely to be of any use to him or the Emperor.'[46]

Thomas now moved his forces towards Sardhana and some kind of 'counter-mutiny' took place, with a portion of the Somru Brigade declaring for the Begum and placing Zaffar Yab Khan under arrest. Thomas now approached the Sardhana cantonment with an escort of only 50 sabres, a battalion of 400 of his infantry following 'with all possible expedition',[47] to support the Begum's partisans. Thomas and his 50 cavalry arriving first, were, for a time, in mortal danger from those troops still adhering to Zaffar Yab Khan, but Thomas's hard-marching battalion following up convinced Zaffar's remaining supporters of the futility of their position, and the Begum was reinstalled to her throne.

Sleeman adds the detail that the European officers now signed a 'covenant' of loyalty to the Begum Somru, somewhat sniffily criticising their lack of education,

42 Sarkar, *Mughal Empire*, vol.4, p.195.
43 Francklin, *Military Memoirs*, p.54.
44 Francklin, *Military Memoirs*, pp.54–55.
45 Sleeman, *Rambles and Recollections*, p.608.
46 Sleeman, *Rambles and Recollections*, p.608.
47 Francklin, *Military Memoirs*, pp.54–55.

> They all affixed their seals to this covenant; but some of them to show their superior learning, put their initials or what they used as such, for some of these *learned Thebans* knew only two or three letters of the alphabet, which they put down though they happened not to be their real initials.[48]

So order was restored within Sardhana, and its disorderly forces brought back to discipline. Zaffar Yab Khan was packed off to Delhi a prisoner, minus any portable wealth he may have had. Bapu Scindia was paid at least part of the money promised to him, and Thomas may have thought that the Begum was in his debt. The new commander of the brigade was none other than Monsieur Saleur, who became the colonel of the Somru Brigade. He had managed to keep out of the mutiny, despite being one of the witnesses to the marriage of Farzana and Le Vaisseau.

The Maratha government seems to have known exactly what was going on: 'The Maratha *sardars* in Delhi were privy to the plot and encouraged it. She was restored to the lordship of Sardhana and sent her worthless stepson into confinement.'[49]

Thomas did not remain long in Sardhana. As usual, there was work for his sword in the service of Appa Khande Rao. Farzana was probably happy to see him go without any fuss.

> There was too much history between them. In 1792 she had spared his life when he might have been hanged for rebellion, a gesture that had felt gratifyingly seigneurial. But when in extremis she had been forced to plead for his help the balance had shifted. He had saved not only her life but her livelihood. She owed him a debt of gratitude that she would never be able to repay; nor would she ever be able to forget the humiliating circumstances under which she had incurred it.[50]

While we may wonder about the actual evidence for Julia Keay's rather emotional conclusion, there is little doubt that Thomas was better away from the Somru Brigade and its recent turmoil. Thomas was a man to seek his own destiny.

Revenue Collection – George Thomas's Way

Once away from the Begum Somru and Sardhana, Thomas was quickly back into the usual round of revenue collection and suppressing those rebellions which arose from the desire of many of the *zemindars* (landlords) to avoid paying their tribute. Money, or lack of it, was a constant trial for Thomas. His troops, as we have seen, were often in arrears with their wages and on more than one occasion Thomas was forced to sell his personal possessions to give them something on account. Thomas's financial straits were

48 Sleeman, *Rambles and Recollections*, p.609.
49 Sarkar, *Mughal Empire*, vol.4, p.195.
50 Keay, *Farzana*, p.240.

not helped by his employer pleading poverty or simply refusing to pay what Thomas was owed.

This led to numerous arguments between the two men over the years, but in the second half of 1795, these tensions seem to have come to a head. Appa Khande Rao, Thomas's employer, plotted to have Thomas killed. To that end, he engaged a body of *goshains* to attack Thomas's camp.

The *goshains* were a type of armed, and often itinerant, religious warrior, quite prepared to hire out their services as mercenaries. The Nawab-Vizier of Oudh had used 5,000 of these men at the Battle of Patna against the British,[51] and numbers of them had been present in the fighting around Delhi during the Ghulam Kadir episode, so it was not difficult for Appa to engage such a band of these itinerant warriors to do his dirty work for him.

Needless to say, Thomas had his own spies in Appa's household to keep him appraised of Appa's plots as,

> The Mahratta Chief afore mentioned, having instigated the *goshains* to attack Mr. Thomas in his camp, to encourage them, offered as a reward for their services the sum of 10,000 rupees.
>
> These particulars were communicated to Mr Thomas by his own *Vakeel,*[52] then resident with Appa. Incensed at the indignity offered him by a conduct so treacherous, he marched against the *goshains*, whom he attacked and defeated with great loss to them and to himself but trifling; after the encounter they fled towards Delhi, and not thinking themselves safe there, continued to retreat until they had crossed the Jumna.[53]

Thomas was obviously incensed by his employer's treachery and threatened to leave his employ, citing his treatment of another European mercenary, one 'Mr Taylor',[54] whom Appa had deprived of his command and thrown into prison in order to extort money from him. Taylor 'was not either to be daunted by threats or cajoled by promises' and so was eventually released.[55] Appa blamed the people of his household for the mistreatment and treachery, citing his own illness and infirmity, and pleading for a personal meeting with Thomas 'to arrange everything to their mutual satisfaction and advantage'.[56]

Thomas declined the invitation, wisely fearing more treachery, though equally he feared reprisals from 'so powerful a chief'.[57] Fortunately, he was, however, directed by Lakwa Dada, the senior Maratha commander, to take his whole force to confront a Sikh raiding party.

51 See Chapter 3.
52 *Vakeel*, an official envoy or emissary.
53 Francklin, *Military Memoirs*, p.44.
54 Mr Taylor seems to have been in Appa's service; see Copestake, *Their Infantry and Guns*, p.47, and footnote 15.
55 Francklin, *Military Memoirs*, p.45.
56 Francklin, *Military Memoirs*, p.46.
57 Francklin, *Military Memoirs*, p.46.

At this time, Thomas, while still technically in the employ of Appa Khande Rao, seems to have been under the command of Lakwa Dada. Appa, because of his precarious financial situation, probably found it politic to 'loan' Thomas to Lakwa Dada, as he was the representative of Appa's overlord Daulat Rao Scindia.

Lakwa was a fine soldier in his own right, and had worked well with de Boigne before the Savoyard had retired, so he had some knowledge of working with and commanding European-style troops. Thomas's rough and ready battalions were not the precise and polished mercenaries of the Army of Hindustan, but were always ready for a fight.

In November 1795, Lakwa had Thomas march to the Seharanpur district to confront a body of some 5,000 Sikh raiders.[58] Despite previously defeating Maratha troops sent against them, they would not face Thomas and beat a hasty retreat. This success caused Lakwa to ask Appa for the use of Thomas to defend the frontier against the Sikh attacks,

> Lakwa, commander of the Maratha forces, hearing of the disgrace sustained by his troops at Seharanpur, as likewise of the subsequent flight of the Sikhs on Mr. Thomas, approach now requested of Appa to permit this enterprising man to raise a body of two thousand men for the protection of the province of Seharanpur, and other parts of the Maratha possessions. To this request Appa, though with difficulty complied, and in consequence the Purgannahs of Panipat, Sonnepat and Karnaul were assigned to Mr Thomas for the payment of 2,000 infantry 200 cavalry and sixteen pieces of field artillery.[59]

Whether these new troops were in addition to those Thomas already had under his command is unclear, but as Thomas had to garrison these additions to his responsibilities, there must have been an increase in his overall troop numbers, even if not in his 'field force', though he does seem to have increased his artillery train.

Thomas already had plenty of experience fighting the Sikhs, gained whilst serving in the Somru Brigade 'Mr Thomas in this place remarks that whilst in the service of the Begum Sumroo he had encountered the Sikh on more than one occasion and had already given them 'samples of his method of fighting'.[60] Thomas would, in the coming years, give the Sikhs many more such samples of his way of fighting.

For much of 1796, Thomas was employed in fighting Sikh raiders 'on both sides of the Jumna',[61] where he seems to have been uniformly successful. But in June 1797, his fortunes took a downward turn, due to the death of Appa Khande Rao. Appa, unable to live longer with the pain, drowned himself in the Jumna. Before his death, Appa had recognised his nephew Vaman Rao as his successor.

For a time, Thomas tried to work with the new 'Rao Sahib' but, 'The death of Appa was on several counts unfavourable to Mr. Thomas's interests; Vaman Rao his nephew

58 Sarkar, *Mughal Empire*, vol.4, p.195.
59 Francklin, *Military Memoirs*, pp.47–48.
60 Francklin, *Military Memoirs*, p.47.
61 Sarkar, *Mughal Empire*, vol.4, p.195.

and successor was a youth vain and inexperienced, and more adapted to the life of an accountant than that of a general.'[62]

Matters deteriorated to such an extent that Vaman demanded the return of all of those *jaghirs* that Appa had given to Thomas to maintain his troops. For Thomas, this was of course an impossible demand, yet Vaman Rao would not negotiate, even when Thomas offered to pay 'a sum of money if left in quiet possession'.[63] Vaman Rao would not agree, and Thomas would have little choice but to go to war with his employer.

Indeed, as Thomas marched his troops into 'his' territory, Vaman Rao had already taken possession of one of Thomas's villages:

> On Mr Thomas's arrival at Kosselli, a large village forming part of his possessions, he perceived it in the hands of the enemy, and Vaman Rao, prepared to defend it encamped under the walls of the fort.
>
> Unwilling to push matters to an extremity, if by any means it could be avoided, Mr Thomas drew off his force to a small distance and gave particular orders to his own people to forbear all acts of hostility on their part.
>
> This mode of conduct was of no avail for the troops of Vaman Rao, coming daily from their own camp, insulted and fired upon Mr Thomas's men by which several of them were severely wounded.[64]

Clearly, Vaman Rao was using the normal Maratha harassing tactics to provoke Thomas into doing something rash or ill considered. Needless to say, Thomas could not let these deliberate provocations continue, lest he lose face with his own troops.

> The enemy reinforced by a large number of the peasantry, and headed by the *zemindars* of their respective villages, were now become so formidable that Mr Thomas resolved to bring the business to an issue. He accordingly attacked them. The affair was quickly decided, the enemy fled in all directions, and the greater part having taken shelter in the fort of Kosselli were followed by Mr Thomas who immediately commenced the siege of that place. Having erected batteries, he ordered the grates for heating shot to be got in readiness, which being done, he fired so successfully with red hot shot that he quickly compelled them to surrender at discretion.[65]

The use of red-hot shot, while not uncommon in eighteenth-century siege warfare, was a difficult and dangerous operation, and argues significant expertise on the part of Thomas's *golandauz*, his gunners and artillery crews. A mistake during loading or a lack of both speed and precision could – and sometimes did – result in the powder charge exploding as the heated shot was rammed home, resulting in an instantaneous but gory

62 Francklin, *Military Memoirs*, p.61.
63 Francklin, *Military Memoirs*, p.62.
64 Francklin, *Military Memoirs*, pp.62–63.
65 Francklin, *Military Memoirs*, p.63.

death for the gunner ramming the shot on top of the double wadding separating the shot from the charge of gunpowder. Should the red-hot shot burn through the wadding and ignite the powder charge too soon, then all manner of carnage in the firing battery could result. Thomas and his gunners were evidently expert enough to avoid such a calamity and caused the fort to surrender.

Despite this, Vaman Rao would not negotiate, and a proposed face-to-face meeting failed because each suspected the other of treachery. Thomas was forced to withdraw, having made his employer seemingly an inveterate enemy.

Thomas was now thrown upon his own resources to maintain his only asset, his army.

7

An Independent Man

George Thomas – The 'Irish Raja'

We now enter the barely believable phase of Thomas's extraordinary career. Yet, here we have marginally more primary sources than Thomas's own recollections as told to Captain Francklin, for by 1797, Thomas is mentioned in the official correspondence of the East India Company. These mentions come from the voluminous official correspondence between the various British residents either at Poona with the Maratha *Peshwa* or with Daulat Rao Scindia, wherever that chieftain happened to be. Thomas is mentioned at least 40 times in this official correspondence.[1]

Initially, however, he had to respond to another raid by the Sikhs, who had struck Thomas's remaining northern *jaghirs*, particularly that of Sonnepat to the north-west of Delhi. This would be sometime in 1797 – dates are uncertain, as are the numbers of troops involved in the ensuing four actions that Thomas fought to disperse these raiders. These actions must have been hard-fought, as Thomas admits to the loss of 500 men, supposedly causing 'double that number' to the Sikh raiders,[2] who then, after some negotiation, agreed to evacuate the province.

Thomas and his *compoo* seem to have had little time for any rest or reorganisation at this juncture – his forces seem to have been constantly on the march from one trouble spot to another. This was, at least in part, due to the distracted state of the Maratha administration in northern India caused by the 'War of the Bais', or 'The Widows' War' as it is sometimes called. The conflict was caused almost entirely by the greed and stupidity of Daulat Rao Scindia, whose actions against Madhaji Scindia's widows and, therefore, his own aunts, had outraged the more conservative of his *sardars*, who had raised the standard of rebellion[3] in support of the outraged ladies. The leader of the rebellion was Lakwa Dada, and several of the other Maratha generals had joined his standard. This led to an inevitable deterioration in the Maratha administration in northern India, as each *sardar* looked to his own advantage.

1 J. Sarkar and G.S. Sardesai (eds), *English Records of Maratha History, vol.8: Daulat Rao Scindia and North Indian Affairs, 1794–1799; vol.9: Daulat Rao Scindia and North Indian Affairs, 1800–1803* (Bombay: Government Central Press, 1943)

2 Francklin, *Military Memoirs*, p.79.

3 Copestake, *Their Infantry and Guns*, pp.107–108.

The frontispiece from Captain Francklin's memoir of George Thomas's campaigns. We have no real idea if this is an accurate portrait of Thomas, and it is very unlikely that he ever wore such a Western-style military costume. It is, however, the only contemporary illustration of this amazing adventurer. (Author's Collection)

Thomas, at this time, seems to have looked to Bapu Scindia, the governor of Seharanpur, for employment. After shooing away Vaman Rao, who had attempted a siege of Thomas's base at Jhajjar, Thomas marched to assist Bapu against a raid by a body of Rohillas, who had been incited to raid the eastern borders of Hindustan by the Sikh *sardar* Nihal Singh, who himself was massing his forces to invade from the west. Nihal declined to face Thomas in battle and Bapu defeated the Rohillas before Thomas's arrival. Thomas therefore marched to Sonnepat, which was still one of his possessions,[4] to inspect its resources and doubtless to 'levy contributions'.

The shifting sands of northern Indian politics and pure bad luck now took a hand. Rumours had been rife that the Afghans were once again to invade Hindustan, and the current Afghan ruler was at this time in Lahore in the Punjab. In fact, the ruler of Afghanistan, Zaman Shah, reached Lahore in January 1797.[5] As this news rippled out across Hindustan, alarm bells rang in all the assorted courts and camps of the various rulers. The consternation caused by this news even put a temporary halt to the 'Widows' War'. The memory of the Maratha defeat of Panipat in 1761 by the Afghans ran deep. Indeed, something close to panic erupted, and new troops were raised, most notably a new brigade – the fourth – for the Army of Hindustan, now commanded by Pierre Cuillier Perron, who had succeeded de Boigne upon his retirement.

It was at this moment that Thomas's much put-upon troops, their pay once again in arrears, refused duty and went on strike. 'Unfortunately, at this critical juncture, Thomas's troops, being in arrears of pay, clamoured for their dues. This, at a time when their service might, at any moment be urgently required, gave the greatest offence

4 Compton, *Particular Account*, p.136.
5 P. Sykes, *A History of Afghanistan*, vol.1 (London: Macmillan & Co, 1940), Indian reprint (New Delhi: Oriental Book Reprint Corporation, 1981), p.373.

and dissatisfaction to Bapu and caused a serious misunderstanding between him and Thomas.'[6]

Seemingly to avoid any conflict, Thomas marched his men away 'in disgust',[7] though how much direct control Thomas had over his force at this point is questionable. Bapu sent some troops in pursuit, and in the ensuing fight, the commander of these troops was wounded, and Bapu's men were defeated.

Further, the Sikh *sardars* serving in Bapu Scindia's forces as mercenaries, always ready to interfere for their own ends, made matters worse. After the action above,

> An amicable arrangement between the parties would now have taken place, had not the Sikhs in Bapu's army, aware of Mr Thomas's intention to enter the Punjab used their utmost exertions to widen the difference. Hostilities being again renewed, an action took place at the passage of the Jumna and though the country people had by this time joined the Marathas, Mr Thomas, by a spirited attack compelled them to leave him a free passage.
>
> Straitened for provisions he proceeded on his route to the North- East frontier; in his retreat, he was followed by Bapu's army, and the troops of the Begum Somru, as also those of Rhagoji the governor of Delhi, had now increased the number of his enemies.[8]

Evidently, Farzana, the Begum Somru, thought she needed to keep an eye on her recent rescuer, ex-confidant, and sometime lover. Whether the Sikhs intrigued against Thomas because of a supposed intention to enter the Punjab, is, possibly, hindsight on the part of Francklin – or perhaps Thomas himself in later years when telling his story to his biographer. The Sikhs' motives were likely to have been more immediate: simply to give Thomas some kind of payback for all the trouble he had given them in the preceding years.

A Freebooter Pure and Simple

Thomas was now in trouble, with enemies all about him. He managed to keep them off until he and his remaining troops reached Panipat, but he simply did not have the military strength to hold that place, so he continued his retreat to his last remaining *jaghir*, that of Jhajjar. This *jaghir* was simply not large enough or rich enough to supply Thomas and his army by itself.

Compton pithily sums up Thomas's predicament,

> Dispossessed of his principal source of income, Thomas was now completely crippled and left with no adequate means to pay his troops, who numbered 3,000 men. He had hitherto occupied a position analogous to other European adventurers

6 Compton, *Particular Account*, p.136.
7 Francklin, *Military Memoirs*, p.82.
8 Francklin, *Military Memoirs*, pp.82–83.

> in the Maratha service, to whom territory was assigned for the upkeep of their corps. But his summary dismissal from his appointment of Frontier Warden and the resumption of his districts by Bapu, left him not only without a master and without a territory, but encumbered by an army heavily in arrears of pay, which had recently mutinied and might at any time mutiny again, and with only the revenues of the comparatively small district of Jhajjar to draw upon.[9]

Thomas would need other sources of income.

To that end, in late 1797 Thomas raided the town of Urika, which was part of the Rajput state of Jaipur, and after his usual speedy assault, extracted a ransom of Rs 52,000 from the *khilladar*. However, much of the town was destroyed by an 'accidental' fire.[10] This foray was only the first of many. 'His attacks were indiscriminate, the occasion of his impecuniosity being the certain signal for a foray on the nearest territory where he could hope to levy a fine.'[11]

It was during this period, sometime in early 1798,[12] that Thomas re-established somewhat friendly relations with Vaman Rao, who still needed an 'enforcer' to collect revenue from refractory *zemindars* who were behind with their tribute. One of Thomas's forays on behalf of Vaman Rao was against a 'thievish tribe' the Meenas, who inhabited an area of Jaipur and had been raiding into Rewari, which was Vaman Rao's territory. Thomas attacked them and 'annihilated this nest of banditti'.[13]

The Conquest of Hariana

> George Thomas, retreating from the Jaipur territory has considerably augmented his force, established himself in the ancient town of Hansi, the fort of which he has had [re-]modelled and strengthened and makes a formidable appearance in the territory of Rewari, either levying contributions or possessing himself of the forts to support his footing in that district.[14]

Thus did Captain Paris Bradshaw, the EIC's assistant resident with Scindia, report the bare facts as he knew them, of George Thomas's conquest of Hariana. Of course, there was much more to this bald announcement than the short letter sent by Bradshaw to the Governor-General in far-away Calcutta.

Francklin tells us that Thomas formed the idea of becoming independent in mid-1798,[15] but the idea must have been older than that, as Captain Bradshaw's letter quoted above is dated 11 May 1798, and tells us that Thomas already had possession of Hansi,

9 Compton, *Particular Account*, p.137.
10 Francklin, *Military Memoirs*, p.83 and Sarkar, *Mughal Empire*, vol.4, p.195.
11 Compton, *Particular Account*, p.138.
12 J.N. Sarkar & G.S. Sardesai, *Poona Residency Correspondence*, vol.8, letter 70.
13 Francklin, *Military Memoirs*, p.84.
14 Sarkar & Sardesai, *Poona Residency Correspondence*, vol.8, letter 70.
15 Francklin, *Military Memoirs*, p.84.

which would become the capital of his 'state' of Hariana. Given the distances and the time for Bradshaw to receive the information, Thomas must have begun his conquest in February or March of 1798 at the latest. This was especially true as, to begin with, all did not go according to plan.

> His first attack was directed against the town and fort of Kanhori, the inhabitants of which were notorious for their thievish depredations. Advancing with celerity, Mr Thomas, according to his usual custom, attempted to carry the place by storm. In this, however, he was not only prevented by the spirited conduct of the enemy, but compelled to retreat with the loss of 300 of his men.[16]

Thomas now began a siege, but the rains and the condition of the ground prevented the use of formal siege works. Thomas's answer was to erect and occupy a chain of posts around the town to prevent help reaching them from outside, but also to prevent the garrison escaping or gathering provisions of which they were somewhat short.

The garrison, however, was made of stern stuff. They made frequent sallies against Thomas's besieging forces, disrupting his siege operations. The garrison would be composed of the usual northern Indian irregular troops, mostly matchlock-armed musketeers with swords as secondary weapons. There may also have been some cavalry, since the inhabitants were apparently notorious for their thieving from their neighbours. Whatever the precise makeup of the garrison, they were adept enough to give Thomas some serious trouble.

> The enemy by frequent sallies endeavoured to interrupt Mr. Thomas's operations. In one of these an attack was made on the redoubt occupied by himself. In the confusion attendant on a business of this nature, the greater part of his people being panic struck ran away. Mr Thomas was thus reduced to a situation truly critical, five men only remained with him of the infantry, to whom he had allotted the particular charge of his firearms, consisting of pistols and blunderbusses of a large size; with these and the assistance of a few horsemen, who had likewise adhered to him, he maintained the post for a considerable time against every effort of the enemy, and at length, by repeated and well directed discharges compelled them to retreat.[17]

Subsequently, the weather improved sufficiently for Thomas to erect a proper battery with heavy guns. This battery opened fire and brought down enough of the wall for Thomas to prepare for a second attempt at a storm, but the enemy evacuated the town during the night and both the town and fort fell the following day.[18]

This costly victory gave Thomas control of much of the southern half of Hariana. It would take him some time to conquer the northern half of the state.

16 Francklin, *Military Memoirs*, p.85.
17 Francklin, *Military Memoirs*, pp.85–86.
18 Francklin, *Military Memoirs*, p.86.

As for the size of the territory that fell under Jehazi Sahib's control,

> As a base for such a rover's life he chose the no man's land west of the Rewari-Delhi –Karnal districts and south of Patiala, which bore the name of Hariana with the city and fort of Hansi for his capital... The tract of land under the rule of George Thomas was oval in shape with ill-defined and ever shifting frontiers. It extended thirty-two to forty-eight miles in different directions. On the north lay the Ghaghar river which separated it from the lands under Sikh occupation, on the west, the country of the predatory Bhati tribe, beyond which lay the deserts of Bikaner. The south was bounded by the Rewari district. In most of the parts of this tract water is scarce. Hence the inhabitants have constructed wells, of 120 to 150 or even 200 feet deep. In the Hissar district there are 300 such wells.
>
> The northern part of Hariana owes its life to the Ghaghar river, which remains lost in sand during nine months of the year but overflows during the rainy season and spreads over the soil a rich fertilizing loam, washed down from the Himalayan foothills, which yields an abundant crop of the finest wheat. The south and west parts are dry and the water has to be drawn up from the very deep wells because the rainfall is scanty and drought frequent. Here in good seasons, they grow millets, pulse, barley and rice. But 'the pasturage is uncommonly luxuriant... The grass of Hariana is of a superior quality, both as to wholesomeness and nourishment. Hence the cattle excel those of other parts'. Even today the Hissar breed of bulls and cows is famous throughout India.[19]

If Thomas could hold these lands and give them peace from other freebooters and bandits, then he would have the foundations to increase his military forces. In this, he seems to have had significant success to begin with. His capital at Hansi, in the centre of his domain, was virtually deserted when he occupied it, yet the population grew. 'But by degrees and by gentle treatment, Thomas attracted nearly 6,000 people to take up their residence in the place, and to these he allowed every lawful indulgence, and guaranteed the protection of their lives, liberty and property.'[20]

In time, Thomas would establish a gun foundry and arms manufacturing at his capital. Francklin here appears to quote him directly:

> Here says Mr. Thomas (with that energy and spirited animation, which distinguished him throughout the scenes of his extraordinary life) Here I established my capital, rebuilt the walls of the city, long since fallen into decay, and repaired the fortifications. As it had been long deserted, at first I found difficulty procuring inhabitants, but by degrees and gentle treatment I selected five and six thousand persons, to whom I allowed every lawful indulgence.
>
> I established a mint and coined my own rupees, which I made current in my own army and country, as from the commencement of my career at Jhajjar, I had

19 Sarkar, *Mughal Empire*, vol.4, p.197.
20 Compton, *Particular Account*, p.142.

> resolved to establish an independency. I employed workmen and artificers of all kinds, and I now judged that nothing but force of arms could maintain me in my authority. I therefore increased their numbers, cast my own artillery, commenced making muskets, matchlocks and powder, and in short made the best preparations for carrying on an offensive and defensive war, till at length having gained a capital and country bordering the Sikh territories, I wished to put myself in a capacity when a favourable opportunity should offer of attempting the conquest of the Punjab, and aspired to the honour of planting the BRITISH standard on the banks of the ATTOCK.[21]

Some of this hyperbole as regards planting the British standard 'on the banks of the Attock' is simply wishful hindsight on Thomas's part, for despite his military skill and love of a fight, it is very doubtful if he would have had the strength to conquer much of the Punjab, even if he had sufficient financial means to do so, which, of course, he did not.

At any event, Thomas tried to give the people of Hariana some kind of peace and security, both of which often seemed decidedly scarce in much of the Indian subcontinent at this time.

The Battle of Fatehpur, February 1799

Thomas was, as usual, short of money to pay his troops, but a possible expedient arrived in the shape of Vaman Rao, his one-time employer. Lakwa Dada, temporarily in favour again with Daulat Rao Scindia, ordered Vaman to collect unpaid tribute from the Rajput state of Jaipur. Vaman Rao did not have the strength to do this formidable task alone, as the Rajputs had the reputation of being the bravest warriors in Hindustan, which, despite the serious defeats that de Boigne had given them at the battles of Patan and Merta,[22] they still held.

In fact, although their bravery was almost legendary, their armies were still essentially medieval in character. The best of their troops were feudally raised cavalry, each clan or family under its own chieftain, the richer men in armour, and all carrying lance and sword, with perhaps an axe or mace as a secondary weapon. Firearms were despised by these 'high-born' warriors – suitable for lowly foot soldiers but not to be touched by Rajput nobles. Rajput armies were often mostly cavalry, with infantry accorded only a secondary role.

They made a fetish of courage and 'honour', which made them fine warriors, but often tactically inept compared to the mercenary regulars they would face. Indeed, their approach to warfare and battle had become rather stylised.[23] Battles tended to open with a cannonade from guns, which were largely immobile once placed. Then,

21 Francklin, *Military Memoirs*, pp.93–94.
22 Copestake, *Their Infantry and Guns*, pp.80–90.
23 R.K. Saxena, *The Army of the Rajputs* (Udaipur: Saroj Prakashan, 1989), pp.348–363, for Rajput battlefield tactics.

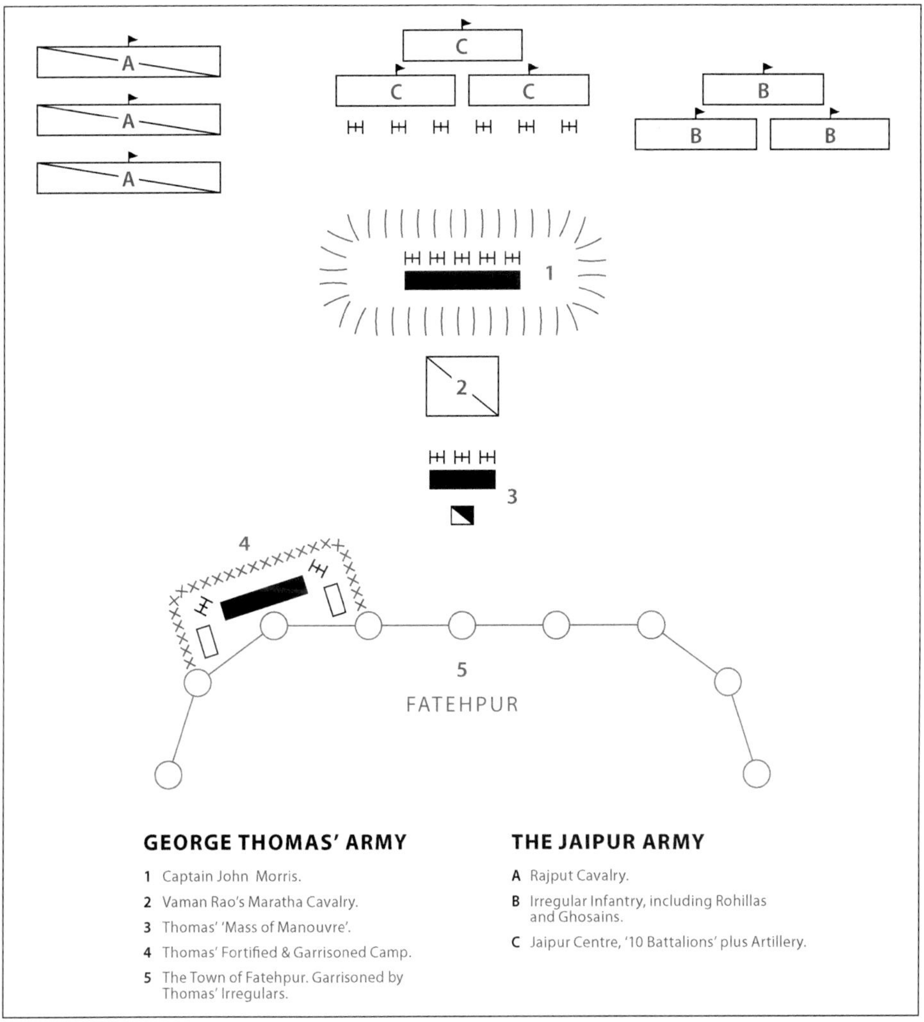

The Battle of Fatehpur. Initial dispositions of the two armies. (Gary Luxton © Helion & Co.)

when the enemy was thought to be weakened sufficiently by this cannonade, the cavalry would begin a – hopefully – decisive charge to contact. Command functions were often non-existent beyond clan leader level, which meant that the finer points of battlefield movement were rarely seen.

However, Vaman Rao had more to contend with than mere reputation. Despite the defeats Jaipur had suffered in recent campaigns, the Rajput state under Raja Partab Singh could still bring formidable numbers of warriors into the field.

> Partab Singh's army consisted of 30,000 cavalry and 18,000 infantry, with a numerous and well appointed artillery. The order to compel the lord of so many

> legions to pay up tribute, quite staggered the little quill-driving copper counting chief, and he immediately wrote pressing letters to Thomas urging him to assist in the proposed expedition.[24]

Despite Vaman Rao's entreaties, Thomas at first declined to take part, being concerned with those parts of Hariana still to be brought under his rule. Vaman Rao was determined upon the expedition, quite possibly because Lakwa Dada had agreed that Vaman Rao could garner ten-sixteenths of any sum gathered into his own purse, with only the remainder being sent to the Maratha coffers, but Vaman simply did not command the military muscle to take on Jaipur alone. He needed Thomas. In the end, Thomas was forced to agree, simply because, as usual, he was short of funds and needed a plundering expedition to 'levy contributions'.

However, there may have been a little more to it than a mere plundering raid. Colonel James Tod's *Annals and Antiquities of Rajasthan*, first published in 1829, cites considerable internal treachery within the Jaipur state, as the prince of Khandela, a feudatory of Jaipur, had been treacherously captured and imprisoned by Partab Singh's prime minister:

> Bagh Singh brother of the captive Prince of Khandela, who was so incensed by the faithless conduct of the court, after the great services they had recently performed, that he determined to oppose by force of arms this infraction of their charter which declared the inviolability of the territory of the confederation so long as the tribute was paid. He was joined by five hundred men of Khetri, which having levied contributions at Singhana and Fatehpur from the traitorous Lord of Sikar, he invited to their aid the celebrated George Thomas then carving out his fortunes amongst these discordant political elements.[25]

It is, therefore, entirely possible that it was this invitation – which Francklin, incidentally, makes no mention of – as well as a promise of some money up front,[26] that persuaded Thomas that the expedition was a viable option.

Whatever the factors governing Thomas's decision process, he joined forces with Vaman Rao for the invasion of Jaipur early in 1799. The two forces united at Karnal. Their combined forces do not seem unduly impressive on paper.

Thomas's *compoo* for this campaign consisted of 1,200 regular infantry, divided into three small battalions of 400 men each, 90 cavalry, 300 Rohilla matchlockmen and 200 Hariana peasantry, which, were probably for camp duties. This small force, however, had 14 guns with crews drilled in the European manner, which would give them a much faster rate of fire than that common in 'unreformed' Indian armies such as the Rajputs.

24 Compton, *Particular Account*, p.146.
25 J. Tod and W. Crooke, *Annals and Antiquities of Rajasthan* (Calcutta, 1829; repr. Delhi: Motilal Banarsidass, 1987), vol.3, pp.1408–1409.
26 Francklin, *Military Memoirs*, p.108.

Vaman Rao's contribution to the invading army consisted of 900 Maratha cavalry, four guns, 600 irregular infantry, and a single battalion of 'regulars' of unknown strength, but unlikely to be more than 500 men. So, at most, Thomas and Vaman Rao could command not much more than 4,000 men to contend with the possibly 40,000-strong army of Jaipur.[27]

At first, all went well. 'The confederates set out from Karnal and entered the Shekahwati district in the north side of the Kachwa kingdom, levying contributions from villages on the way. Bagh Singh of Khandela and other disloyal barons of that district welcomed and subsidised the invaders out of spite for their liege lord the Raja of Jaipur.'[28]

As Francklin tells the tale, 'The offer was accepted, and the troops marching forward compelled several others to similar exactions. For near a month the united armies continued their progress without interruption, but the Raja of Jaipur who had in the interim been collecting his troops, now marched to the relief of his possessions.'[29]

Thomas and Vaman Rao were shortly to be in deep trouble, not that Partab Singh was actually leading his army – that role he had delegated to his favourite Rodoji Khawas,[30] who would have something around 30,000–40,000 men under his command, all to crush Thomas and Vaman Rao and their paltry 4,000.

However, before we credit either side with an incredible skill or equally incredible stupidity, perhaps we might take account of the difficulties of generalship in an age and place where maximum speed was that of a fast horse or camel. 'To credit the commanders of those days therefore with wonderful strategic insight or with extraordinary crassness is equally unreal. They and their armies wandered about in a slow frustrating version of blind man's buff occasionally blundering into each other by chance.'[31] This is, perhaps, a somewhat harsh judgement by a professional soldier-turned-author of a later age, but, based on the evidence of many campaigns as it is, the statement has more than a kernel of truth.

In the event, Thomas became aware of the much larger Jaipur forces closing in on his army. Vaman Rao thought the game was up and advocated retreat. Thomas disagreed, and while we may doubt the veracity of the words Francklin put into his mouth saying that retreat would be, 'a dishonour to himself and his progenitors who never turned their backs on an enemy'.[32]

There were reasons enough for carrying on. The terrain they were moving through was largely desert, and food, and especially water, were extremely scarce. The army was running short of both. The troops were tired and needed rest, so a long and arduous retreat was out of the question without some kind of resupply. That supply could only come from the nearby town of Fatehpur. Without the resources of that town, Thomas

27 Francklin, *Military Memoirs*, p.109.
28 Sarkar, *Mughal Empire*, vol.4, pp.195–196.
29 Francklin, *Military Memoirs*, p.109.
30 Sarkar, *Mughal Empire*, vol.4, p.196.
31 Bidwell, *Swords for Hire*, p.137.
32 Francklin, *Military Memoirs*, p.110.

and Vaman Rao were finished. Without food and water, the troops could not go much further, and once the gun bullocks and baggage animals began to die, the guns and ammunition would be stranded in the desert. Fatehpur was, in effect, their last hope. 'In the end Vaman Rao agree to risk an engagement, and with this determination marched to Fatehpur, a prosperous and important town in the Shekwati district where there was a prospect of finding a supply of grain sufficient for the troops and securing a strong defensive position.'[33]

However, on arriving outside the town, Thomas found the gates shut against him and the walls manned. Worse still, just outside the town, a body of 400 men was overseeing the filling in of the only available well.

> The possession of this remaining well, now became the object of contention betwixt Mr Thomas and a body of 400 men who had been detached from the city, for the express purpose of filling it up; Mr Thomas, who perceived no time was to be lost, ordered his cavalry to charge, the action was at first obstinate, but two of the enemy's *sirdars* being killed, the rest retreated and the well was happily preserved. This was of great importance, as except for this single supply, no water was to be procured but from a considerable distance.
>
> The service on this day was uncommonly severe, as Mr Thomas had completed a march of five and twenty miles over a deep sand which in most places was above the ankles of his men, he was therefore glad to encamp and afford some repose to his fatigued troops.[34]

If the infantry were fatigued after such a march, then the gunners and the bullocks hauling the guns and tumbrils must have been in a considerably worse condition.

The town governor now offered Thomas a *lakh* of rupees (Rs 100,000) as a ransom. Vaman countered in a typically Maratha manner with a demand for 10 lakhs, which was, of course, utterly out of the question. Negotiations were therefore broken off. Thomas could not waste time in further fruitless banter, as the Jaipur forces were now nearing Fatehpur, so the following morning he stormed the town. 'In the early hours of the next morning, he formed up a storming party, escaladed the walls and quickly made a lodgement in the town. It surrendered at once on the promise of being spared a sack.'[35]

Time was now of the essence. Thomas needed every minute to prepare his position for the upcoming attack by the far larger Jaipur forces. In this, he was helped by the dilatory conduct of his enemy, who were not exactly speedy in their approach. Perhaps Rodoji Khawas thought he had these importunate raiders at his mercy, therefore he could take his time while they contemplated the fate that awaited them.

Whatever the reasons, Thomas was given enough time to fortify his position. The sandy terrain made European-style entrenchments impossible, so Thomas used what he had to hand.

33 Compton, *Particular Account*, p.147.
34 Francklin, *Military Memoirs*, p.111.
35 Bidwell, *Swords for Hire*, pp.138–139.

> In the neighbourhood were an abundance of large thorn trees which are common in the west of India, a sufficient number of these were cut down and by Mr. Thomas's direction piled one upon another in the front and flanks of his camp, his rear being secured by the city of Fatepur. To render it more impregnable the branches of the trees being closely interwoven with each other were then made fast with ropes thus forming CHEVAUX DE FRIZE to keep off the cavalry, and lastly a large quantity of sand was thrown between the branches which pointed outward towards the enemy.[36]

This fortified camp and the walls of Fatehpur gave Thomas a firm foundation around which he could manoeuvre if he chose to do so. Fatehpur was garrisoned by his Hariana irregulars, stiffened by 100 Rohillas.[37] Other irregulars must have been left to garrison the camp and man the chevaux-de-frise, though this is not stated. Indeed, other than the Maratha horse, we know nothing of the position or activities of the rest of the troops under Thomas's command. Some – in addition to those mentioned – must have been in Fatehpur and others may have been in the camp, but this is no more than 'informed speculation'.

Thomas also took the time to fill up the nearby wells outside of the city. Although not stated specifically, this must have included the well that he had fought for only a few days previously.

After leaving a battalion of his regulars with four 6-pounder guns to guard the camp, even assuming the Maratha infantry were there, it is clear that Thomas placed no reliance in them. Thomas had a force of no more than 800 regular infantry in two battalions, 200 Rohilla irregulars, and his own troop of about 80 or 90 cavalry, together with 10 guns to face the mass of the Jaipur army.

The Maratha cavalry, which Bidwell describes as 'perfectly useless',[38] were, of course, Thomas's eyes and ears in the days immediately prior to the coming battle, and thus far from useless. It must have been they who brought the news of the approach of the Jaipur force and they who informed Thomas of its encamping within four cos (approximately 6–8 miles, or 10–13 km) of Fatehpur. Thomas's filling of the wells had given the Jaipur army the same water problem, but on a larger scale, that Thomas had undergone on his initial approach to Fatehpur a few days previously.

To secure the wells, Rodoji Khawas sent forward an advance guard, some 7,000 strong, both horse and foot.

> For two days he allowed them to proceed with their work uninterruptedly but on the third morning, he with two battalions of infantry eight pieces of artillery and his own cavalry marched out with a resolution to attack their grand park of artillery, leaving directions to the battalion that remained behind to attack and disperse the advanced party before mentioned; On his departure he left a written

36 Francklin, *Military Memoirs*, pp.113–114.
37 Francklin, *Military Memoirs*, p.119.
38 Bidwell, *Swords for Hire*, p.136.

> paper for Vaman Rao requesting that chief to follow with the remainder of his cavalry and the infantry he had with him to provide for the security of the camp.[39]

A night march is never easy, and this one was no exception. A tumbril, or ammunition cart, was 'upset' on the road, and righting and reloading it took considerable time, so that the new day was dawning when Thomas's force arrived in sight of the enemy camp. Worse yet, the Rajputs were assembled, ready to receive Thomas's attack.

Failing in his hope for a night attack on the Rajput camp, Thomas's force now fell in with the advance guard sent to clear out the wells by Rodoji. Thomas attacked this force, causing it to fall back 'with considerable loss'[40] on its main body. Pausing only to fill in the wells once more and to collect the horses and cattle left by the retreating Rajputs, he retired upon Fatehpur without further inconvenience.

There was a curious upshot to this action. Thomas had, on the previous night before his departure, said nothing of his plan to Vaman Rao, leaving only a written paper containing his instructions. He did this to avoid letting his intentions be known as, 'from his experience of the Marathas, who he well knew, if acquainted with his plans could keep nothing secret but would by divulging them put the enemy on their guard.'[41]

One is forced to wonder if somehow, despite Thomas's precautions, the news of the attack had 'been divulged', as the Rajputs were, by Thomas's own account, 'on their guard'. We can never know this for sure, of course, but it is at least a possibility. The following day, the Jaipur army finally approached Fatehpur in battle array. The delay doubtless being caused in part by having to dig out the wells yet again.

Thomas now moved out with his 'field force' of two battalions of infantry, 80 or so cavalry, 200 Rohillas, and 10 field pieces to take on an army roughly 10 times his own size or perhaps a little more. The catch-all figure of 40,000 men is mentioned by Bidwell,[42] but it is unlikely that all of those were present, much less effective. A considerable number of men must have been left in the camp, as the Rajputs were aware of Maratha cavalry in the vicinity, and while these horsemen were not always to be relied on as battle cavalry, they were excellent raiders and plunderers and a large, unguarded camp would be far too tempting a target for them to ignore.

Other numbers for the Rajput army given in Francklin are surely inflated by Thomas's memory:

> Their right wing, consisting of their whole force of Rajput cavalry was destined to the attack of his camp, and so certain were they of victory, that on perceiving the stockade we have before described, they laughed at the idea, that a few bushes, as they were pleased to term them, could for a moment, retard their progress or resist the impetuosity of the attack; the left wing consisted of 4,000 Rohillas, 3,000 *goshains* and 6,000 irregular infantry commanded by the chiefs of their respective

39 Francklin, *Military Memoirs*, p.115.
40 Francklin, *Military Memoirs*, p.116.
41 Francklin, *Military Memoirs*, p.115.
42 Bidwell, *Swords for Hire*, p.140.

> districts, advanced at the same time with hasty strides and loud shouts to take possession of the city, the loss of which by cutting off the supply of water, would have been attended with the most serious consequences.
>
> The third or main body was composed of 10 battalions of infantry, 22 pieces of artillery and the *sillah posh* or body guard of the Raja consisting of 1,600 men armed with matchlocks and sabres.[43]

Even if we assume that the '10 battalions' had only 400 men each, this still gives the Rajputs a total of over 18,000 infantry, which is surely far too many. Unfortunately, no numbers of any kind are given by Francklin for the Rajput cavalry, though there must have been several thousands of these Rajput 'knights'.

Nevertheless, even reducing these numbers by 50 percent, it is clear that the Jaipur army still massively outnumbered Thomas and Vaman Rao's total force by five to one or more, and that Thomas's own force, which would take the brunt of the coming action, may have been outnumbered by as many as 10 to one. However, he was not without some advantages. To begin with, his artillery was far superior in terms of manoeuvrability and firepower, gun for gun, than the Jaipur guns. His *golandauz* – gunners – were trained in the European method, which gave them an advantage in speed with which they could reload and fire their pieces twice as fast as the undrilled Rajput gunners. His infantry was also trained in the European method to fire by volley and reload quickly. They could also move about the battlefield while retaining their order and formation – something which was beyond most Indian irregular infantry. Further, Thomas's small force had a unified command structure. Thomas was able to react much faster to events on the battlefield than the larger, more unwieldy Rajput force he was facing. However, Thomas could not afford any mistakes. His force was too small to survive a full-blooded onslaught by his opponent.

Thomas made his dispositions with some care. As the Jaipur army moved slowly forward, the right and left wings of the host moved somewhat faster than the centre, so that they almost surrounded Thomas's force. To Thomas's front, some distance from his defended camp, was a ridge or large sandhill. Upon this eminence, Thomas placed 11 companies of infantry and seven guns under the command of the otherwise unknown Captain John Morris, an English officer in his service.[44]

Vaman Rao's 900 or so Maratha horse were placed behind Morris's command. Thomas himself kept under his own hand five companies of infantry, three guns, and his cavalry, so perhaps 350 men all told. This small force Bidwell describes as Thomas's 'mass of manoeuvre',[45] and it was this force that would fight much of the battle. What is important here is that Thomas's forces occupied a central position between the aforementioned ridge occupied by Morris's command and the walled town of Fatehpur, garrisoned by some of Thomas's irregulars, against which rested Thomas's fortified and garrisoned camp. Within the confines of that space, Thomas had almost complete

43 Francklin, *Military Memoirs*, pp.117–118.
44 Bidwell, *Swords for Hire*, pp.141–142; Francklin, *Military Memoirs*, p.118.
45 Bidwell, *Swords for Hire*, p.142.

freedom of movement to strike the comparatively ponderous Jaipur forces where and how he would.

Thomas's account of the ensuing action is rather confusing in parts, but we also have Bidwell's professional soldier's analysis, which unravels much of the confusions. In essence, the combat breaks down into four segments.

The opening attack on Thomas's forces was made by the Rajput cavalry of their right wing. They advanced in 'close and compact order',[46] but were frustrated by the 'few bushes' and the fire of the guns and infantry holding the camp against them. They were further incommoded by Thomas's own force, which, from its position behind the ridge, could engage the Rajput cavalry in flank and rear.

> the enemy as thus placed between two fires and could neither charge him or attack the camp, they consequently began to draw off, but perceiving he had but few cavalry and those being in his rear on a sudden made a furious charge on them by which the person who commanded, and several other brave men were instantly cut to pieces, and it was not until the advance of two companies of grenadiers, who after having given their volley, charged with bayonets that the enemy thus exposed, were compelled to retreat.[47]

In the meantime, over on the other flank, the Rajput infantry – the *goshains* and Rohillas – had mounted a rather half-hearted attack on the city itself, which Thomas's own Rohillas and Hariana irregulars had no real trouble fending off, as they had fortified themselves in the tallest houses, which overlooked the walls of the town. This lacklustre assault was easily beaten off, so that the attacking infantry retired and awaited some artillery support. This support finally arrived in the form of a six-gun battery, which, after some delay, began to fire upon the city. At this, Thomas took his 'mass of manoeuvre' across the field, behind the ridge still held by Morris, who seems to have done a sterling job occupying the Jaipur centre and thus keeping it out of the action. This manoeuvre allowed Thomas to attack the Jaipur infantry and the six-gun battery now firing on the city. The infantry do not seem to have put up much of a fight, and were soon in rout. The Jaipur artillery seem to have seen him coming, as four of the guns made their escape, but two 24-pounder guns remained, perhaps stuck in the sand. They would make an important addition to Thomas's artillery train, if he could capture and hold on to them.

However, the Rajput main body in their centre now seemed, finally, to have decided to intervene, rather than simply watching and being fired on by Morris on his ridge. Thomas, therefore, joined Morris, adding his three guns to Morris's seven, and began to fire upon this main body.

> Their main body had by this time become a confused mass, without order, regularity or method. The enemy notwithstanding, was determined to risk the issue of the

46 Francklin, *Military Memoirs*, p.118.
47 Francklin, *Military Memoirs*, pp.118–119.

> day on a general charge on Mr. Thomas's main body, but their general was not met on this occasion with equal ardour by his troops; and Mr Thomas perceiving them at a stand, commenced a heavy fire of grape from his guns, when after sustaining much loss the enemy retreated.[48]

Thomas now ordered a pursuit, in which Vaman Rao's Maratha cavalry, who had seemingly been cowering behind Morris's main body, unsure of where to flee, were delighted to join in.

They had done nothing in the preceding hours of fighting, except bleat for reinforcements, which Thomas sent from the troops in his fortified camp. This force, four infantry companies and two guns seemingly joined Thomas,[49] after which no more is heard of them as a separate body. So, we can deduce either that they returned to the camp or that they remained with Thomas adding to his 'mass of manoeuvre'. Both options are possible, though the latter – adding themselves to Thomas's force – is perhaps the more likely. The extra 200 or so infantry and especially two more guns would give Thomas that little extra 'punch' when dealing with the Rajput attacks. Then, when Thomas later joined Morris with a possible maximum of 12 guns to bring to bear on the stalled Jaipur main body, it is little wonder that under such a hail of fire they began to retreat.

Rodoji Khawas, the Rajput general, had singularly failed to command his army in this fight, and now all seemed lost. However, Ranjit Singh, the chieftain of Chaumun, 'to redeem what the cowardice and ill-conduct of the general-in-chief had lost',[50] formed his clansmen into a *ghol*. This dense, close order body of horsemen was almost the Rajput cavalry's only tactical formation. As Vaman Rao's cavalry began the pursuit, Ranjit charged them and straight away sent them scuttling back to where Thomas was attempting to draw off the two 24-pounder guns. The routing Marathas, in their panic, rode down some of Thomas's infantry, and the pursuing Rajputs got in amongst the now disordered foot soldiers and began to put them to the sword. Though the infantry fought on,

> … many of them, even in the agonies of death, seized hold of the bridles of the enemy's horses; the moment was critical, and to Mr Thomas pregnant with great mischief. With the only gun that remained, which he loaded up to the muzzle, and about 150 of his followers; who bravely determined to conquer or die with him, he waited the event with fortitude; after permitting the enemy to approach within 40 yards, he gave his fire accompanied at the same time by a volley of musketry, with such considerable effect, that great numbers of the enemy were instantly knocked down. This first effort, being followed by two other discharges, completely routed the enemy. And drove them from this well contested field.[51]

48 Francklin, *Military Memoirs*, pp.119–120.
49 Francklin, *Military Memoirs*, p.118.
50 Tod, *Annals and Antiquities of Rajasthan*, vol.3, p.1409.
51 Francklin, *Military Memoirs*, p.121.

This last charge of the Rajput horse had been costly. Ranjit Singh, leading the charge himself, was desperately wounded, and the two chieftains of the Khangarot clans, Bahadur Singh and Pahar Singh, along with many of their men, were killed by Thomas's discharges of grapeshot and canister. However, the two 24-pounder guns were recovered by the Rajputs, so in some way this persuaded them that they had not been entirely defeated.[52]

In fact, while Thomas had certainly avoided outright defeat – despite admitting to the loss of some 300 of his men (including the courageous Morris)[53] – it is hard to see what he had actually achieved beyond bare survival. His now reduced force still held Fatehpur, but the enemy had not been dispersed, and despite perhaps being rather battered, had merely retreated to their own camp some distance off and were awaiting reinforcements.

Negotiation seemed the only way out of the trap in which Thomas and Vaman Rao now found themselves. To that end, Thomas sent envoys to the Rajput camp on the following morning, proposing a truce to collect the wounded. This was accepted, and further negotiations were put in train. Rodoji offered Rs 50,000 and an unmolested retreat for Thomas and Vaman Rao to go away and leave him in peace. Rather unwisely, Vaman Rao declined this offer, saying that as Daulat Rao Scindia's representative, which technically he was, he wished to settle the whole matter of unpaid tribute. Rodoji declined, pointing out that this was impossible without consulting his master, the Raja of Jaipur. In the meantime, reinforcements had arrived to strengthen the Jaipur forces, including a contingent from the Raja of Bikaner. Thus, Thomas and Vaman Rao's position was growing worse almost by the day.

Indeed, they were, in effect, under siege, as their foraging parties were attacked, though the Rajputs avoided any major action.[54] To cap it all, messages arrived from Daulat Rao Scindia via the French officer Pierre Cuillier Perron, now commander of Scindia's regular forces, to desist from the whole enterprise and leave Jaipur alone. Retreat was now the only option.

Thomas began the retreat, 'The next morning before daybreak the troops began to file off, but were scarcely got in motion, when the enemy's whole force came up to the attack; while it continued dark, great confusion prevailed, but on the appearance of day light, Mr. Thomas, having formed his men, compelled the enemy to retreat with great loss.'[55]

This night action was doubtless very confused, and the Jaipur attack was only beaten off with the coming of dawn. Yet, worse was to come. The ensuing retreat must have been something of a nightmare. The weather was hot, water and fodder were short, and marching through the sand was tiring to say the least. Added to these mere bodily difficulties, the Rajputs were soon in pursuit again, with cavalry threatening to charge when occasion offered, and rocket men who were at times showering the retreating troops with their erratic and frightening missiles.

52 Tod, *Annals and Antiquities of Rajasthan*, vol.3, p.1409.
53 Francklin, *Military Memoirs*, p.122.
54 Bidwell, *Swords for Hire*, p.147.
55 Francklin, *Military Memoirs*, p.125.

> They still continued to hang on his rear, and annoy him with the fire of artillery, assisted by an immense quantity of rockets. From the rapidity of his march, the enemy's heavy guns were soon obliged to remain behind and the rocket and the matchlock men alone continued the pursuit. The day was extremely hot and the troops suffered severely from a total want of water.[56]

The march continued all day, until Thomas's little army arrived at a village, which he does not name, where water was to be had from its two wells. The following day was more or less the same, except that the retreat appears better organised, with Thomas having his artillery as part of the rearguard, the fire from the guns having some success in keeping the Jaipur cavalry at a distance. This continued until the army arrived, 'at a large town, in the neighbourhood of which he was gratified with the sight of an ample supply of water from five wells.'[57]

Thomas took the opportunity to rest his tired men, especially as the Rajputs had now halted their pursuit. Once the troops were rested, Thomas began raiding once more. 'Mr. Thomas recommenced hostilities on the enemy's country, and by a succession of exactions and fines obtained money sufficient to defray his expenses and satisfy his troops for their arrears.'[58] These raids brought the Rajputs to the negotiating table once more, and a 'sum of money' was paid and hostilities therefore ceased.

It is interesting to note here that both Thomas and Vaman Rao ignored the orders sent from Daulat Rao Scindia, Vaman's supposed overlord, via Perron, to desist from these attacks on Jaipur. Thomas evidently saw himself as owing allegiance and obedience to no man, least of all to Perron or Daulat Rao.

Once the hostilities with Jaipur were concluded, Thomas was free to return to Hariana, but rather than return directly to his base, he decided to punish the Raja of Bikaner for his temerity in aiding the Jaipur Raja. Surut Singh, the Raja of Bikaner, had an army estimated at 8,000 men, consisting of both mercenaries and feudal levies, of which two-fifths were cavalry. The Raja also had several European officers who trained his troops.[59] Nevertheless, he declined to meet Thomas in the field and 'confined his defence to strongly garrisoning his frontier towns'.[60] Thomas was rarely averse to storming a garrisoned town, and so it proved. The town of Jeitpur, 'seven marches north-east of the Raja's capital and defended by 3,000 men',[61] was stormed by Thomas and forced to pay a large ransom for the security of its inhabitants and their property. The fate of that town intimidated other towns and villages in the surrounding country, so that the mere appearance of Thomas's troops caused them to disgorge a ransom. Surut Singh had little choice but to attempt negotiation. The net result was that Thomas extracted two lakhs of rupees (Rs 200,000) from the Raja. Half of this was paid in cash and half in promissory notes, which, quite naturally, the Raja later refused to honour. With his

56 Francklin, *Military Memoirs*, p.125.
57 Francklin, *Military Memoirs*, p.126.
58 Francklin, *Military Memoirs*, p.127.
59 Compton, *Particular Account*, p.156.
60 Compton, *Particular Account*, p.156.
61 Compton, *Particular Account*, p.156.

money bags now comparatively full, Thomas now made his way back to Hariana and his capital, Hansi. He would not remain there long.

Begum Somru, Jehazi Sahib, and the Widows' War

Thomas's memoirs, as written by Captain Francklin, are frequently less than exact regarding dates and times. It is quite possible that when Thomas was telling his story to his biographer, he put some of the events in his crowded life in the wrong order. This may be one of those times.

The battle of Fatehpur took place in February 1799, and Thomas's raids into Bikaner followed on swiftly from this action. Francklin next has Thomas conducting a campaign against the Sikhs of Patiala and Jhind (see Chapter 8). However, we have no less a source than the British resident with Daulat Rao Scindia, the experienced Colonel John Collins, informing the Governor-General in Calcutta, in a letter dated 28 April 1799, that Thomas was already campaigning in Malwa against Lakwa Dada, who had taken up the cause of Madhaji Scindia's widows.[62] Now, Thomas may have been able to act with some speed, but the distances involved and the shortage of time must at least allow for the possibility that Thomas simply misremembered the precise order of his actions when telling his story to Francklin in the months before his death.

To say that the political and personal cross-currents of the 'Widows' War' are 'complicated' is something of an understatement. Fortunately, we are only concerned with that part of this particular conflict that took place in the northern areas of Daulat Rao Scindia's territories. Of course, this included Hindustan and those imperial lands which the Marathas administered. The major cities and forts of Delhi, Agra, Gwalior, and Aligarh all had Maratha governors, as did many smaller places. The outrage caused by Daulat Rao's mistreatment of Madhaji's widows led to a widespread rebellion amongst the more conservative Maratha nobles.

The fighting began in February 1799, as Collins reported in his letter to the Governor-General of 18 February, 'Lakwa Dada has assembled about twenty thousand irregular horse and foot with which force he plunders the Maharajah's districts with impunity.'[63]

The revolt would spread quickly, and the governors of Aligarh and Agra had both declared for the rebels by early March 1799. The Raja of Datia brought his men into the field and was attacking Daulat Rao's supporters around the city of Gwalior. In addition, Jagu Bapu was advancing on Ujjain, Daulat Rao's capital.

Things looked decidedly bleak for Daulat Rao, but he was not without allies and adherents. The most effective of these was, of course, Pierre Cuillier Perron, who was now commander-in-chief of the Army of Hindustan, that disciplined body of European-trained Indian mercenary troops that had been created a decade ago by Benoît de Boigne. De Boigne had, by now, retired, and his command had been taken up by Perron. The on-and-off threat of a renewed Afghan invasion had prompted Perron to add a fourth

62 Sarkar, *Poona Residency Correspondence*, vol.8, letter 136.
63 Sarkar, *Poona Residency Correspondence*, vol.8, letter 122.

Pierre Cuillier Perron in old age. Perron, a sometime foundry worker and deserter from the French navy, succeeded Benoît de Boigne as commander of the Army of Hindustan. He had considerable influence over Daulat Rao Scindia and would become instrumental in the eventual destruction of George Thomas. (Public Domain)

brigade to the three already in existence, bringing this army to a paper strength of 40 battalions (10 per Brigade) and over 200 artillery pieces.[64] This was, indeed, a formidable force, but it was often difficult to concentrate more than two brigades in one place. In another letter, Colonel Collins gives the dispositions of Perron's battalions as he knew them as of 4 March 1799:

> The Corps commanded by Mr. Perron are as follows:- Four battalions besieging Agra which fortress is in the possession of Visram Bhow the brother of Balooba Tantia.
>
> Two battalions at Muttra under Colonel Sutherland. Two battalions in Malwa opposing Lakwa Dada and Jagu Bapu. Two battalions under Major Pedron blockading Aligarh, a fort adjacent to Koil and which is commanded by an adherent of Lakwa Dada. One battalion stationed near Gwalior to assist the troops of Ambaji in opposing the Datia Raja.
>
> A large division of Ambaji's force has been detailed to cover Malwa. that Subah being threatened with an invasion by Lakwa Dada and Jagu Bapu; and the other corps in his employ, with an exception of one battalion of infantry and two thousand cavalry with him at Agra are employed against the Raja of Datia who has excited an insurrection of a serious nature in the district of Gwalior.[65]

Colonel Collins put forward a plan to fish in these troubled waters by trying to detach some of the rulers – such as those of the Rajput states – from Scindia's grasp, and they were not the only rulers that Collins recommended to the Governor-General: 'Begam Samroo who lives under constant apprehension of the effects of Scindia's violence and

64 For details of the organisation of the Army of Hindustan, see Copestake, *Their Infantry and Guns*, Chapter 5.

65 Sarkar, *Poona Residency Correspondence*, vol.8, letter 123.

rapacity, and George Thomas who is disgusted with him on account of his being lately deprived of two purganas that were given to Filose would both most readily avail themselves of your Lordships protection from which they might derive great advantages.'[66]

In the event, the British did no more than watch events with interest, but the same letter notes that Thomas's force is within 50 cos (roughly 75 miles) of Delhi and Begum Somru's force no more than 30 cos (45 miles) from that city.

Thomas, meanwhile, had found a new employer, as Daulat Rao Scindia was having trouble containing the spreading rebellion in favour of Madhaji Scindia's widows. Indeed, in March 1799, Collins was reporting to the Governor-General in Calcutta, 'The disturbances in the district of Gwalior have increased in so great a degree that Ambaji finds it necessary to send a reinforcement to the troops now there, and letters from Malwa assert that in consequence of an amicable accommodation between Bala Rao and Lakwa Dada that the former Chief had consented to withdraw his forces from that province.'[67]

Ambaji, as Scindia's main commander in Hindustan, therefore needed all the troops he could get, especially since Perron was still stuck besieging Agra. To that end, Ambaji sent one Khamgar Khan as his emissary, offering Thomas Rs 50,000 per month to enter his service with his troops. At that time, Collins believed Thomas to be 'employed in reducing refractory *zemindars* in Mewat',[68] rather than campaigning against the Sikhs. Collins's more immediate evidence in this case is more believable than the possibly failing memory of Thomas in the months before his death.

Whatever the actual course of events, Thomas, 'Having at present no particular destination he closed with the terms and agreeably to the instructions of Ambaji prepared to lead his army to Udaipur to encounter Lakwa.'[69]

At this time, in early April 1799, the British resident with the *Peshwa*, William Palmer, in Poona, estimated Lakwa Dada's forces, 'By a newspaper which I received yesterday from Lakwa Dada's camp I find that he is about 40 kos north of Ujjain. I cannot exactly learn his force but from my recollection of his original strength and the subsequent junction of confederates it amounts to 15 or 16,000 men and he has a good train of artillery.'[70]

Hindustan was now in more than its usual state of disorder. The Raja of Udaipur attacked Ambaji's possessions in Ajmer, which had formerly been part of Udaipur territory, but the attack was defeated, so the watchful Colonel Collins tells the Governor-General in his letter of 5 April 1799: 'after a sharp conflict by Ambaji's sebandis and some new levies raised by Golabji Kadam an officer in his service. But it would appear from the enclosure no 1 that Ambaji still entertains apprehensions for the safety of his pergannahs in the province of Ajmer.' *Sebandis* or *Seebundies* were irregular infantry,

66 Sarkar, *Poona Residency Correspondence*, vol.8, letter 123. Filose was the commander of another mercenary *compoo* in Scindia's service.
67 Sarkar, *Poona Residency Correspondence*, vol.8, letter 125.
68 Sarkar, *Poona Residency Correspondence*, vol.8, letter 128.
69 Francklin, *Military Memoirs*, p.140.
70 Sarkar, *Poona Residency Correspondence*, vol.8, letter 130.

usually used for revenue collection. Collins continues in the same letter: 'Intelligence from Delhi states that Begum Samroo has perpetrated great outrages in the pergannahs subject to Shah Nizam-ud-Din the governor of Delhi and that Jote Pant amil (on the part of Ambaji) of Saharanpur and Panipat had deserted the interests of his master and was likewise committing depredations in Shah Nizam- ud-Din's jaghir.'[71]

Jote Pant seems to have been the deputy governor of Saharanpur, but he was in rebellion against Ambaji. Indeed, at this time, Collins's letters often contain news regarding Ambaji's problems with Lakwa Dada and the other rebels. It also seems that Perron was spinning out the siege of Agra for his own purposes.[72] There seems to have been considerable jealousy on the part of Maratha officers towards Perron and some of the other mercenaries,

> Lakwa Dada, in a private letter to his family mentions the impolicy of intrusting Mr. Perron with the fortresses of Delhi and Agra and also observes that the existing disturbances in Scindia's territories may be hereafter adjusted to the satisfaction of all parties by mutual concessions but that this Frenchman will not easily be prevailed on to relinquish any command from which he derives either influence or emolument.
>
> Though their apprehensions may be ascribed to self interest, yet bearing in mind the insolent conduct of the French officers in the Deccan and their interference in matters totally distinct from the military profession, I think it is reasonable to suppose that many other Maratha *sardars* are equally desirous, with Ambaji and Lakwa Dada of reducing the consequence which these Europeans have obtained in Scindia's Government.[73]

Collins also adds, in the same letter, his opinion that Begum Somru is 'inclined to favour the party of the Bais' – that is, the rebels – despite a rumour that she had agreed to assist Ambaji with three battalions of her sepoys.

It was in this atmosphere of uncertain loyalties and jealousies that Thomas joined Ambaji Rao sometime in mid-April 1799. Ambaji's troops in Mewar under Golaba Kaddam had recently been defeated by Lakwa Dada, 'with great slaughter... In consequence of this event Ambaji, who is exceedingly alarmed thereat, has pressingly urged Mr. George Thomas to proceed by rapid marches to Ajmer.'[74]

Indeed, there had been an action in which the army of Ambaji's son, usually known as the Bhow, had been defeated by Lakwa largely because some of the Bhow's troops had been 'tampered with' or bribed. There seems to have been two *compoos* under Indian officers in this army in Ambaji's service, '8 battalions under Colonel Kaleb Ali and four under Khutub Khan these had been joined by 2 battalions of Sutherland's Brigade under Captain Butterfield' – with James Skinner as the only other European officer.[75]

71 Sarkar, *Poona Residency Correspondence*, vol.8, letter 131.
72 Sarkar, *Poona Residency Correspondence*, vol.8, letter 131.
73 Sarkar, *Poona Residency Correspondence*, vol.8, letter 132.
74 Sarkar, *Poona Residency Correspondence*, vol.8, letter 133.
75 Copestake, *Their Infantry and Guns*, pp.108–110.

Thomas, however, was having troubles of his own, as at the commencement of his march, his troops once again broke into mutiny over their arrears of pay. In response, Thomas charged the mutineers with his cavalry and expelled the ringleaders from his camp. This was not the end of this affair. Sometime later, the mutiny broke out once more. Thomas, again seizing the ringleaders, put them in irons and chose one of them for execution using the old Mughal punishment of being blown from a gun. This was apparently the last mutiny Thomas had to contend with.[76]

Thomas's force for this campaign was somewhat larger than that he had commanded at the Battle of Fatehpur, being in total six battalions of infantry, 150 cavalry, 300 Rohilla irregulars, and 22 guns.[77] In total, perhaps 3,000 men or a little more. In addition, Ambaji had some troops of his own, though their numbers are never stated. The combined army was joined by four battalions of the First Brigade of the Army of Hindustan, under Colonel Robert Sutherland (Compton says the Second Brigade, but this must be an error, as Sutherland did not command the Second Brigade until the following year),[78] which Perron had sent out as early as mid-March 1799.[79] Colonel Collins, the British resident with Daulat Rao Scindia, sent this intelligence to Lord Mornington, the Governor-General, in a letter dated 25 March of that year. Sutherland was still en route in late April, as Collins reported to Mornington in his letter of 3 May 1799.

> Mr Perron has detached four battalions under the command of Mr Sutherland towards Ajmer by the route of Jaipur. This movement renders the situation of Lakwa Dada still more critical and his ruin which must equally involve the Raja of Udaipur, seems inevitable unless he can give Bala Rao a total defeat previous to the arrival of the troops that are now advancing against him.[80]

These four battalions were in addition to the two sent earlier under Captain Butterfield, who had been roughly handled by Lakwa in an earlier engagement. Assuming Sutherland's battalions were near full strength, these four units should have added around 2,500 bayonets and 20 guns to Ambaji's army.[81] This force now proceeded to the borders of Udaipur to confront Lakwa Dada.

Thomas gives Lakwa Dada a considerably superior force: 'The force of Lakwa at this period amounted to 9,000 cavalry, 6,000 regular infantry, 2,000 Rohillas and about 5 or 6,000 mercenaries together with 90 pieces of artillery.'[82]

He gives no more than these bare details, but it is interesting to note that the regulars may have included a *compoo* commanded by William Henry Tone, brother of the Irish revolutionary leader, Wolfe Tone. William Henry's *compoo* was certainly present in the

76 Francklin, *Military Memoirs*, pp.148–149.
77 Francklin, *Military Memoirs*, p.155.
78 Compton, *Particular Account*, p.161 and Smith, *Regular Corps*, p.52.
79 Sarkar, *Poona Residency Correspondence*, vol.8, letter 126.
80 Sarkar, *Poona Residency Correspondence*, vol.8, letter 137.
81 For details of Army of Hindustan organisation, see Copestake, *Their Infantry and Guns*, pp.60–66.
82 Francklin, *Military Memoirs*, p.155.

campaign that led to Lakwa's final defeat in 1801, where it was strong enough to lose 16 guns to the Third Brigade of the Army of Hindustan.[83] There is no certainty that Tone was present for this earlier campaign, but it is at least a possibility.

Lakwa, a general of considerable skill, had taken up a strong position covering a narrow pass into Udaipur, through which he had sent his heavy baggage and stores. He was sure of the friendship and protection of the Raja,[84] so he really only needed to protect his baggage long enough for the cumbersome collection of elephants, camels, cattle, and carts to negotiate the narrow pass into the safety of Udaipur. 'A plan of attack was now concerted by Mr. Thomas and Mr. Sutherland and the ensuing morning named for carrying it into execution; that very night however Mr Sutherland, without assigning any cause, to Mr. Thomas's utter astonishment, thought proper to decamp and leave him to conduct the operations against Lakwa with his own troops.'[85] The sudden departure of Sutherland improved Lakwa's circumstances significantly, so that he began to manoeuvre against Thomas and Ambaji.

> Mr. Thomas leaving Ambaji with his troops to protect the baggage, advanced against Lakwa in order of battle; but the action was at that time prevented by the coming on of a most tremendous storm of rain, thunder and lightning, which induced Lakwa to halt; Mr. Thomas's position being favourable for cavalry to act, of which the enemy's force chiefly consisted, and far superior in number, he was desirous of changing it, and accordingly moving more to the left, he took post on a rising ground from whence he would have nothing to apprehend from an attack of horse; when the storm was over Lakwa again advanced towards Mr. Thomas, but seeing his advantageous position, and having lost a number of men in his approach from the fire of Mr. Thomas's artillery he thought it proper to draw off the field.[86]

It now became clear why Sutherland had retired, as *vakils* (envoys) from Lakwa's camp came in with letters from Daulat Rao Scindia, ordering a cessation of hostilities. Indeed, by 29 May 1799, Colonel Collins was reporting to the Governor-General that some kind of reconciliation had taken place.[87]

This did not mean the end of the fighting. In the ensuing council of war between the various *sardars* of Ambaji's army, Thomas took the position that he had been retained by Ambaji to bring the province of Mewar back under Ambaji's authority. Without Ambaji's direct order to the contrary, he would continue in this task.[88] To begin with, a sort of uneasy truce existed, while the two armies marched northward and awaited new instructions. Thomas did not trust Lakwa, and, indeed, he had some reasons not to do so. Thomas was aware that the Maratha general was expecting reinforcements from

83 J. Baillie Fraser, *Military Memoirs of Lieut.-Col. James Skinner, C.B.* (London: Smith, Elder & Co., 1851), vol.1, p.186.
84 Francklin, *Military Memoirs*, p.149.
85 Francklin, *Military Memoirs*, pp.149–150.
86 Francklin, *Military Memoirs*, pp.149–150.
87 Sarkar, *Poona Residency Correspondence*, vol.8, letter 145.
88 Francklin, *Military Memoirs*, p.151.

Ajmir, but also that some of Ambaji's officers had been bribed.[89] The net result was a resumption of hostilities some 15 days later.

This time, the two armies were encamped some distance apart, separated by a *nullah*, or dry watercourse.

> Between the camps there ran a *nullah*, the north side of which was occupied by the army of Lakwa, and the troops of Ambaji and Mr. Thomas were stationed on the south; Ambaji, in order to prevent the advance of Lakwa's artillery, who endeavoured to open upon him, fortified an advanced redoubt on the north side of the *nullah* but too far detached from his main body to receive succour in case of an attack; for its defence were stationed 3 battalions of sepoys, 6 pieces of cannon and 1,000 *goshains*. To support these 5 battalions were posted a short distance in the rear.[90]

The weather now intervened, as a heavy rain caused two tanks or reservoirs to overflow, thus filling the *nullah* and making it impassable. This cut off any communication between the redoubt and Ambaji's camp. Lakwa saw his moment, and attacked the now isolated position with some vigour. 'His men, advancing to the assault, were up to their necks in water, which resolute conduct infused such terror into the men in the redoubt, that being panic struck they surrendered without firing a shot. The *goshains* alone refused to submit, and after a brave tho' fruitless resistance were cut to pieces.'[91]

This defeat caused large-scale desertions in Ambaji's forces. However, despite Thomas's constant references to Ambaji, it is clear from Colonel Collins's letters that the actual commander was Nana Ganesh, Ambaji's *dewan* or minister. It would not be a stretch to say that Nana Ganesh's army seems to have fallen apart. Indeed, although Thomas's narrative blames Lakwa's 'intrigues', it looked as if the defeat caused local rulers, such as the Raja of Shahpura, to join what they saw as the winning side. Thomas was cut off from his supplies and forced to retreat some 20 cos (approximately 30 miles or 48 km) to his supply base at a place he names as Singanah.[92]

Colonel Collins, catching up with the news from his camp at Fatehgarh, writes in a letter dated 22 June 1799: 'My latest advices from that province mention that Mr Sutherland, George Thomas and Nana Ganesh, Ambaji's Dewan had advanced within five cos of Lakwa Dada.'[93]

A later inclusion in the same letter notes that Perron has recalled Sutherland from Ajmer, while Ambaji has directed Thomas to withdraw from the vicinity of Lakwa's camp. The implication here is that, despite Thomas's narrative, Ambaji is not yet present with his army in Mewar. However, by 12 July 1799, Collins writes:

89 Francklin, *Military Memoirs*, p.152.
90 Francklin, *Military Memoirs*, p.156.
91 Francklin, *Military Memoirs*, pp.156–157.
92 Francklin, *Military Memoirs*, p.157.
93 Sarkar, *Poona Residency Correspondence*, vol.8, letter 151.

> Lakwa Dada having frequently written to me in most friendly style since his late reconciliation with Scindia, I had no hesitation in soliciting the interposition of his authority and advice with Pertab Singh on the present occasion; and I am free to confess that I have greater expectation of deriving advantage from the influence of this chief than from the promised exertions of Ambaji whose power is on the decline at Jaipur.[94]

Collins further notes in the same letter that, 'The disputes in Ajmer between Lakwa Dada and Ambaji's sardars appear at length to be amicably adjusted. Ambaji and Mr. Perron still continue at their respective cantonments'. Again, Colonel Collins was just a little behind the times, as hostilities had erupted again, as we have seen.

> The renewal of hostilities is solely ascribable to Lakwa Dada who, on the 15th of this month made a vigorous and in some degree successful attack on the troops of Nana Ganesh and Mr. George Thomas. From that day until the 20th instant, which is the date of my last advices from Ajmer the parties have been alternately negotiating and fighting.[95]

Indeed, the fighting seemed to accelerate, as Collins gets some details of the loss of the redoubt. It differs somewhat from Thomas's account:

> Accounts from Mewar state that on the 9th instant [9 August 1799] a body of Lakwajee's troops about five thousand in number, carried by assault one of the batteries of Nana Ganesh which was defended by two battalions of sepoys under the command of Bunead Singh and Bakhtawar Singh both of whom were wounded and made prisoners. Nana Ganesh lost in this action killed and wounded 800 men, five pieces of cannon with their ammunition carts and much baggage.
>
> It is said that Mr. George Thomas was prevented from assisting the troops of Nana Ganesh on this occasion by the overflowing of a *nullah* which ran between his camp and the assaulted battery.[96]

The two accounts are sufficiently similar to be accounts of the same action, and, once again, the relative immediacy of the account given by Collins tends to support its veracity.

However, moves to achieve a political solution were once again afoot, and after considerable negotiations involving Ambaji, Perron and Daulat Rao, as well as Lakwa Dada, some kind of agreement appeared. Lakwa would eventually evacuate Mewar but keep Ajmer. Ambaji kept all his territories around Gwalior. The ink would be barely dry before the 'Widows' War' started again, but none of that would be Thomas's problem.

94 Sarkar, *Poona Residency Correspondence*, vol.8, letter 156.
95 Sarkar, *Poona Residency Correspondence*, vol.8, letter 159.
96 Sarkar, *Poona Residency Correspondence*, vol.8, letter 163.

As far as Thomas was concerned, this meant the end of his employment. His mistrust of Lakwa continued. He refused an order from Scindia to join the now-combined forces of Ambaji and Lakwa, fearing some kind of treachery. Thomas, therefore, began to march northward,

> Refusing therefore compliance with the demand he commenced his march northward.
>
> Lakwa, now throwing off his mask wished to send a force after Mr Thomas to punish him, but was not able to raise a supply of money sufficient for the purpose. Mr. Thomas continued to levy contributions through the Ajmir province through which he directed his march.[97]

In total, Thomas plundered, by his own admission, two lakhs of rupees (Rs 200,000) on this march before returning to Hariana and his base at Hansi to rest his weary army.

Far away on the other side of Delhi, Farzana, the Begum Somru, had not had such an active part in the 'Widows' War'. Yet, for a while, she had been in considerable jeopardy, as she was, as we have seen, suspected of being in sympathy with the widows – the Bais. This may, indeed, have been true, but her first priority, above all others by far, was to hold on to what she had. This would not be easy in the unsettled state of Hindustan in 1799.

After the death of Le Vassault and George Thomas's rescue of Farzana from the mutineers and her consequent reinstatement at Sardhana,[98] the Somru Brigade needed a new commander. The chosen officer was Colonel Saleur, who was either French or Swiss.[99] Saleur added new battalions in 1797 and 1798, bringing the total once more to six.[100] The Begum would need them all.

Sardhana appears as something of an oasis of peace in 1798–99, when the 'Widows' War' was causing the Maratha administration in northern India to fall apart. Covetous eyes were cast upon the Begum's *jaghirs*, not least by Ambaji Ingle, that same chieftain who was employing George Thomas against Lakwa Dada. Colonel Collins's letter to the Governor-General, dated 11 May 1799, lays out the position as he then saw it:

> I have the honour to apprize your Lordship that Ambaji Rao was at Garh Muktesher on the 6th instant and that Mr Perron marched from Aligarh on the 2nd of this month in the same direction.
>
> Several intelligent persons conceive that these commanders entertain hostile designs against Begum Somru, on account of her late evasive conduct. I cannot however believe that Ambaji will make any immediate attempt to dispossess the Begum of her *jaidads*, as such an aggression might cause the defection of Mr George Thomas, whose services are at present indispensably required for the support of Bala Rao in the subah of Ajmer.[101]

97 Francklin, *Military Memoirs*, p.161.
98 See Chapter 6.
99 Compton, *Particular Account*, p.387.
100 Sleeman, *Rambles and Recollections*, p.610.
101 Sarkar, *Poona Residency Correspondence*, vol.8, letter 139.

A week later, Collins was writing of the Begum's troubles once again:

> My public agent at the Court of Delhi assures me that is was the general belief, and public talk in the city that Ambaji and Mr. Perron were determined on depriving Begum Somru of her *jaidad*. He also writes that the Begum being perfectly aware of their hostile designs, had put the fortress of Sardhana into a respectable state of defence and, leaving a strong garrison there was advancing towards Kotana a ghat on the Jumna where the Begum may be speedily reinforced by those Sikh sardars whom, it is supposed, she has attached to her views and interests.[102]

Collins, amongst his many other 'intelligence' tasks, was keeping an eye on the movements of the Begum Somru and her forces. A few days after his previous letter, on 22 May 1799, he notes, together with other news: 'Begum Somru is at Kotana where she has assembled the greatest part of her forces, She lately transmitted to Ambaji a letter from Daulat Rao Scindia to his address, in which the Maharaja enjoins his chiefs not to molest the Begum under any pretence, as she was an old adherent of his family.'[103]

How effective this order was is open to some doubt. The Begum obviously distrusted both Ambaji and Perron. In May 1799, both of these commanders were engaged in the siege of the fort of Parichitgarh whose owner, 'Nainsook a Gujar Chief had committed many acts of aggression against the government of Scindia in Hindustan.'[104]

Collins reported on 6 June 1799 that the Begum was advancing on the fort of Parichitgarh and gives the strength of her field army:

> Advices of the 1st instant from Parichitgarh mention that Begum Somru had arrived within three cos of this fort with five Battalions of sepoys complete, two hundred troopers, twenty-five pieces of cannon and forty European artillerymen. This report was made to Mr Perron by an hiccarah whom he sent to examine into the state and situation of her troops.
>
> The nearer approach of Begum Somru has alarmed both Ambaji and Mr. Perron whose present force is by no means considerable. Possibly, however, the Begum entertains no hostile designs against those commanders, and only means to secure her own person from any attempt of violence or treachery.[105]

Farzana, evidently, did not mean to be threatened or trifled with by either Ambaji or Perron. At all events, she remained with her troops and seemed ready to fight, if there was no alternative. Her 'field army' was not large. Assuming 500–600 men per battalion, plus the cavalry and gun crews, this would give a total of no more than 3,500 fighting men.

102 Sarkar, *Poona Residency Correspondence*, vol.8, letter 141.
103 Sarkar, *Poona Residency Correspondence*, vol.8, letter 142.
104 Sarkar, *Poona Residency Correspondence*, vol.8, letter 142.
105 Sarkar, *Poona Residency Correspondence*, vol.8, letter 148.

Collins's next two letters to the Governor-General explain the situation further. First, his letter of 10 June 1799:

> The spirited conduct evinced by Begum Somru has induced Ambaji to submit to the humiliation of sending his son to her camp for the purpose of gratifying her pride or softening her resentment, and it is supposed that this visit will be productive of an interview and reconciliation between the Begum and the Maratha Chieftain.
>
> I do myself the honour to enclose the translation of a letter from my native agent in Ambaji's camp, the contents of which will satisfy your Lordship that Begum Somru neither fears nor respects Mr. Perron. In fact she considers this officer in the light of a determined enemy, who would deprive her of her *jaidad* were his power proportionate to his enmity.[106]

And his letter of just seven days later:

> Ambaji and Mr. Perron seem to have established their quarters at Khatauli, one of the disputed Mahals, and the troops of the Begum Somru are encamped within a cos of the same place. Outlying piquets covered by artillery, are posted from each camp and every precaution denoting apprehended treachery has been taken by both parties. My native agent in the camp of Ambaji, writes that if Mr Perron does not soon relinquish his demands on the Begum, hostilities are unavoidable, as she is positively determined not to surrender the Mahals until her accounts are fairly settled and the balance liquidated.[107]

In the event, no fighting seems to have occurred, and news of the Begum's movements disappears from Collins's intelligence reports for a while. The on-off negotiations between Lakwa Dada and Daulat Rao Scindia calmed the situation, at least for a few months. Indeed, Lakwa was reinstated as Daulat Rao's deputy in Hindustan, and all seemed well.

As for Farzana, the Begum Somru, Collins notes in his letter of 21 September 1799, 'Begum Somru appears to be in high favour at the Durbar of Daulat Rao Scindia, She shortly expects to receive a Khelat from the Maharaja and to be ordered to join and assist Lakwa Dada with her troops.'[108]

A *khelat* (also *khillut*), a 'Robe of Honour', was a mark of favour from a ruler to a loyal subject. Farzana had received other such robes earlier in her career from the Mughal Emperor himself. But times had changed, as the Marathas were now the de facto rulers of Hindustan. With little other choice if she was to retain her lands, Farzana was now firmly in the orbit of Daulat Rao Scindia.

106 Sarkar, *Poona Residency Correspondence*, vol.8, letter 149.
107 Sarkar, *Poona Residency Correspondence*, vol.8, letter 149.
108 Sarkar, *Poona Residency Correspondence*, vol.8, letter 171.

8

The Sailor and the Sikhs

George Thomas and his Campaigns against the Sikh States

Even before his conquest of Hariana, Thomas had spent a good deal of his time campaigning against the incursions of the Sikhs into Hindustan. This had begun as a junior officer in the *compoo* of the Begum Somru, then as governor of Tappal, and later as a sort of 'Frontier Warden', protecting the borders of Hindustan against Sikh raids.

By the end of the eighteenth century, raids by the growing forces of the Sikh *misls* had become an uncomfortable fact of life on the northern and western frontiers of the rump of the Mughal Empire. As we have seen,[1] at times even Delhi was not safe, so the frontiers needed all the protection they could get.

The decline in the power of the Mughal Empire after the death of the Emperor Aurungzeb in 1707 had left a power vacuum in the Punjab, the 'Land of Five Rivers', which had been filled at various times by Afghans and latterly by the rising power of the Sikhs.

Sikh Armies in the Eighteenth Century

The militarisation of the previously peaceful Sikh farming communities began as a reaction to the religious persecution perpetrated by their Mughal rulers, most especially by the Emperor Aurungzeb. A book such as this is not the place to comment upon the Sikh religion, but suffice it to say that the faith of the Sikhs became the reason for their militarisation. From peaceful farmers, they became warriors to protect their faith and their people.

From the early years of the eighteenth century, the Sikhs began a guerrilla war against their Mughal oppressors, slowly 'liberating' parts of the Punjab from the Mughals and the Afghans. These early forces were more guerrilla war bands than organised armies, but, by the middle years of the eighteenth century, a more permanent organisation – and therefore an increased capability – was apparent in their forces. In March 1748, the Sikh military force, the Khalsa, was formally divided into 12 divisions, or *misls*,

1 See Chapter 4.

each with its own kettledrum and standard. These *misls* were almost entirely cavalry,[2] as infantry and artillery were of little use to a force whose tactics were based around the sudden attack, and equally sudden retreat when threatened by superior numbers.

Name of *misl* and leader	Number of Cavalry
Bhangi – Hari Singh Dhillon	10,000
Ramgarhia – Jassa Singh Ramgharia	3,000
Singhpuria – Nawab Kapur Singh	8,000
Shahidi – Baba Deep Singh	2,000
Ahluwalia – Jassa Singh Ahluwalia	3,000
Dalewalhia – Gulab Singh	7,500
Nishanwalia – Dasausunda Singh	12,000
Kanhiyha – Jai Singh	3,000
Karorasinghia – Karora Singh	12,000
Nakai – Hira Singh	2,000
Phulkea – Baba Ala Singh	5,000
Sukarchakia – Charhat Singh	2,500

The table above gives an impressive number for the totals of cavalry the Sikhs could raise. The titles of each *misl* came either from the village where they were first raised, or from the name of their leader.[3] Each *misl* was, to an extent, a 'commonwealth', with each warrior having some say in the running of that war band, and being free to leave to join another, perhaps more successful group.

As for the men themselves, 'Fighting and riding were the only qualifications required from an individual who came to seek recruitment under a chief, and possession of a horse and a matchlock was his best recommendation, though in many cases they were assured of these things by the leader from the proceeds of his spoil.'[4]

Tactically, they made much use of the matchlock musket, similarly to other northern Indian cavalry, attacking the enemy in waves, firing their muskets, and then retiring to reload. They would charge home sword in hand if the enemy became disordered by their fire. Richer men might wear armour, but at first this was quite rare, though successful plundering of the Mughals and other enemies must have increased the availability of such items as the eighteenth century wore on. As the various *misls* conquered territory and were able to hold it, infantry and field artillery would rise in importance. The infantry would garrison forts, and sometimes appear in the field, especially when defending their home from raiders such as Thomas. Such foot soldiers would be mainly armed with the usual matchlock musket, with tulwars as a secondary weapon, though poorer men might have only spears or even agricultural tools to defend their homes.

2 Mann, *The British and the Sikhs*, p.35, from which the table of *misl* strengths also comes.
3 R. Kumar (ed.), *Military System of the Sikhs* (New Delhi: Commonwealth Publishers, 2004), p.13.
4 H.R. Gupta, *History of the Sikhs*, vol.1, as quoted in Kumar, *Military System*, p.13.

'A Sikh showing his weapons to a Lady'. A mid-nineteenth-century watercolour by an Indian artist, showing a Sikh warrior. Thomas would encounter many men armed as this man, both horse and foot, in his campaigns against Jhind and Patiala. (Anne S.K. Brown military collection)

Of course, by no means all of the quoted numbers would be in the field at once, even from the same *misl*. The various *misls* would sometimes squabble amongst themselves, though they could usually be relied upon to unite against a common enemy, such as the Mughals or Afghans. The *misls* do not seem to have been monolithic organisations, but included 'sub- chieftains', who might, for a time or for a specific task, go their own way. The state of Jhind, for example, was, in 1799, ruled by Bhag Singh of the Phulkea *misl*.[5] Also, as we have seen, Sikh cavalry served as mercenaries in Mughal and even Maratha

5 J.D. Cunningham, *History of the Sikhs* (1849; repr. Milton Keynes: Lightning Source UK, [n.d.]), p.111.

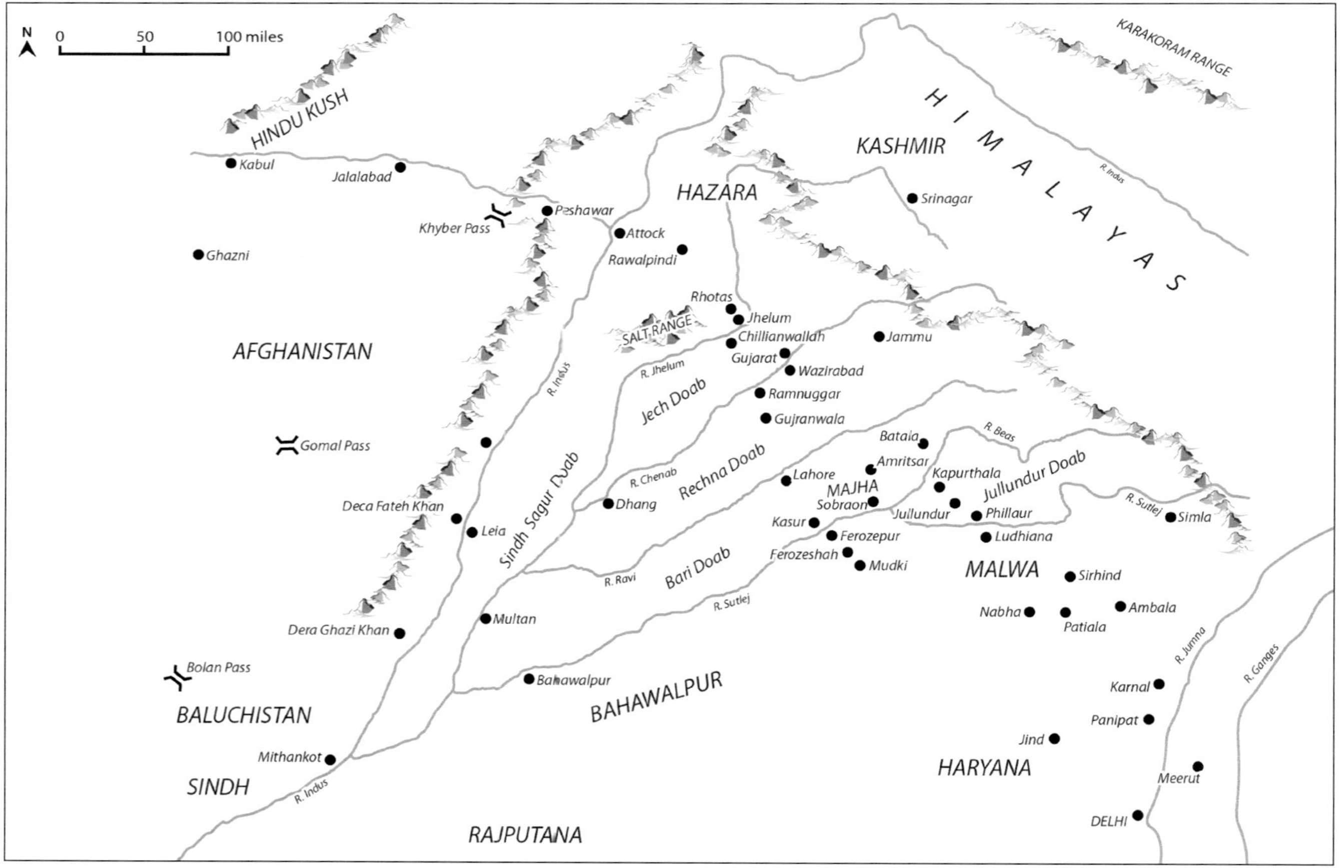

The Punjab and the Cis-Sutlej states. Thomas campaigned against the states of Jhind and Patiala more often than others. His stated ambition to conquer the Punjab can be seen as mere boasting once the comparative resources are taken into account. (George Anderson © Helion & Co.)

armies. By the late eighteenth century, much of the Punjab was under Sikh control, and on the southern bank of the Sutlej River, several Sikh states such as Jhind and Patiala had been carved out of territory that had recently been Mughal. Sikh raids had reached Delhi and had temporarily occupied Panipat and Sonnepat, to the north-west of Delhi, until they were pushed back by a temporary resurgence of the imperials. In 1795, Thomas was then given these two *purgannahs* as *jaidad* to pay his troops and guard the frontier.[6]

So, by the time Thomas struck out on his own, he already had considerable experience in fighting the Sikhs, and they already had some experience of him. It would be the 'cis-Sutlej' states, to the north and west of Thomas's Hariana, that would become targets for the Irish Raja's rapacity.

The 'Irish Raja' goes to War

> In 1799 Thomas invested the town of Jhind which belonged to Bhag Singh of the Phulkea confederacy. The old Chief Baghel Singh, Krora Singea and the Amazonian sister of the imbecile Raja of Patiala relieved the place, but they were repulsed when they attacked Thomas on his retreat to Hansi.[7]

This seems to have been little more than another of Thomas's plundering raids to 'levy contributions' to keep his army in the field. Thomas's memoirs do, however, put the case somewhat differently:

> Mr Thomas now marched to Jhind a town on the frontiers of Harianah and Punjab belonging to Bhag Singh. This chief had from Mr Thomas first entering the province behaved towards him in a hostile manner, for which Mr Thomas now determined to retaliate. On his arrival at Jhind, the capital of Bhag Singh he attempted to storm the place, but was driven back with the loss of 400 men; undismayed even at a check so unexpected, Mr Thomas having fortified his camp agreeably to his usual custom, formed the blockade of the place, by which means, there being 3,000 persons within the town, he expected to compel them to a surrender.[8]

In this expectation, Thomas was, however, to be disappointed. The blockade lasted three months, without any sign of a surrender as, 'the sister of Sahib Singh of Patiala, a woman of a masculine and intrepid spirit attended by a large force arrived to succour the place; with her also came Bhagel Singh and other chiefs of the Sikhs.'[9]

In the ensuing engagement, Thomas was, despite early success, defeated and forced to raise the siege after losing two redoubts to the enemy. The Sikhs followed his retreat,

6 See Chapter 6.
7 Cunningham, *History of the Sikhs*, p.111.
8 Francklin, *Military Memoirs*, p.137.
9 Francklin, *Military Memoirs*, p.137.

gathering strength as they did so. Thomas now faced a force which he estimated at 10,000, joined by Sahib Singh of Patiala himself, with 'several pieces of heavy artillery'.[10]

Thomas was able to fend off several Sikh attacks, and, although he gives no details, the assumption is that he used his usual combination of infantry and guns to do this, as he had in his retreat after the Battle of Fatehgarh the previous year. Whatever the precise details, eventually the Sikhs drew off, but only, it seems, to threaten Hansi, Thomas's capital.

> ...but the enemy having repeatedly attacked him, and as often been repulsed, now of their own accord drew off, and directed their march towards Hansi. Hoping to intercept him before he could reach that place, in their route they encamped at Narnound a town 20 cos to the northward of Hansi. Here Mr Thomas resolved to attack them. For this purpose he marched all night and arriving by daybreak, in their camp, gave them a complete defeat. Their tents baggage, the howdahs of their elephants, the bazar with 1,000 saddles and about 200 horses fell into his hands, but his troops, dispersing on all sides in search of plunder, prevented his becoming master of their artillery and elephants.[11]

Meanwhile, Sahib Singh's 'amazonian sister' had been left behind in Jhind when the main Sikh force set off in pursuit of Thomas. When the beaten Sikhs returned to the town, that martial lady was so disgusted with their defeat that she closed the gates of the town in their faces and offered to take the field herself.[12] Apparently shamed by this, the Sikh army returned to the offensive and found Thomas 'encamped near a large town'.[13]

> but whilst deliberating on the mode of attack, their own camp was suddenly assaulted during the night by a numerous and daring banditti, who sounded their trumpets with such loud alarms, that the Sikhs thinking that the whole force of Mr Thomas was at hand abandoned their camp, with precipitation. This circumstance, tho' it occasioned no real loss to the Sikhs; had great effect on the minds of the country people and lessened their ideas of Sikh prowess.[14]

Here, Thomas seems to have escaped a possible defeat by something close to a miracle, though he gives no more details of these 'banditti'. Both sides now agreed to a return to the status quo as it had been before Thomas's siege of Jhind. The exception was Sahib Singh of Patiala, who refused to sign the treaty and, furthermore, imprisoned his sister, possibly in revenge for shaming him. However, Thomas, not for the first time in his career, played the knight errant, 'Mr Thomas, deeming it his duty to interfere, on this occasion, by threats, compelled him to release her.'[15]

10 Francklin, *Military Memoirs*, p.138.
11 Francklin, *Military Memoirs*, pp.138–139.
12 Francklin, *Military Memoirs*, p.139.
13 Francklin, *Military Memoirs*, p.139.
14 Francklin, *Military Memoirs*, p.139.
15 Francklin, *Military Memoirs*, p.140.

This was not to be the end of the enmity between Thomas and the Raja of Patiala. On 31 January 1800, Colonel John Collins, still the British resident with Scindia, is once again writing to the Governor-General with his usual collection of news and intelligence. There is much concerning Maratha revenue collection, but also this:

> My private agent in Delhi informs me that Mr. George Thomas has invaded the territories of Sahib Singh the Raja of Patiala. This Raja it seems, has seized and confined the person of his own sister, Sahib Kaur, a lady who possesses considerable influence among the Sikh *sardars*. It is not unlikely that Mr. Thomas may have been invited to cooperate with her party.[16]

Indeed, that is precisely what had happened, though the order of events is a little confused, as Thomas spent a good part of 1799 embroiled in the 'Widows' War' in the service of Ambaji Ingle, fighting Lakwa Dada.[17]

If we take the dates of Colonel Collins's letters as a very rough calendar, then Thomas must have attacked Patiala either at the end of 1799 or very early in the new year of 1800. This attack was more than simply another plundering raid.

Thomas's narrative tells us of a tribe he refers to as the Bhatties, who seem to have been, like him, great raiders and plunderers of their neighbours' territories.[18] In response, the Rajput Raja of Bikaner had built a fort, which he garrisoned with cavalry, who mounted counter-raids into the Bhatties's country: 'In this fort, exclusive of the garrison, he stationed a large body of cavalry, who so much annoyed the Bhatties by frequent sallies, in which they took such numbers of cattle, that the inhabitants entertained thoughts of emigrating from their own country altogether.'[19]

However, help, for a price, was at hand: 'When Mr Thomas reached the frontier of Bikaner, the chiefs of the Bhatties, hearing of his arrival, were desirous of entering into a treaty with him and in order to secure him in their interests, offered the sum of 40,000 rupees if he would reduce the fort abovementioned.'[20]

This Thomas promptly did, using his artillery to batter the walls and make a breach, after which the garrison capitulated. They were allowed to march out with the 'honours of war', and then Thomas handed over the fort to the Bhatties. Needless to say, this was not the end of the matter, 'Several other places were taken possession of and several other actions took place, by which, and the unhealthiness of the climate, Mr. Thomas's troops were reduced to one-third of their original strength.'[21]

At this unfortunate juncture, one of the Bhattie chiefs, who 'was at variance' with his brother chief, began to attack Thomas's weakened force, which caused Thomas to fortify his camp to resist their onslaughts. Thomas gives no details to Francklin of these

16 R. Sinh (ed.), *Poona Residency Correspondence*, vol.9: *Daulat Rao Scindia and North Indian Affairs, 1800–1803* (Bombay: Government Central Press, 1943), letter 2.

17 See Chapter 7.

18 Francklin, *Military Memoirs*, pp.163–173.

19 Francklin, *Military Memoirs*, p.172.

20 Francklin, *Military Memoirs*, pp.172–173.

21 Francklin, *Military Memoirs*, p.173.

battles, saying only that, 'By night the enemy made frequent attacks but unsuccessful in all attempts, at length gave up the point and withdrew their army.'[22]

Indeed, we are supposed to believe that after this piece of hard service, and with an army that was barely a third of what it had been, Thomas,

> Took possession of the town of Futtehbad and several others, which he burnt and would now in all probability, have got possession of the whole country, had not the enemy at this time, received assistance from their neighbour, the Sikh Chief of Patiala. That Chief, having sent 1,000 cavalry to their aid, and concluded a treaty of alliance, Mr Thomas did not deem the present moment favourable for a prosecution of hostilities. He therefore returned to Jhajjar in order to afford some relief to his people from the distempers they had contracted in the course of the campaign.[23]

Sahib Singh, the Raja of Patiala, clearly saw Thomas as a menace.

Thomas now needed to rest his troops before his next foray, but also to restore order to the districts of his domain that were in rebellion against his rule: 'At this time Mr. Thomas received intelligence that several of his districts, particularly those in the vicinity of Hansi, were in a state of actual rebellion and had plundered the merchants resorting to that place of a very considerable sum of money and other valuable effects.'[24]

Thomas would have to put down these rebellions, yet by 22 February 1800, Colonel Collins has received the following information regarding Thomas, which he communicated to the Governor-General in Calcutta in his letter of that date: 'The troops of Mr George Thomas have evacuated the territories of the Patiala Raja after committing great depredations, and are now employed in the siege of Sersah a fort belonging to the Pathans in the Zilla of Ballogestan [Registan?] and in levying contributions on the Talukdars in that quarter.'[25]

Put simply, Thomas was plundering any town or landowner who could supply his army with the wherewithal to continue in the field. These plundering expeditions evidently had considerable success, as by July 1800, Colonel Collins is again reporting to the Governor-General news concerning Thomas:

> Yusuf Ali Khan who was detained a whole day in the camp of Mr George Thomas at Sossnah by the late heavy rains, states his present force to consist of seven battalions of infantry, five hundred cavalry, twenty field pieces of artillery and four howitzers, the whole well equipped, regularly paid and in strict subordination. Mr Thomas treated Yusuf Khan with great kindness and furnished him with a strong escort to Jhind a Sikh city distant about sixty cos from Delhi.[26]

22 Francklin, *Military Memoirs*, p.174.
23 Francklin, *Military Memoirs*, p.174.
24 Francklin, *Military Memoirs*, p.191.
25 Sinh, *Poona Residency Correspondence,* vol.9 letter 3.
26 Sinh, *Poona Residency Correspondence,* vol.9 letter 19.

So, by July 1800, Thomas's troops were evidently in better condition than they had been earlier in the year. Thomas, after restoring order within his domain, which seems to have taken some weeks, prepared once again to attack the Sikh states on the southern bank of the river Sutlej. This would be Thomas's last expedition against the Sikhs, and its results would have serious consequences for the Irish Raja.

The force for this expedition was not large. Thomas gives it as 5,000 men and 36 guns.[27] Information passed by Colonel Collins in his letter of 16 May 1801 gives Thomas's strength as: '...six battalions of sepoys, five hundred cavalry and a large train of artillery.[28] This would mean – after deducting the cavalry and, say, 500 men to move, service, and crew the 36 guns – that Thomas's battalions were each somewhat over 600 men strong. If he had a few hundred Rohilla mercenaries in his army, as he often did, then the sepoy battalions would perhaps be a little weaker. This was quite a small force to attempt any major conquest, but more suited to one of his usual large-scale marauding expeditions to 'levy contributions'.

Compton makes much of Thomas's statement to Captain Francklin that he intended the conquest of the Punjab. With these slender resources, that would have been quite beyond his means. One suspects that his statements to Francklin that, 'Having offered to advance and take possession of the Punjab and give up his army to the direction and control of the English; to take the country and become an active partisan to their cause',[29] were merely the pipe dreams of a defeated man. Thomas's account, as given to Captain Francklin in the months before Thomas's death, is the only English account of this campaign other than the bare notices in the letters and intelligence reports of Colonel Collins. Secondary sources, such as Compton's *Particular Account of the European Military Adventurers of Hindustan*, written almost a century later, merely paraphrase Francklin's earlier work. Thus, for the details of Thomas's penultimate campaign, which was his last offensive, we have to rely on Thomas's own account given to Francklin, who, as his biographer, is considerably biased in Thomas's favour as a fellow 'Englishman'.

By 1800, the Punjab was just beginning to come under the control of Ranjit Singh, the greatest of the Sikh leaders. He took control of Lahore in 1799 and would make it the capital of a Sikh empire that would, in time, stretch beyond the Punjab. Thomas's 'conquests' over the Sikhs were mostly illusory and confined to the Sikh states on the south bank of the Sutlej River. To these states, Thomas was a constant threat as a raider and plunderer, but he never actually conquered or held any of them. With the slender resources he had, and his constant need to 'levy contributions', anything resembling a stable conquest was impossible.

Whatever Thomas's motives actually were can never be known, but this penultimate campaign began with the usual quest for cash to pay his troops. This foray was against a town Thomas calls Bulhalli, which was in 'rebellion' against him and had a garrison

27 Francklin, *Military Memoirs*, p.215.
28 Sinh, *Poona Residency Correspondence*, vol.9 letter 252.
29 Francklin, *Military Memoirs*, pp.247–248.

of some 3,000 men. Thomas besieged the place, rather than storm it, as 'thinking the number and bravery of the garrison the event might prove doubtful'.[30]

Thomas's grip on the town tightened,

> Having erected a chain of redoubts well-fortified and supplied with artillery he completely encircled the place, encompassing the whole by a ditch 12 feet in depth. As no provisions could enter the town, the garrison after some days, experienced distress, they made repeated sallies but having to cross the ditch before they could reach the redoubts on the plain they became exposed to the whole fire of the trenches and were in consequence defeated in every successive attack.[31]

Thomas's cavalry scoured the surrounding countryside, bringing in some 3,000 head of cattle, and making sure that no assistance could come to the town from its neighbours or, as Thomas seemed to think, from Mr Perron.[32] Eventually, the town, by this time under considerable privation from lack of food and water, agreed to capitulate and hand over the sum of Rs 30,000. With this transaction, completed with the taking of hostages to ensure compliance, Thomas returned to Hansi, 'where he employed himself completing his ammunition and stores'.[33] No doubt, some of the loot from his recent plundering helped in this regard.

Once Thomas had re-supplied and refreshed his army, he set out on his next expedition. His initial target was, once again, the Sikh state of Patiala, whose Raja, at least from Thomas's point of view, had broken a treaty by aiding another of Thomas's many enemies. He was therefore ripe for 'punishment' 'for his treacherous conduct'.[34]

Thomas's narrative gives the Raja's force as 1,500 cavalry and 1,000 infantry. The Raja, Sahib Singh, once again in disagreement with Sahib Kaur, his martial sister, was besieging her in a fort. As Thomas and his army approached, the Raja, wisely declining to fight a larger force, retreated to the town of Sunam, 'a large town situated 20 cos to the westward of Patiala'.[35] Thither Thomas followed him, intending, no doubt, to storm and loot the town. Sahib Singh, however, was not without allies, and his son-in-law Tara Singh came to his relief with a considerable force. This gave Thomas little choice but to begin a retreat. Still worse for Thomas, the local peasantry were gathering to the Raja's standard, and as he retired, 'numerous bodies of cavalry continued daily to hover about the skirts of his army, during the march, by which he sustained great annoyance.'[36]

It is here pretty obvious that Thomas's attentions were decidedly unwelcome. Thomas's narrative makes it clear that the towns and villages in this part of north-west Hindustan were all fortified to a greater or lesser extent 'in consequence of the continual state of

30 Francklin, *Military Memoirs*, p.192.
31 Francklin, *Military Memoirs*, pp.192–193.
32 Francklin, *Military Memoirs*, p.193.
33 Francklin, *Military Memoirs*, p.194.
34 Francklin, *Military Memoirs*, p.194.
35 Francklin, *Military Memoirs*, footnote p.194.
36 Francklin, *Military Memoirs*, p.195.

warfare in those parts',[37] with no thought as to the possible irony of that statement. Thomas was not, of course, solely responsible for the unsettled state of the country, but his constant raiding certainly did not make for a lasting peace.

However, Colonel Collins, reporting to Calcutta in his letter of 8 April 1801, seemed to think that Thomas was in trouble:

> Advices from the Punjab state that Mr George Thomas is completely surrounded by the Sikhs. It seems that this officer rashly adventured to invade the territories of the Patiala Raja neglecting the necessary measures for preserving a communication with his own districts. It is therefore likely that he will be obliged to submit to the most humiliating conditions, should the Sikhs be disposed to grant any, in order to secure a safe retreat.[38]

In the event, Colonel Collins was here somewhat misinformed, as although Thomas was much outnumbered, he stormed the town of Belad, defended by a wall nine feet thick and a ditch 20 feet deep, losing a mere 80 casualties. His largely Muslim troops seem to have got out of hand here and committed some atrocities upon the Sikh inhabitants of the town, 'and in the heat of racial conflict, despite all his attempts to stay the slaughter, no less than 500 of the garrison were put to the sword.'[39] Those of the townspeople and garrison who survived were ransomed 'by a large sum of money'.[40]

Thomas had bought himself some time in which to defeat his enemies in detail. To that end, he took up a position between the towns of Patiala and Sunam, but did not remain long there, as he saw a chance to punish Tara Singh for his temerity in aiding his father-in-law. Thomas proceeded to march upon Tara Singh's capital of Maler Kotla, but his advance guard was ambushed as they passed through a patch of jungle along the route. The ambush was quickly driven off, but this may have been a feigned flight designed to draw Thomas away from a tempting target, 'Hurrying forward Thomas found his advance guard had been attacked by a superior force of the enemy just as they were emerging into an extensive open plain and presently discovered that this was a ruse to draw his observation from a large and populous town named Bhat, situated close at hand and belonging to Tara Singh.'[41]

Needless to say, the discovery of Bhat and the prospect of the resources that might be acquired from the town led Thomas to immediately attack, despite the place having a 3,000-strong garrison.

> Mr Thomas nevertheless resolved to storm it. The walls of the fort were 12 feet thick and 30 in height; four strong bastions well fortified with cannon commanded the town below as well as the plain adjoining, it was in all respects a place

37 Francklin, *Military Memoirs*, p.196.
38 Sinh, *Poona Residency Correspondence,* vol.9 letter 248.
39 Compton, *Particular Account*, p.175.
40 Francklin, *Military Memoirs*, p.196.
41 Compton, *Particular Account*, p.175.

> difficult of access. Mr Thomas himself at the head of a select body of his troops, entered nearly opposite the centre of the town, while Mr. Hopkins the son of a field officer in the East India Company's service, now in Mr Thomas's employ, led on his party to storm the eastern angle; the affair was desperate and though the town was soon set on fire, the enemy made a brave and determined resistance. Mr Hopkins gallantly advancing to the attack, stormed in the quarter assigned him, though at the moment of success he was unfortunately shot through the body and several other officers were killed or disabled, the enemy still keeping up a tremendous fire from the fort. The affair presented a doubtful aspect; a large body of cavalry making their appearance without the town, Mr Thomas's troops, though in possession of the place, whether from the excessive heat occasioned by the surrounding flames, or the severe fire they sustained from the enemy in the fort were inclined to retreat; at that critical instant, Mr Thomas, having with the greatest presence of mind, brought up a 6-pounder close to the gate of the fort by repeated discharges almost demolished it, the enemy then gave up the contest and by submission saved a further effusion of blood on both sides. The lives of the people within the fort were granted but Mr Thomas compelled them to pay him 50,000 rupees.[42]

This victory seems to have given the *killadar* of Maler Kotla a change of heart, along with those of the population who were not Sikhs, although it is equally likely that the *killadar* was simply trying to avoid a similar fate for his own town and fort: 'Although Tara Singh was a Sikh a great portion of the population of Maler Kotla were Mohammedan, who when they heard of the capture of Bhat showed a disposition to join Thomas and eventually paid him a contribution and united their troops with his.'[43]

Thomas puts this a little differently, but with the same result:

> The chief of Maler Kotla now thought proper to change sides and being like other Pathans adopted the practice of his countrymen by connecting himself with the party from whom he expected to derive most advantage.
>
> He agreed to pay Mr Thomas a sum of money, and moreover, sent a body of troops under the command of his nephew to join him.[44]

In the meantime, the Sikh leaders had finally decided to combine against Thomas. Sahib Singh of Patiala offered the hand of his daughter to the son of Kurram Singh of Shahabad, as a condition of an alliance against Thomas. This move seems to have prompted other Sikh leaders of the Cis-Sutlej states to combine against Thomas. However, events now took a strange turn.

42 Francklin, *Military Memoirs*, pp.197–198.
43 Compton, *Particular Account*, p.176.
44 Francklin, *Military Memoirs*, p.198.

A late-nineteenth-century illustration, supposedly of a Sikh. He could equally, with small changes in dress and turban, be almost any northern Indian irregular warrior. Men such as these fought both for and against George Thomas. (Author's Collection)

The Rani and the Impostor

> A circumstance now arose that turned the scale much in the enemy's favour.[45]
> Adjoining the Maler Kotla country was the territory of Rai Elias, a youth who had recently succeeded his father, Rai Kalian in his inheritance. Rai Elias's district ran contiguous with the Sutlej river and included the important cities of Ludhiana and Firozpur. In consequence of his tender age, his mother had assumed the reins of government, but from inexperience and the disadvantages of her sex, proved wholly unable to rule a country producing a revenue of five lakhs of rupees and surrounded by enemies eager to prey on it. Taking advantage of her weakness the Sikhs had attacked her son's districts in the previous year, and had taken possession of a great portion of them, only a few strong forts remaining to the Rani.[46]

Being Muslims, the Rani and her son appealed to Zaman Shah, the ruler of Afghanistan, who, in 1799, was in Lahore settling the government there after the Sikhs had defeated and killed the Afghan governor of that city. Presented with something of a *fait accompli* after the recent Sikh victories, Zaman Shah appointed Ranjit Singh as the new ruler of Lahore.[47] Zaman Shah returned to Afghanistan after only a few months in Lahore. In the coming years, Ranjit Singh would extend his power over the whole of the Punjab and beyond. This made the possibility of any permanent conquests by Thomas extremely unlikely. In the short term, Zaman Shah's inability to help the Rani and her son would cause her to appeal to Thomas as a last resort, soon after his capture of the town of Bhat.

Matters were, however, complicated by internal Sikh politics. One Sahib Singh – not to be confused with the ruler of Patiala – set himself up as some kind of religious prophet and '...by fraud and artifice imposed on his countrymen'.[48] He gathered a large following, invaded the Rani's country, and laid siege to Ludhiana. The Rani now offered Thomas a *lakh* of rupees, plus an annual tribute of Rs 50,000, to rid her lands of Sahib Singh and guarantee the security of her son's inheritance. 'Lovely woman in distress never appealed in vain to this susceptible Irishman and whether it was the Witch of Sardhana, the Amazon of Patiala or the Widow of Ludhiana, it needed but a woman's cry to bring him to the rescue.'[49]

While we may doubt, in our more cynical age, the precise truth of Compton's statement here, and rather look to the *lakh* of rupees on offer, Thomas kept to the agreement. He sent a deliberately haughty response to the letter sent by the impostor Sahib Singh, who had threatened Thomas: 'In this letter arrogating to himself the title of successor to Nanak and sovereign of the Sikh nation he commanded implicit obedience to his commands.'[50]

45 Francklin, *Military Memoirs*, p.199.
46 Compton, *Particular Account*, p.177.
47 Sykes, *History of Afghanistan*, vol.1, p.380.
48 Compton, *Particular Account*, p.177.
49 Compton, *Particular Account*, p.177.
50 Francklin, *Military Memoirs*, p.208.

Needless to say, Thomas was less than impressed with this missive and replied with a demand for money before he would make peace, ordering the impostor to leave the Rani's territory without delay:

> Meanwhile the young Raja despairing of profiting from a longer stay with the chief of Patiala, of his own accord took leave and came straight to Mr Thomas's camp. 'The comely appearance (says he) of this youth, his fallen condition, and above all the confidence he showed in placing his whole reliance on one against whom he was lately leagued in enmity altogether influenced me in his favour and determined me to use every exertion in support of his cause.'[51]

It soon transpired that the impostor's forces were something of a paper tiger, and they retreated as Thomas advanced. Having no artillery of their own, they were able to outmarch Thomas's men, although at times it was a close run thing, 'So rapid was his march that in one place he found the bed, palanquin, tent and baggage belonging to the impostor, who by a timely retreat saved himself from being made prisoner and never afterward occasioned any disturbance.'[52]

The Rani and her son were now re-established in their territory, but they would not allow Thomas to leave, as they wished for his continued protection. Thomas was now in something of a quandary, as the Raja of Patiala and other Sikh leaders were attacking his forces and preventing them from foraging for supplies. Neither side wanted to force a major engagement, but rather continued the war in, 'a desultory manner, the Sikhs wished by annoying his foraging parties to cut off the supplies from his camp, this mode also prevented him from making collections.'[53]

Since much of this 'desultory war' was being carried on within the Rani's domain, Thomas, needing more supplies of ammunition, decided to retire towards Hansi, in the hope of drawing the Sikh cavalry after him. In this, he was successful, as the Sikh forces followed him, their superior numbers of cavalry harassing his column during his retirement.

> The Sikhs, as he had foreseen, harassed him on the march, but their attempts proving ineffectual to do him any essential injury, only incited him to retaliate, by destroying their villages as he passed along. Directing his march towards Hansi, he perceived, not without satisfaction, that the whole of the Sikh army were following him, by which means the country of his youthful ally would at least for the present be free from their depredations.[54]

Thomas continued his depredations by storming the fort of Kanhori, which belonged to Lal Singh of Kaithal, who had, along with Bhag Singh of Jhind, 'agreed to a cessation of

51 Francklin, *Military Memoirs*, p.209.
52 Francklin, *Military Memoirs*, p.209.
53 Francklin, *Military Memoirs*, p.210.
54 Francklin, *Military Memoirs*, pp.210–211.

hostilities during his absence; to abstain from the invasion of his territories, and allow him to prosecute the war against his enemies.'[55]

Apparently, they had not done as they were forced to agree to, and had joined the Sikh forces pursuing the Irishman's column. Thomas, in consequence, decided to punish them for their 'treachery'. Kanhori was his first target in this reprisal, which he stormed putting the whole garrison to the sword. He then installed his own garrison with the intention of using the fort as a base and stores depot for further attacks on the Sikh states. Thomas also took hostages to ensure the 'peaceful behaviour' of the local inhabitants.[56]A second fort, Retara, also belonging to Kaithal, surrendered at Thomas's appearance, its 500 man garrison apparently fearing to receive the same fate as the garrison of Kanhori. They were allowed to go free on payment of a large ransom.[57]

The onset of the hot weather had forced the Sikhs to give up their pursuit, due to a lack of water for man and beast, and they remained encamped around Kaithal.

Thomas now returned to Hansi, as it had come to his attention that Bapu Scindia had invaded Hariana at the behest of General Perron in Delhi. On Thomas's approach, Bapu and his Maratha cavalry fell back to Delhi.[58] Thomas was seemingly beset by enemies on all sides, yet he still took the time to punish Bhag Singh of Jhind by attacking his fort and town of Safidun. The siege did not go according to plan.

The fortifications were made of brick with walls of 'uncommon height'.[59] Thomas erected three redoubts, placing six cannon, 6-pounders and 12-pounders, in each redoubt, and began to batter the walls to effect a breach. Some kind of breach was quickly made, but some 400 of the 700-strong garrison sallied out to attack Thomas's advanced posts and some sharp hand to hand fighting must have taken place as 'most of the party, among whom were some chiefs of distinction, were put to the sword.'[60] Thomas next tried an assault, but the scaling ladders were too short, and the remainder of the garrison defeated this attempt. Thomas lost 450 men during this botched operation, and Captain Hopkins, possibly the best of his few European officers, was wounded once again. Thomas began a retirement, but the surviving garrison, in hardly better shape, thought it prudent to abandon the fort and attempt to cut their way out and flee to a nearby forest. Thomas, possibly sighing with relief, let them go and, returning, took possession of the fort. He had more luck than he deserved, for the main Sikh army lay some 27 miles (43.4 km)[61] away at Kaithal, yet did nothing to help their hard-pressed comrades.

Thomas now moved his forces towards the main Sikh army, but neither side wanted to continue the war, and the Raja of Patiala and some of the other Sikh leaders sent *vakils* – that is to say, envoys – to Thomas's camp to discuss peace terms. A treaty was finally agreed to and Thomas's version of this makes fascinating reading,

55 Francklin, *Military Memoirs*, p.211.
56 Compton, *Particular Account*, p.180.
57 Compton, *Particular Account*, p.180.
58 Compton, *Particular Account*, p.180.
59 Francklin, *Military Memoirs*, p.213.
60 Francklin, *Military Memoirs*, p.213.
61 Compton, *Particular Account*, p.181.

> Mr Thomas on his part was sincerely inclined to put an end to the war, as he was well informed, that the army of Mr. Perron was on its march from Delhi, for the avowed purpose of affording aid to the Sikhs. They likewise had recently been informed that disturbances prevailed in their own country and therefore hastened to conclude the present negotiations. It was agreed therefore that the Sikh should pay the sum of 135,000 rupees and renounce all pretentions to the country of Rai Kalian. That the Raja of Patiala should be reconciled to his sister, with whom he had been so long at variance, that this lady should be reimbursed her property that had been confiscated. That certain districts should be ceded to Mr Thomas and finally the Raja of Patiala should keep two battalions of infantry in constant pay for the defence of the Punjab frontier as a mutual safeguard to either party.[62]

One is forced to wonder how much of this treaty either side really intended to honour.

Thomas had, by now, become painfully aware that Perron and the Marathas had seen enough of his turmoil and depredations on their frontiers. Indeed, the British were also becoming aware of moves by General Perron and some of the Sikh *sardars* to control George Thomas. This was reflected in a letter dated 12 December 1800 sent by Mir Usuf Ali Khan from Lahore to his employer, Colonel John Collins,

> Just now a singular event has occurred here. Raja Bhag Singh, the uncle of Ranjit Singh living in constant dread and alarm from George Thomas has long devotedly prayed for the arrival of Mr Perron in this quarter, and this occurrence lately taking place by the approach of Mr Perron to Karnal, all the Sardars in that vicinity influenced by their fear of Mr Thomas sent letters *nazars* and presents to Mr Perron on which occasion Bhag Singh in particular gave his personal attendance. Mr Perron by acts of conciliation relieved Bhag Singh's mind from the solicitude felt in respect to Mr Thomas and afforded him the fullest satisfaction.[63]

Clearly, with General Perron and many of the Sikh chiefs now in alliance, Thomas's days as an independent warlord looked to be decidedly numbered.

62 Francklin, *Military Memoirs*, pp.214–215.
63 Sinh, *Poona Residency Correspondence,* vol.9 letter 240A.

9

Jehazi Sahib at Bay

The War with General Perron

With hindsight, it was inevitable. Thomas's poisonous hatred of the French and Pierre Cuillier Perron's ego were bound to clash.

To General Perron, commander of the largest and most efficient army outside of British India, Thomas was an annoying upstart with ideas above his station, a loose cannon outside of the *subahdar* of Hindustan's control. A man whose depredations caused constant turmoil. To Thomas, Perron was simply another Frenchman getting in his way.

Their seeming distaste for each other may have gone back some time. They may have encountered each other as early as the 1780s, when Thomas was a junior officer in the Somru Brigade and Perron equally junior in the French mercenary Lestineau's *compoo*, but this is uncertain.

We can say with a little more certainty that Thomas's relationship with the Army of Hindustan was not always a happy one. He had found Major Gardiner too formal in siege work for his taste.[1] Sometime later, during the first phase of the 'Widows' War', Thomas had been left in the lurch when Colonel Robert Sutherland departed overnight with his six battalions the night before a proposed joint attack on Lakwa Dada.[2] It is no wonder that a man of Thomas's temperament was somewhat suspicious of the Army of Hindustan.

Colonel Collins, the British resident with Scindia, was in no doubt. His 26 July 1800 letter to Calcutta includes his opinion of Perron's attitude to Thomas:

> Though I can have little doubt that Mr. Perron is jealous of the growing power of Mr. George Thomas and would willingly crush it whenever a convenient opportunity occurred, yet I am inclined to think he will if possible, avoid coming to immediate hostilities with that officer as well on account of the force he commands which is far from contemptible as in consideration of Mr Thomas's connection with Begum Somru who now accompanies Mr Perron and whose assistance is of importance in this juncture.[3]

1 See Chapter 6.
2 See Chapter 7.
3 Sinh, *Poona Residency Correspondence,* vol.9 letter 19.

It was clear to Collins that the situation between Thomas and Perron would need watching. Indeed, through the next few months, the relationship between these two, such as it was, deteriorated. Perron's objective at this point seems to have been to bring all of the mercenary *compoos* operating in Hindustan under his control in the name of his master, Daulat Rao Scindia. In this, he was having some success, as the Begum Somru was, according to Collins, travelling with him at the time he wrote the above-quoted letter. The same letter indicates that Dudrenec, another French officer, had already, or was about to, come over to Perron from the service of Jaswant Rao Holkar, which was indeed the case, though he did not bring his *compoo* with him. He would, in time, command the Fourth Brigade of the Army of Hindustan.[4]

Collins also forwards to the Governor-General in Calcutta an 'Extract of a letter from Colonel Collins's private agent in the Camp of Ambaji, dated 20 Safar, 13 July 1800', from which the following is taken:

> Mr Perron has represented to Ambaji Rao that Shambu Nath the Dewan of Imam Baksh Khan has entered into a confederacy with the Sikhs and Mr George Thomas and excited commotion in Hindustan, and that Mr Thomas being of the same nation with the gentlemen to the eastward, has acquired considerable consequence through their countenance and is the promoter of disturbance. That as there are two expeditions to be forwarded and that as he Ambaji would not oppose Mr G. Thomas and punish Sikhs, he would therefore furnish battalions under Mr Louis and two of the big guns with which he advised Ambaji to pass expeditiously to Ujjain marching through and previously settling Mewar, that he himself as a first object would proceed against Mr Thomas.[5]

Shambhu Nath was, indeed, raising disturbances in Hindustan with an army of perhaps 15,000 men, of which some 5,000 were Sikh cavalry, though without any help from Thomas. In the event, Shambhu Nath was defeated by elements of the Third Brigade, under an Indian officer named Ashraf Beg. On the appearance of more of the Third Brigade under the command of Lewis Ferdinand Smith, Shambhu Nath fled, taking his Sikh mercenaries with him.[6]

The 'Mr Louis' in Collins's letter was Major Louis Borquien, at that time an officer in the Third Brigade of the Army of Hindustan. He would take over that brigade later in the year from the ageing Pedron. It would be Borquien who would initially command the forces sent against Thomas. However, to begin with, Perron would try negotiation.

Collins, once again, writes his intelligence report to the Governor-General on 12 August 1801:

> I learn from Syed Reza Khan that Mr George Thomas has consented to join and serve Mr Perron in consideration of a monthly stipend of forty thousand rupees

4 Smith, *Regular Corps*, p.52.
5 Sinh, *Poona Residency Correspondence*, vol.9 letter 19A.
6 For details of this smart little campaign, see Copestake, *Their Infantry and Guns*, pp.117–118.

> with permission to retain the fortress of Hansi, All other perganas which he possesses to the north-west of Delhi are to be relinquished in favour of M. Filose to whose *jaidad* they appertain. Syed Reza also affirms that a treaty to this effect has been signed by M Perron, on the part of Daulat Rao Scindia, and that Mr Thomas is, in consequence, shortly expected.[7]

Collins, for once, was somewhat misinformed, as events would bear out. Of this proposal, Thomas was somewhat mistrustful. Captain Francklin informs us,

> To preserve the thread of our narration, it will now be necessary that repeated letters has lately been sent by Scindia to Mr Thomas to induce him to act in conjunction with Mr Perron against their common enemies.
>
> In answer he represented that Mr Perron and himself, being subjects of different nations, then in a state of actual hostility against each other, it was impossible that they should ever act in concert, or with cordiality. He was moreover convinced, that as a Frenchman and possessed of a national enmity against him, Mr Perron would always be induced to represent his actions in a light most unfavourable to his interests.[8]

Francklin further tells us that Thomas would have gone into Scindia's service with an independent command under a Maratha general. Scindia replied that this was not possible, as it would set 'an unfavourable precedent'.[9]

The negotiations were spread over some time, and eventually Perron requested a personal interview. Thomas agreed, though it is clear from Francklin's narrative that Thomas did not trust Perron in the slightest, and, indeed, expected treachery on the part of the French officer.

> In his master's name therefore Mr Perron requested an interview. The fort of Behadur Ghur was the place named for the meeting, on his approach to that place, Mr Thomas was informed that Mr Perron had put to death a Sikh chief who had lately revolted from Scindia and of whose person he had got possession of by treacherous means.
>
> This intelligence induced Mr Thomas to observe the greatest circumspection in the approaching interview.[10]

With such a level of mistrust, the likelihood that the interview would go well was very small indeed. The meeting took place in August 1801, outside the fort of Bahadurghar.

Captain Lewis Ferdinand Smith, an English officer in the Third Brigade of the Army of Hindustan, and who was present, takes up the story:

7 Sinh, *Poona Residency Correspondence,* vol.9 letter 27.
8 Francklin, *Military Memoirs,* pp.219–220.
9 Francklin, *Military Memoirs,* p.220.
10 Francklin, *Military Memoirs,* p.221.

> I was employed to bring Thomas to terms and to an interview with his rival – Perron offered him sixty thousand rupees a month for his party, the rank of Colonel and the fort of Hansi, if Thomas would take service with Scindia and serve under Perron's order. Thomas to gain time agreed to Perron's terms, and with some difficulty I brought them to an interview; but they soon became mutually distrustful and separated to commence hostilities.[11]

It is unlikely that either Thomas or Perron ever wished the interview to succeed. Thomas had the most to lose, moving from being an independent ruler to being merely another colonel under Perron. Thomas, with his combative nature, must have thought he would be better fighting it out. Thomas's version of the meeting is a little different.

> Mr Thomas took with him on this occasion 300 cavalry and two of his most approved battalions being determined to afford no opportunity to his enemies to effect his ruin by treacherous means.
>
> In the month of September after some previous negotiation between the parties, Mr Perron and Mr Thomas met for the first time, at the town of Behadur Ghur; Mr Thomas having received recent information that the affairs of Scindia presented an unfavourable aspect and that the chief was unequal to the contest with Jaswant Rao Holkar, hoped the present interview would be productive of an amicable adjustment of all former differences and establish the future tranquillity and good understanding of both parties.
>
> In this however he was deceived, for at the second days meeting he was much surprised by a demand, equally sudden as unexpected to give up the district of Jhajjar entirely to the Marathas; in lieu of this, he was to receive for the support of his battalions, the monthly sum of 50,000 rupees and henceforth to be considered as the immediate servant of Daulat Rao Scindia.
>
> Although this proposal might have been forseen Mr Thomas gave it a positive denial; and perceiving the nature of the design formed against him, was aware, that he should be required to act against Holkar in the present war, and if it proved unfavourable to the interests of that chief, and his authority was subverted; Scindia would not only discontinue the payment of the monthly sum now offered to Mr Thomas but compel him to accept of any terms the Maratha Government might think proper to impose.
>
> For these reasons, Mr Thomas, without further discussion on the subject, abruptly broke up the conference and marched away in disgust.[12]

Colonel Collins, or rather his agent in Perron's camp, had a slightly different take on events. Collins's letter of 10 September 1801 to the Governor-General in Calcutta states the position as he knew it at the time:

11 Smith, *Regular Corps*, p.22.
12 Francklin, *Military Memoirs*, pp.222–223.

> Mr George Thomas having greatly risen his demands on Mr Perron after their late interview, the negotiation pending between them has been broken off, even at the moment when it was generally supposed that the terms of the proposed treaty has been mutually agreed on. The former has fallen back to Jhind which country is again suffering his violence and rapacity; and the latter marched to Jhajjar in order to establish the authority of M Filose in that district which form part of his *jaidad*.[13]

Not being defended, Jhajjar fell immediately. Colonel Collins – or his informant – was mistaken in saying Thomas had returned to Jhind for yet another plundering expedition. Thomas had more immediate concerns. He needed to prepare for the coming war. 'On arrival at Hansi, Mr Thomas lost no time in completing his ammunition and other stores; his intention was first to attack Mr Louis, but Captain Smith having lately invested the fort of Georgeghur, by which means the collections in that district were interrupted he resolved to proceed to its relief.'[14]

'Mr Louis', again, is Major Louis Borquien, at this time commanding the Third Brigade of the Army of Hindustan. As we shall see, he was not the most competent of Perron's commanders. 'Captain Smith' is Lewis Ferdinand Smith, whose book *Sketch of the Rise, Progress and Termination of the Regular Corps formed and Commanded by Europeans in the Service of the Native Princes of India* is one of the main contemporary sources for our knowledge of the various mercenary forces in Maratha service.

The Irish Raja's Last Campaign

Thomas was now in serious trouble. He simply did not have the resources to fight Perron on anything like equal terms. The Begum Somru, despite the 'connection' mentioned by Collins above, had more sense than to help a lost cause such as Thomas's appeared to be. As we shall see,[15] her objective was simply to hold what she had, doing whatever had to be done to achieve this. Aiding Thomas would have seen the destruction of her forces and the loss of her *jaghirs* to Perron or Ambaji Ingle. This was not the time for any sentimentality.

Thomas seems to have thought that the civil war between Scindia and Holkar would perhaps give him some kind of chance of an alliance with Holkar, but in this he was mistaken. As always, Holkar had his own interests at heart and no alliance was forthcoming. Worse, several Sikh chiefs, including the rulers of Jhind and Patiala, offered Perron Rs 50,000 per month if he would send troops against Thomas.[16]

Thomas was on his own.

13 Sinh, *Poona Residency Correspondence,* vol.9 letter 29.
14 Francklin, *Military Memoirs*, p.224.
15 See Chapter 10.
16 Francklin, *Military Memoirs*, pp.225–226.

True to his usual method, Thomas moved swiftly and with some decision. His first objective was to relieve the fort of Georgeghur, besieged by a detachment of Borquien's brigade under Captain Lewis Ferdinand Smith.

> I was ordered with three battalions to lay siege to Georgeghur, a small fort some 40 cos [approximately 60 miles/96 km] from Hansi – Thomas and his forces were encamped under the fort of Hansi. Borquien was ordered with seven battalions and five thousand horse to lie between me and Hansi to cover the siege of Georgeghur which would have fallen within a week; but with singular ignorance Borquien encamped at Gin, 10 cos further from me than Thomas's army – the consequence was obvious – three days after I laid siege to Georgeghur I was attacked by Thomas with eight battalions, compelled to raise the siege and retreat to Jhajjar four cos to the east of Georgeghur. Favoured by the obscurity of night, I was not completely cut off and made good my retreat with the loss of one gun and one third of my force killed and wounded – how I escaped total destruction I do not yet know – why Thomas did not follow my retreat I cannot say, for if he had continued the pursuit, I must have lost all my guns and my party would have been completely destroyed.[17]

Francklin, in his biography of Thomas, gives a somewhat different version of the same events. This was Thomas's own version when he dictated most of the memoir to Francklin a year or so later:

> Here he was informed that Captain Smith having got imperfect intelligence of his advance. Had withdrawn his guns from the batteries and struck his camp.
>
> Mr Thomas having ordered the cavalry to proceed with all expedition, continued his march with the infantry towards Georgeghur, where, on his arrival late in the evening, he learnt that Captain Smith had retreated.
>
> Early on the ensuing morning Mr Thomas commenced the pursuit but Mortuza Khan the commander of his second regiment, who had received orders to proceed in advance, and cut off the retreat of Captain Smith, most unaccountably lost his road and the soldiers being fatigued did not come up with their colours; with the only battalion that remained, Mr Thomas, on reaching the rear of Captain Smith's line of march commenced the attack; Captain Smith, in order to cover the retreat of his artillery and baggage, drew up to receive Mr Thomas and after a slight cannonade continued his route; at this time Mr Thomas's second regiment made its appearance of which from the causes before stated not more than 70 men had yet come up, and they advancing incautiously into a field of Joar on the right without having previously reconnoitred were suddenly attacked by a battalion of the enemy; his men being so few in number, made but a feeble resistance and before they had time to unlimber the enemy took possession of four of their guns.[18]

17 Smith, *Regular Corps*, p.23.
18 Francklin, *Military Memoirs*, pp.225–226.

Smith makes no mention of even the temporary capture of any of Thomas's artillery in his rather terse account of his retreat, so perhaps he was not aware of this local counter-attack by one of his battalion commanders. In the event it did not matter as,

> Mr Thomas, hearing of this disaster, immediately advanced to the relief of his troops; he was attended on this occasion by Afalut Khan, a native officer formerly in the service of the East India Company, they charged the enemy with vigour, sword in hand, and after a severe conflict in which the commandant of the enemy was taken prisoner, gave them a complete defeat.[19]

Thomas's men, exhausted by their exertions, could pursue no more, and although Thomas sent his cavalry after Smith's retreating force, they seem to have achieved little more than to pick up the abandoned small arms of the retreating soldiers.

Thomas says that Smith lost 700 killed and wounded, which tallies remarkably well with Smith's admission that he lost one-third of his force. Smith's three battalions would have numbered around 2,100 men, or perhaps a little less. Smith made good his escape to Jhajjar, and Thomas halted 'two miles distant from that place'.[20]

Thomas did not remain still for long. Despite the tiredness of his troops, he quickly retired to Georgeghur upon learning that Borquien was approaching with the rest of the Third Brigade. Sensibly, Thomas had no wish to be caught between two forces, even if one of those forces was that which he had recently defeated.

Colonel Collins, far away in his camp at Fatehgarh, writes to the Governor-General in Calcutta in his letter of 23 October 1801 what he knows at that time of the recent events concerning George Thomas:

> Since my last address to Your Lordship of the 8th instant I have learnt that Mr Hearsey with the corps that were left under his command at Hansi, had effected a junction with Mr George Thomas, It appears also from my advices that Major Louis attempted to intercept the reinforcement but without success, owing to a judicious movement on the part of Mr George Thomas who joined Mr Hearsey in time to support his detachment; the engagement that followed was bravely contested on both sides, but the advantage seems to have been with Mr Thomas, since he effectually protected a large convoy of ammunition and provisions which he conducted to his camp without loss.
>
> Notwithstanding this success the situation of Mr George Thomas still must be considered as critical, as Major Louis, since the action above mentioned has been joined by some thousands of Sikh cavalry and four battalions of sepoys under the command of Mr Perron and Bapuji Scindia.[21]

19 Francklin, *Military Memoirs*, pp.225–226.
20 Francklin, *Military Memoirs*, p.227.
21 Sinh, *Poona Residency Correspondence*, vol.9 letter 31.

James Skinner. Both he and his younger brother, Robert, were with the Third Brigade for the campaign against George Thomas. His memoir, despite his exaggeration of the numbers of troops involved, is still a major source for this campaign. (Public Domain)

Collins's informants had given him a rather superficial account of the main events of the campaign – correct in many respects, but incorrect in some details. For example, Perron did not take the field himself, but as Collins acknowledges later in the same letter, 'M Perron is still at Koil, from whence he constantly supplies the camp of Major Louis with ammunition and stores of every description.'

Equally, Francklin does not mention Hearsey in the earlier part of the campaign narrative at all, so we must conjecture that, as Smith tells us, he was attacked by eight battalions. Subsequently, Hearsey's convoy was escorted from Hansi by another two battalions, as Thomas had 10 battalions for the upcoming battle with Borquien's brigade.

We are fortunate that there are other sources – such as Smith and Skinner, who were both present – to give us a rather more detailed selection of accounts upon which to base a reconstruction of the next stage of the campaign.

The Battle of Georgeghur, 30 September 1801

There are three contemporary English accounts of this battle, all by participants who were involved in the combat – Thomas's own account as given to and written by Francklin; Lewis Ferdinand Smith's account in his rather short but essential *Sketch of the Rise, Progress and Termination of the Regular Corps formed and Commanded by Europeans in the Service of the Native Princes of India;* and James Skinner's account, originally written in Persian and given to his friend and biographer, James Baillie-Fraser, some years later. With these three accounts, a reconstruction of the course of the battle is just about possible.

Thomas gives the force under his command, 'His force consisted of 10 battalions of infantry 50 pieces of cannon 600 Rohillas and about 500 cavalry not exceeding in the aggregate 5,000 men of which number only 4,000 could be brought into action.'[22]

22 Francklin, *Military Memoirs*, p.228.

Some of Thomas's 10 battalions must have been very thin, averaging less than 400 men each, possibly less than 300 in some cases. Fifty guns would require 400–500 men alone just to work them, but we can only assume that the gunners were not included in the infantry total. If they were so included, and Thomas's statement that only 4,000 men could be brought into action is taken at face value, then Jehazi Sahib may have had as few as 2,500 infantry in the coming battle. Unusually for Thomas, he also had the assistance of three other European mercenary officers, as Skinner saw during the abortive negotiations between Thomas and Perron, 'We saw his troops, who looked well but were not over-disciplined; his artillery was very fine and the bullocks particularly good and strong. The only European officers he had were Captains Hearsey, Hopkins and Birch and there were some Europeans acting as sergeants in his artillery.'[23]

Whatever the actual fighting strength of Thomas's force, the army he faced was far more formidable, at least on paper. To begin with, after the relief of Georgeghur and Smith's retreat to Jhajjar, his rather battered force was joined, on 28 September, by 2,000 cavalry, commanded by his brother, Captain E.F. Smith.[24] This somewhat relieved Smith's anxiety about his position, as he expected Thomas to attack him.

Smith then tells us, 'On 29th September 1801 Major Borquien with the 3rd Brigade reached Georgeghur after a surprising march of 40 cos in thirty-six hours. The brigade arrived about midday – the troops were harassed, fatigued and famished. With destructive imbecility, Borquien ordered the troops, consisting of seven battalions, to storm Thomas's entrenched camp at four o'clock in the afternoon.'[25] Smith obviously thought little of Borquien's military talent.

However, it is clear that Thomas had fortified his camp. This is not, however, confirmed by Thomas's own, somewhat confused narrative as told to Francklin:

> On the ensuing morning the enemy prepared to attack him. His situation was, at this time critical; the battalions who had before retreated from Georgeghur now came back and took post within cannon shot to the eastward of his encampment; the force under Mr Louis was stationed to the South West; whilst the enemy's numerous cavalry attacked him in front.[26]

James Skinner, then a captain in the Third Brigade and under Borquien's command, has a slightly different view of the events leading up to the battle:

> It appeared that Smith, on hearing of Thomas being within five cos of him, had raised the siege and commenced his retreat, leaving this one battalion under command of a native Poorun Singh, a brave old soldier, as a rearguard. Thomas with five battalions overtook this single one; and while Smith with the battering train gained Jhajjur, a fort belonging to us, Poorun Singh drew up his men and

23 Fraser, *James Skinner*, p.216.
24 Smith, *Regular Corps*, p.24.
25 Smith, *Regular Corps*, p.24.
26 Francklin, *Military Memoirs*, pp.227–228.

> a fierce fight took place. The brave old fellow charged the two first of Thomas's battalions which came up and drove them off, capturing four pieces of cannon, Thomas himself then headed his five battalions and came on but was again repulsed. Unfortunately, Poorun Singh was wounded and fell from his horse, which threw the battalion into confusion and as Smith though only two miles distant, would not come back, they all fell victims being cut to pieces by Thomas.[27]

This is obviously an account of the same rearguard action as recounted by Smith and by Thomas, who was, of course, the attacker in this case. As for Borquien's approach march, Skinner's view is more detailed and less vitriolic than that of Smith: 'and we marched without halting, except two or three hours at a time to refresh the men and cattle, so that we reached Jhajjur on the third day. There we halted for one day to rest and next morning moved on to Baree, within two cos of Georgeghur. Borquien then went to reconnoitre the place and I accompanied him.'[28]

Skinner's account, therefore, contradicts Smith's statement regarding Borquien's 'destructive imbecility', telling us that not only did Borquien rest his men for a day at Jhajjar, but that on the following day he – with Skinner – reconnoitred Thomas's position. This argues for at least a basic military competence on the part of Borquien and his officers. Skinner then describes Thomas's position: 'We found that Thomas had drawn up in one line, having Georgeghar on his right flank, and a large village which he had fortified; on his left he had a small fort or ghuree in which he had stationed 1,000 Rohillas and four pieces of cannon. His rear was likewise defended by a large village.'[29]

This is the only description of the battlefield, other than Francklin noting that Thomas, 'drew up his army on a loose sand which deadened the shot and prevented their rising after the first graze.'[30] The loose sand prevented the solid iron cannon shot from bouncing through the ranks, as it would have done on firmer ground. This doubtless gave Thomas's men at least some protection. Thomas's description of his dispositions is rather confused, to say the least, 'Of this force 5 battalions were opposed to Mr Louis, two others were assigned for the battalions opposite the centre of his line, and three to sustain the shock of the enemy's horse.'[31]

It is possible to deduce from this that Thomas's narrative assumes that Borquien was in command of the main body of the assault, so five battalions were directly opposed to this, with perhaps two more as a reserve in the centre of his line. The remaining three battalions were, therefore, in and around the large village in Thomas's rear, watching the two thousand horse, who, from Thomas's perspective, must have posed a significant threat.

The force facing him was considerably larger. There were nine infantry battalions left in the Third Brigade, of which two – presumably those survivors from the

27 Fraser, *James Skinner*, p.218.
28 Fraser, *James Skinner*, p.219.
29 Fraser, *James Skinner*, p.219.
30 Francklin, *Military Memoirs*, p.228.
31 Francklin, *Military Memoirs*, p.228.

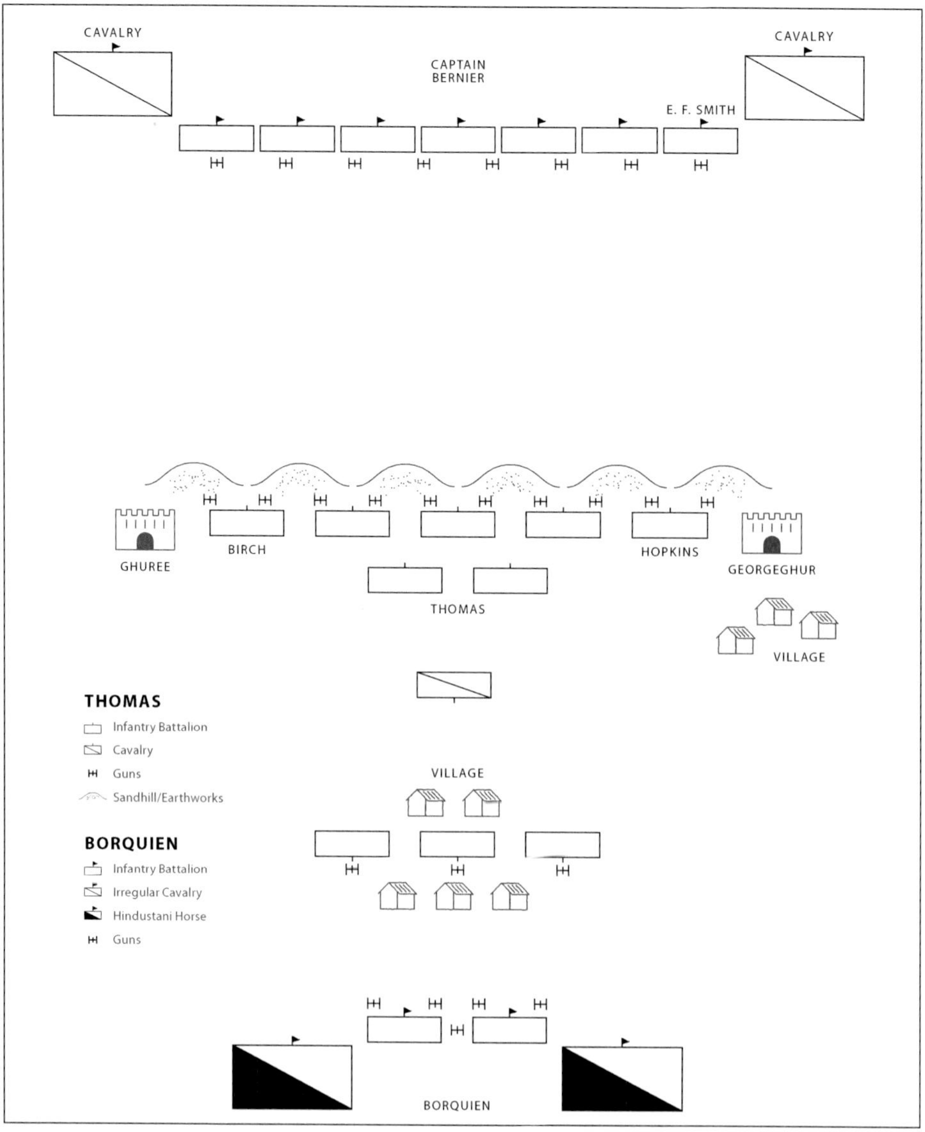

The Battle of Georgeghur. Initial dispositions of Thomas's and Borquien's forces. (Gary Luxton © Helion & Co)

previous action – took no part, as we shall see. The remaining seven battalions, if at full strength,[32] would have totalled a little less than 5,000 men, including the crews for their 35 guns and howitzers. Skinner says that there were 28 guns with these seven battalions, so they were certainly somewhat under establishment – perhaps the preceding forced

32 For the organisation and establishment of an 'Army of Hindustan' brigade, see Copestake, *Their Infantry and Guns*, Chapter 5.

march had thinned the ranks a little. It is also possible that the howitzers, which were often part of each battalion's allotment of artillery, at one howitzer per battalion, were simply not used. At all events, Thomas was somewhat outnumbered in infantry, but his defences more than made up for the disparity.

Thomas was hugely outnumbered in cavalry, of which Borquien's army may have had as many as 5,000, as the original 2,000, which Skinner calls 'regular Hindustani Horse',[33] had been joined by some thousands of Sikh cavalry, doubtless eager for revenge for the depredations Thomas had committed in Jhind and Patiala. However, they appeared to take little part in the coming fighting: 'The cavalry were on our flanks but took good care to keep out of cannon reach.'[34]

Two battalions with two 18-pounders and 'some horse which were sent to try his rear'[35] were separated from the main assault force and were under Borquien's direct command, as Smith rather disparagingly says, 'He did not lead the attack himself but prudently remained with the cavalry two thousand yards in the rear of George Thomas's line.'[36]

This is Smith's only mention of the force to Thomas's rear, and it must be the same force as mentioned by Skinner. Apart from the inherent unlikelihood of two separate forces, there were simply not enough troops. The two 18-pounder guns must have slowed down the progress of Borquien's command, as it does not seem to have taken much further part in the action. Perhaps they attacked the large village that defended Thomas's rear, but if so, no mention is made of such an attack by any of those present. Yet, they had some effect, as Francklin recounts, 'A strong detachment of the enemy who were stationed in Mr Thomas's rear prevented his receiving any support from the troops opposed to them.'[37]

This 'strong detachment' would be the two battalions, probably with their own guns, plus the two 18-pounders and the 2,000 'Hindutani Horse' mentioned by Skinner and Smith. Therefore, this detachment would have perhaps 1,000 or so infantry, and a total of 10 or 12 guns, including the two 18-pounders, plus the 2,000 Hindustani Horse. It was with this force that Borquien remained during the action.

The main assault on Thomas's line would, therefore, be made by the remaining seven battalions of the Third Brigade. However, no mention is made of the commander of the assault. Skinner, however, may be implying that the assault was actually commanded by Captain Bernier when he says, 'had it not been for Captain Burnear, a Frenchman, we should certainly have lost the day for the Major was not seen at all during the battle – and our being saved from total destruction was entirely owing to the exertion of Captain Burnear who was a brave and able soldier.'[38] The man was the same Captain Bernier who had previously served in the Somru Brigade.[39]

33 Fraser, *James Skinner*, p.217.
34 Fraser, *James Skinner*, p.219.
35 Fraser, *James Skinner*, p.219.
36 Smith, *Regular Corps*, p.24.
37 Francklin, *Military Memoirs*, pp.229–230.
38 Fraser, *James Skinner*, p.223.
39 See Chapter 6.

Borquien's Third Brigade of the Army of Hindustan was a veteran formation. It was originally raised by Benoît de Boigne and had been on campaign almost constantly since its formation in 1795.

Smith describes the assault:

> The seven battalions of de Boigne with calm intrepidity, advanced with their guns through heavy sand exposed to a dreadful and well directed fire of fifty-four pieces of cannon, and attacked Thomas's ten battalions in their entrenchments; but they were repulsed with the severe loss of above one thousand and one hundred men killed and wounded which was nearly one-third of their number.[40]

Smith gives Thomas too many guns, as his own admitted total was only 50, and some must have been with the three battalions covering his rear. Smith may be forgiven a hint of bitterness here, as his younger brother, Captain E.F. Smith, commanding the left wing of the assault, was killed in this action.[41] That the assault was severe and bloody is confirmed by Skinner,

> At three p.m. we moved to the attack, in open columns of companies... Having come within gunshot we formed line, under a heavy cannonade of thirty-five pieces. [Skinner seems only to count the guns facing him rather than the full total of Thomas's artillery] The cavalry were on our flanks, but took good care to keep out of cannon reach. Our right had come into a line with Thomas's left, when the word was given to wheel into line and thus we moved to the attack. Both parties fought well, and disputed the day with great courage. About four p.m. we came within musket range, but found that Thomas had thrown up sand banks in his front, which brought our line to a halt. Both musketry and cannon now showered on us like hail, and the men began to fall by hundreds. Two of Thomas's battalions now moved out in columns of companies, under command of Captain Hopkins, a gallant officer. They formed just in front of our left wing, and gave their fire exactly as if they had been at a review: when all had formed, they gave a volley and came to the charge, which completely succeeded in driving back our left wing. However our golundauze kept to their guns; and the gallant Hopkins, having his leg shot off, by one of our six pounders, whilst advancing at the charge, the battalions gave way as soon as he fell, and ran back taking their leader along with them. Our left wing then rallied and resumed their position, but the fire was so murderous that our whole line was ordered to sit down; as for Thomas's men, they were sheltered by the sand hillocks in his front.[42]

40 Smith, *Regular Corps*, p.24.
41 Smith, *Regular Corps*, p.25.
42 Fraser, *James Skinner*, pp.220–221.

This was obviously warm work for both sides, though Thomas's sand 'fortifications' gave his men considerable protection. Not only that, but the attacking battalions had significant trouble moving their guns through the sand,

> Their slow progress through the heavy sand which lay in front of Thomas's line. Owing to the guns, which they would not leave in their rear, occasioned not only their defeat but their dreadful carnage. Thomas's loss was not so great, as the guns of de Boigne's battalions were mostly dismounted by their recoil on the sand, when fired, which snapped their axel trees.[43]

Thomas's own account, as related by Francklin, despite being a little confused, adds more details, especially regarding a counter-attack led by Captains Hopkins and Birch,

> Mr. Lewis's division came on briskly having their guns at the drag ropes [this would be the main assault where Thomas assumed Borquien would be]. Mr. Thomas by a rapid discharge of round and grape shot from his artillery, at first threw them into confusion, and had he been able at this moment to prevent his troops from giving way, would have entirely defeated the enemy, but the centre of his line, being at that time hard pressed by the enemy's cavalry, gave way and no effort could prevent the remainder from following their example.
>
> This rendered an immediate and spirited advance necessary to support; for this purpose Mr Thomas ordered Mr. Hopkins with the right wing and Mr. Birch with the left to advance and charge with bayonets their respective wings, which service they performed with no less gallantry than success.
>
> The enemy halted, and began to retreat, but a heavy fire being still continued, from their numerous and well served artillery, Mr. Thomas's people fell in great numbers, which the enemy's cavalry perceiving charged a second time.
>
> They were not only repulsed with loss, but pursued by Mr. Thomas's horse a considerable distance from the field of battle, at this time intelligence was brought to Mr. Thomas who was on the left wing that Mr. Hopkins had received a severe contusion, by a cannon shot, which broke his leg, this circumstance so disheartened his men, that they fell back in disorder and increased the confusion in the centre of his line.
>
> A strong detachment of the enemy, who were stationed in Mr. Thomas's rear prevented his receiving any support from the troops opposed to them, and he could only spare one battalion to support the centre. This body, however conducted themselves with so much gallantry, that could Mr. Thomas have afforded the additional aid of 100 resolute men, they might have advanced, and would, in all probability, have decided the fate of the day.[44]

43 Smith, *Regular Corps*, p.24.
44 Francklin, *Military Memoirs*, pp.228–230.

Neither Smith nor Skinner make any mention of a cavalry attack by Borquien's troops. Indeed, Skinner says that the cavalry stayed out of artillery range on the flanks of the main assault. However, Thomas's account does confirm both Smith and Skinner regarding the position of a force in Thomas's rear, though it says nothing of its composition. Perhaps – and this is speculation – the cavalry action described was an attempt by the Hindustani Horse in Thomas's rear to have some effect on the main battle. If this was so, then Thomas's cavalry seem to have beaten any attempt by Borquien's cavalry to interfere in the action. Another possibility is that cavalry from the wings of the main assault advanced to cover the retirement of those seven battalions of the Third Brigade, and Thomas's memory has magnified this into a charge which needed to be fended off by his own cavalry. Either, or even both, are possibilities in the confusion of battle.

Borquien's assault faltered, and the battle shuddered to a stalemate.

> In this way we remained all night; for neither could Thomas come out to attack us nor could we attack him. At sunrise we hung out a flag of truce; the firing ceased and we were allowed to clear the field, which took us till twelve at noon. The flag was then pulled down. And we retired out of cannon reach. But Thomas was so well sickened that he would not follow up the blow.[45]

Thomas held his position, but only just, and as night fell, the fighting died down. Quite who was in the worst position at the close of that day's combat is open to debate.

Skinner's view is interesting, despite his inflation of the numbers involved:

> This was the severest battle I had ever seen; our troops were nearly equal as to infantry – we had about 8,000 men. Thomas had thirty-five pieces of cannon, we twenty-eight; the cavalry did not come into play. Our loss in killed and wounded was between 3,000 and 4,000; out of seven European officers we had two killed Lieutenants Smith and McCulloch and two wounded Captains Oliver and Rabella. Twenty-five of our tumbrils were blown up by the enemy's shot, and fifteen of our guns dismounted. Thomas had about 2,000 killed and wounded and Captain Hopkins who died of his wounds. Had Thomas possessed another officer like him he would have gained the day.[46]

What is obvious is that both parties had been severely mauled. In the following days, however, it soon became clear that Thomas had lost some of his usual offensive spirit.

> We had always heard that Thomas was a brave active and clever soldier and an able general; but we were surprised that he now permitted us to remain for fifteen days without attempting to attack us or to make good his retreat to Hansi, for there was no doubt on our minds that, had he tried either plan, he would have succeeded.

45 Fraser, *James Skinner*, pp.220–221.
46 Fraser, *James Skinner*, p.221.

> The state of our guns and the spirits of our soldiery was such, that had Thomas shown any inclination to move towards us we should have got out of his reach.[47]

Skinner makes it clear that the Third Brigade was in no fit state to resume active operations, but, of course, Thomas had his own problems directly resulting from the battle. The loss of Captain Hopkins seems to have hit him rather hard, for, according to Skinner, 'Thomas now gave up all the management to Captain Hearsey who joined him a few days after the battle, and to his native officers, while he himself took to drinking.'[48]

Yet, Thomas was not entirely devoid of finer feelings. Francklin makes a point of giving us this illustration of another side to Thomas's character, with regard to the death of Captain Hopkins,

> To do Justice to the memory of my friend I cannot on this occasion, forbear to mention, that after the death of the gallant youth, Mr Thomas, with a liberality of spirit which reflect the highest credit on his character sent the young man's disconsolate sister (she became an orphan by her father's death) a present of 2,000 rupees, with a promise, if that was not thought sufficient to supply her wants to extend his benevolence, though out of the remains of a ruined fortune of his own.[49]

This act of kindness seemingly happened during the time Captain Francklin knew Thomas personally, while writing his 'Military Memoirs', and accords with Thomas's earlier rescues of 'damsels in distress'.

Thomas's own version of events after the battle is, as one might expect, a little different, both as regards his own losses in the action and the events in its immediate aftermath. On the balance of probabilities, Captain Hearsey probably joined Thomas before the battle, as outlined above:

> In this action the enemy lost 2,000 men and 30 pieces of artillery. Mr Thomas's loss was 700 men and 20 pieces of cannon rendered unfit for further service; the cause of this loss in artillery, was occasioned partly by his cannon being dismounted by the enemy's shot and partly by the breaking of their axle-trees as the carriages of the guns, instead of recoiling as usual after the discharge, from the nature of the soil, being a deep and heavy sand stopped short and broke.[50]

Thomas was now in dire straits. Colonel Collins's letter of 23 October, quoted above, tells us that his enemies were being reinforced. The four battalions of sepoys Collins mentions were not commanded by Perron himself, but were in fact four battalions of the Fourth Brigade, under the aged but competent Colonel Pedron, who superseded Borquien.[51]

47 Fraser, *James Skinner*, p.223.
48 Fraser, *James Skinner*, p.224.
49 Francklin, *Military Memoirs*, p.231.
50 Francklin, *Military Memoirs*, pp.230–231.
51 Smith, *Regular Corps*, p.25.

By 30 October 1801, Collins was reporting again to Calcutta,

> ...it appears by the Delhi Akbars that this fortress [Georgeghur] is already completely invested on all sides by the numerous bodies of cavalry and infantry which Major Louis [Borquien] has drawn together, and that all kinds of provisions bore an exorbitant price in the camp of Mr. Thomas; but the position taken by this officer is very strong, and the redoubts that cover his encampment have been erected with so much military skill, that his enemies have abandoned all hope of subduing him by force, and trust the accomplishment of their objects by the slow yet certain effects of famine.[52]

Thomas's enemies were closing in, and, while one may doubt Francklin's statement that 'thirty thousand men and a train of 110 pieces of artillery had now surrounded Mr Thomas on all sides',[53] at least as regards numbers, there is no doubt that the 'Irish Raja' was now surrounded by enemies, including many of the Sikhs whose lands he had 'levied contributions' upon the year previously. Famine would eventually do its work, yet other methods were available:

> His native officers had been bribed over to Perron's interest, fresh forces arriving, and Thomas unable or unwilling to retreat to his fort he was surrounded at Georgeghur; Colonel Pedron arrived, superseded Borquien and blockaded Thomas and his diminished troops, They sustained the blockade for seven weeks and at last were conquered by famine, The troops came over to Pedron or dispersed and Thomas escaped with great difficulty with his European officers Captain Hearsey and Lieutenant Birch who adhered to his fallen fortune, with commendable inflexibility, to Hansi, and left his enemy in possession of fifty-four pieces of cannon, his camp and baggage.[54]

Smith's laconic and rather brutal description of Thomas's disaster glosses over the details. Thomas's men were deserting in numbers, and some of his officers had apparently been bribed. 'A body of Rohillas who were stationed in the posts that commanded the water used for the supply of the camp suddenly went over to the enemy; Mr Thomas instantly appointed others to guard the posts thus abandoned, but to his sorrow soon found that the spirit of desertion had seized upon the Mussulman [Muslim] troops in general, the cavalry alone excepted.'[55]

Thomas seemed to waver between making a breakout and holding out in the hope of help from his one-time enemy, Lakwa Dada. Perhaps Thomas was unaware that Lakwa had been defeated by Perron at the Battle of Seonda in May 1801 and would eventually

52 Sinh, *Poona Residency Correspondence,* vol.9 letter 33.
53 Francklin, *Military Memoirs*, p.232.
54 Smith, *Regular Corps*, p.25.
55 Francklin, *Military Memoirs*, p.238.

die of wounds received in that action.[56] Indeed, some of the battalions of the Third Brigade now facing Thomas had been present in that campaign. It is equally possible that Thomas, when telling Captain Francklin of his career, simply used Lakwa Dada's non-appearance, or indeed that of any of his other supposed 'allies', as an excuse for his defeat. The plan of a breakout was abandoned, as the troops simply would not countenance such a desperate scheme. Indeed, as the blockade continued, it became clear that Thomas's army was falling apart, and a council of war of the remaining officers advised surrender.[57]

Matters became worse when Shahtab Khan, the *khilladar*, or governor, of Thomas's fort of Georgeghur, which was in effect the anchor of his fortified camp, defected to the enemy. By this time, hunger was taking its toll, and 'not a seer of rice or grain could be procured'.[58] Thomas decided on a last, desperate throw of the dice – he would break out with his still-loyal cavalry and ride for his capital of Hansi.

Colonel Collins received the news of Thomas's flight a few days later, and communicated it to Calcutta in his letter of 14 November 1801,

> I have now just received advices mentioning that on the night of the 10th instant Mr Thomas fled from Georgeghur with his cavalry, towards the fort of Hansi; that the whole of his artillery and baggage had been captured and his sepoy-corps completely plundered; that the fortress of Georgeghur was in the possession of Mr Louis whose cavalry were gone in pursuit of Mr Thomas.[59]

In fact, Borquien's pursuit was not very effective, for although Thomas 'fell in with a party of the enemy who attacked him with vigour',[60] he was able to break contact and continue to Hansi with at least some of his surviving cavalry.

Jehazi Sahib's Last Stand: The Siege of Hansi, November–December 1801

Thomas and his exhausted followers arrived in his capital, something over 14 hours after his escape from the besieged camp.[61] The situation in Hansi was not one to inspire confidence. Thomas, however, does seem to have recovered something of his old fighting spirit, as he busied himself strengthening his position. 'Two pieces of artillery were all that remained in the fort fit for service. The dilatory march of the enemy to invest the town, afforded Mr Thomas sufficient time to cast and mount eight additional cannon. The enemy advancing by easy stages, possessed themselves of the wells in the neighbourhood of Hansi and at length commenced the siege.'[62]

56 Copestake, *Their Infantry and Guns*, pp.119–122.
57 Francklin, *Military Memoirs*, pp.237–238.
58 Francklin, *Military Memoirs*, p.240.
59 Sinh, *Poona Residency Correspondence*, vol.9 letter 34.
60 Francklin, *Military Memoirs*, p.241.
61 Fraser, *James Skinner*, p.225.
62 Francklin, *Military Memoirs*, p.242.

The slowness of the enemy's approach gave Thomas time to construct three redoubts, one covering each of the three gates into the town of Hansi. Thomas's most loyal remaining troops, 300 Rajput irregulars, were garrisoned in the fort itself. His other men, about 900 assorted irregulars, mostly garrisoned the redoubts. However, the desperate situation was not to the taste of some of Thomas's remaining men,

> The Rajputs who still adhered to Mr Thomas by this time reduced in their numbers to 300 were stationed within the fort; the remainder of his force consisting of about 900 men, were distributed for the defence of the city and the out posts, aware of his very critical situation Mr Thomas himself remained within the fort, taking care to keep a strict guard during the night.
>
> The troops destined for the security of the outposts had scarcely occupied their respective stations, when, in a manner most dastardly and treacherous, they delivered them over to the enemy, and the fort and city were thus left to be defended, by a handful of men.[63]

Assuming that the fall of Hansi was a foregone conclusion, Colonel Pedron returned to Aligarh. James Skinner was less than happy about this, 'Pedron completed the 3rd brigade from the five battalions of the 4th which he had brought with him from Aligarh; but it was unfortunately Borquien under whom we were ordered to attack Hansi. The 3rd brigade with a large battering train, 500 regular Hindustani horse and about 5,000 Sikhs marched for that place while Pedron went back to Aligarh.'[64]

Thomas had found the time to block up or pollute all the wells for a considerable distance around Hansi, thus slowing the approach of Borquien's army, and buying time to strengthen his defences. Clearing out these wells was no easy task, as Skinner is at pains to tell his readers,

> When we reached Sewannee seven cos south-west of Hansi, we received information that Thomas had choked up all the wells within six cos around the place. Bursee four cos in our front, had five pukka wells; and Hansi was three cos distant from Bursee. I was ordered with two battalions and all the pioneers to clear out one of these wells, – and this I affected in two days, after which the troops marched and all the rest were cleared out. We discovered too, that the little tanks of water near Hansi had been defiled with pork and beef.[65]

Polluting wells and tanks with animal carcases – offensive to both Hindus and Muslims, as well as being a disease risk – was by no means uncommon in Indian warfare. Clearing out the large, and often deep, wells of northern India would take time. Skinner's pioneers obviously knew their work. Nevertheless, the advance to Hansi was slow, giving Thomas

63 Francklin, *Military Memoirs*, pp.242–243.
64 Fraser, *James Skinner*, pp.225–226.
65 Fraser, *James Skinner*, p.226.

more time, perhaps, than he expected, but it was not too long before Borquien's force was before Thomas's capital.

Thomas's own account of the siege is perfunctory at best, concentrating rather on the treachery of his Rohilla mercenaries than his own actions. Smith gives the action barely a couple of lines, although he was certainly there. We are left, therefore with the account of James Skinner for details of the action. Reading Skinner's memoir, as recounted by Baillie-Fraser, it is clear that he had a habit of exaggerating numbers, a prime example being, 'Thomas had still about 5,000 foot and 200 horse',[66] which is a huge over-estimate, to say the least. Had Thomas possessed even half of this force, surely he would have made a more active defence. As it was, with only about 1,200 men – of which only 300 were trustworthy – he was hard-pressed to defend the walls of the town of Hansi and leave a reliable garrison in the fort.

Equally, if Skinner was even remotely correct about Thomas's numbers, why were the garrisons of the three redoubts Thomas built to defend the gates of the town so small? As Skinner himself tells us:

> Borquien reconnoitred the fort several times. Thomas had still about 5,000 foot and 200 horse, with two 24 four 12 and 6 six pounder guns; and he had fortified strongly three outworks about a hundred yards from the town. One to the south-east at the Bursee gate, was defended by sixty men; another at the Kootub gate to the south by 100 men; and one on the west towards Hissar with 200 men.
>
> At three in the morning Borquien ordered these three works to be attacked. Two battalions under Lieutenant MacKenzie were directed to assault that towards the Bursee gate; two others under my command to that at the Kootub gate; while Captain Bunnear [Bernier, a capable French officer who had previously served in the Somru brigade] with two more was ordered to that at the Hissar gate. We arrived at our destinations near daybreak and led on the respective columns. MacKenzie and I both succeeded without much trouble, the enemy's parties running into the town. But Captain Bunnear having got between the out work and the town, and thus cutting off their retreat, the men resisted obstinately, and beat back the party. Bunnear rallied them but in so doing was killed in the ditch – on which his men rushed on, carried the place, and put the whole of the enemy party to the sword.[67]

Thomas's out works were captured and the besieging force could now erect the siege batteries and emplace their heavy guns without interference. Thomas simply did not have enough trustworthy troops to mount any kind of sortie against the besiegers: 'During the siege of the town nothing was done to interrupt us by Thomas though the garrison kept up their fire from musketry and cannon pretty well.'[68]

Once the heavy guns were emplaced and were able to open fire, and the walls were breached, the assault would go in. Each of the three storming parties was 1,500 men

66 Fraser, *James Skinner*, p.226.
67 Fraser, *James Skinner*, pp.226–227.
68 Fraser, *James Skinner*, p.227.

strong. One was commanded by Skinner, a second by his younger brother, Robert, and the third by Lieutenant MacKenzie. The date set for the assault was 3 December 1801.

Skinner takes up the story,

> At dawn of day, on the 3rd of December, the signal of attack was given. Mackenzie was opposed to Captain Hearsey: my brother to a native, Ellias Beg; and I had to contend with Captain Birch. Both Mackenzie and my brother made good their way in, after some resistance; but Birch, who defended his post well, beat me back twice with great loss. Burning powder choppers [chopra? – chopped hay bales], powder pots, and everything he could get hold of were showered upon us; but our greatest loss was from the powder pots [these pots would be primitive grenades] which greatly disheartened the men: however, after a desperate struggle I drove them from the breach. Just as I had got up, I saw Birch about twenty yards from me taking aim at me with a double barrelled gun, the contents of which, both barrels, he fired at me; but 'the sweet little cherub' saved me from them. I immediately levelled my javelin, and, putting my shield to my breast, darted it at him, and took off his hat, on which he set off and joined his men, who were now leaving the wall and retreated about two hundred yards behind houses.
>
> All my storming party had now got in, and we moved towards the chowk or centre of the bazar where we saw our columns. The fight now became desperate. Thomas had come down from the fort with 1,000 of his chosen men, attacking the column commanded by Lieutenant Skinner, drove it back to the walls of the town. I immediately hastened to my brother's assistance, and beat Thomas back to the gate of the fort.
>
> All our columns now having joined in the chowk, Thomas made another attempt, bringing up a six-pounder, and, after great resistance, drove us out of the chowk. We were then joined by our reserve of a battalion, with a couple of six-pounders, and, in spite of a very obstinate resistance, by Thomas, drove him back to the fort. About noon we had a complete possession of the town; but it cost us dear, as the slaughter on our side was very great, for several times we had to come to the sword [that is hand to hand with the sword]. My brother got a cut at Thomas but his armour had saved him.[69]

The fighting was evidently fierce and bloody, and not infrequently hand-to-hand. Thomas and his remaining men were not ready to give up just yet. Borquien brought up reinforcements, which must have included some of the Sikh cavalry, dismounted, as Skinner mentions '3,000 dismounted troopers and two battalions'[70] as the reinforcement to the troops already in the town. Thomas was evidently still active in the defence of the fort, even after the town had fallen to Borquien: 'Mr Thomas's remaining troops fighting with the most determined valour. Three different times the enemy were repulsed

69 Fraser, *James Skinner*, pp.228–229.

70 Fraser, *James Skinner*, p.230.

with loss, but numbers at length prevailing Mr Thomas could no longer persuade his men to continue the conflict.'[71]

Once again, Thomas blames the treachery of his remaining Muslim troops for the fall of the fort, and certainly they had a part to play, as they were in contact with Borquien's men on the outside: 'Borquien began to intrigue with Thomas's men, and wrote them letters promising them six months pay and permanent service if they would give up the fort and Thomas. These letters were rolled upon arrows and shot into the fort from our trenches, they were answered in the same way by Thomas's men.'[72]

Most of Borquien's remaining European officers were 'British or country-born', in other words, like the Skinner brothers, of British fathers and Indian mothers, and they found Borquien's intrigues distasteful. They, therefore, persuaded Borquien to offer 'honourable' terms to Thomas if he would surrender. To that end, Captain Smith went into the fort under a flag of truce:

> Borquien had subdued the garrison with gold, which in India is more irrefutable than in Europe. I came forward once more to assist Thomas to mitigate the severity of his misfortunes and dissipate the dangers with which he was environed – I advised him to an honourable surrender before the garrison delivered him up to his enemy with eternal disgrace to themselves and ignominy to him. He followed my counsel, surrendered the fort on 1st January 1802 and with his family and private property was conveyed to the Company's frontiers under my protection.[73]

There was a little more to the surrender than Smith's bare narrative. This included a surprising amount of conviviality between Thomas and the European officers of Borquien's army. Wine seems to have been taken in some quantity. This almost got out of control when Borquien – in his cups – suggested a toast to the success of Perron's arms,

> At this we all turned up our glasses; and Thomas on hearing and seeing this burst into tears, and putting his hand to his sword called out to Borquien that it was not to him but to his own ill fate that his fall was due, and (drawing his sword) – 'One Irish sword' said he 'is still sufficient for a hundred Frenchmen,' Borquien, in terror at this, jumped from his chair and ran out of the tent, calling for his guard.[74]

The affair almost turned into a brawl, as Thomas's own guards rushed into the tent to protect their general, but they were calmed by Skinner and the other officers. Bloodshed was avoided and Thomas eventually calmed down and was persuaded to put away his sword. Borquien, to his credit, then re-entered the tent and, shaking Thomas by the hand, apologised for what he had said.

71 Francklin, *Military Memoirs*, p.243.
72 Fraser, *James Skinner*, p.231.
73 Smith, *Regular Corps*, p.26.
74 Fraser, *James Skinner*, p.234.

Once the fort was formally surrendered, Thomas, with his family and personal property, was escorted into British territory by a battalion of the 3rd Brigade, commanded by Captain Smith.

The Last Months of George Thomas

Once safe in British territory, Thomas travelled to Berhampore, where he seems to have spent time telling his remarkable story to Captain Francklin, who would publish it in 1803. Now a broken man, Thomas seemingly planned to return to 'his native country',[75] but got no further in his travels than Berhampore, where he died on 22 August 1802, aged only 46.

Thomas had finally been brought down by Perron, specifically by Perron's commander on the spot, Major Louis Borquien.

There is something of the classical tragic hero about Thomas and his rise to fame and sudden fall from grace. Captain Lewis Ferdinand Smith fought against him and obviously respected and possibly liked him. His opinion of Thomas is worth recording:

> This man was one of the most uncommon characters I have ever seen; and I knew him well; he was bold, indefatigable, active, cautious, and possessed a strong natural sense; he formed a considerable party from his own personal exertions unassisted by the power or treasure of any prince – without money and without country – opposed by all and supported by none, he raised a strong party which was nearly destroying the gigantic power of Perron.[76]

Compton certainly saw him as such a hero, and his other later biographers seem to have more or less followed that trend,[77] but that is perhaps to miss the point. Certainly, Thomas was an uncommon man with drive and determination above the ordinary. He was also a product of the times and the places he lived in. The Royal Navy of the eighteenth century produced hard men. Once Thomas deserted that service, he put himself beyond the pale, and he was forced to shift for himself. He was not beyond becoming a bandit, first with the Poligars in the south and possibly on his journey north to Hindustan, in order to survive. His mercenary service with the Somru Brigade may have given him a veneer of respectability of a sort, but it was his ability to fight that made his name in the mercenary business of late-eighteenth-century India. Being able to fight was a valuable commodity in an era of constant warfare. Thomas fought constantly throughout most of his career. In that, he was no different in most respects from the people who employed him or the people he fought against. His men followed him because he was usually successful and he treated them well when in funds, paying

75 Francklin, *Military Memoirs*, p.245.
76 Smith, *Regular Corps*, p.20.
77 Compton, *Particular Account*, has a fine Victorian style biography of Thomas, written at the height of the British Raj. Compton could hardly do other than see Thomas as a hero.

them whenever he could – in hard times even selling his own property to give them something on account. Yet, at times, perhaps most of the time, he was little more than a robber baron 'raising contributions' to finance his sometimes rickety war machine. In that respect, he was little different from the Maratha warlords he was often employed by. He survived as long as he did because he was useful, but also because there were larger wars for Perron to fight. Once 'Mr Thomas's Party' became large enough for Perron to realise it was a possible threat, then, at a time of Perron's choosing, Thomas was to be either controlled or destroyed. Thomas, with an almost pathological hatred of the French, chose to fight and was therefore destroyed.

10

A Christian Princess

The Last Years of The Begum Somru

The defeat of Lakwa Dada at the Battle of Seonda in May 1801 finally brought an end to the 'Widows' War'. That did not mean the end of conflict in Hindustan. The 'Widows' War' was quickly followed by a major civil war between the Maratha houses of Scindia and Holkar.

Farzana, the Begum Somru, is mentioned much less by such astute intelligence gatherers as Colonel John Collins in this period. While she appears quite often in the official correspondence for 1794–1799,[1] she appears with significantly less frequency in the period 1800–1803.[2] Yet, Collins is still concerned that General Perron wishes to deprive the Begum of her territories. In his letter of 18 August 1800, he informs the Governor-General, along with much other intelligence:

> My Agent at the court of Delhi apprizes me that Mr. Perron had actually formed a plan for seizing the person of Begum Somru whenever she repaired to the citadel in order to pay her respects to His Majesty Shah Alam. It appears, however, that the Begum had received timely notice of this treacherous design, and had in consequence, retired to her own camp for security.[3]

A resurgence of disturbances in Hindustan as part of the 'Widows' War', and the financial troubles that this caused for Perron, as various 'rebels' withheld their tribute due to Daulat Rao Scindia, caused the French general to march with three battalions of sepoys and 500 cavalry to extort the three lakhs of rupees (Rs 300,000) that Partab Singh, the Raja of Jaipur, owed in tribute.[4]

As for the Begum, she still had the support of the emperor and of Scindia. Because her *jaghirs* were awarded directly from the emperor, Perron's attempts to take them from her came to naught.[5]

1 Sarkar, *Poona Residency Correspondence*, vol.8.
2 Sarkar, *Poona Residency Correspondence*, vol.9.
3 Sinh, *Poona Residency Correspondence,* vol.9 letter 21.
4 Sinh, *Poona Residency Correspondence,* vol.9 letter 24.
5 Sarkar, *Mughal Empire*, vol.4, p.207.

Begum Somru and her household. This painting by an Indian artist shows Farzana in the centre, with the officers and court functionaries around her. In the background, sepoys of the Somru Brigade in their blue coats and red turbans act as guards. There are also four Europeans in the picture, three of whom wear differing military uniforms. See also the front cover of this book. (Public Domain)

She seems to have been able to keep out of the wider Holkar-Scindia civil war, which at first seemed a continuation of the 'Widows' War', but became a wider conflict once Jaswant Rao Holkar began to meddle.[6] For the little information we have on Farzana's movements, or indeed lack of the same, we must rely on the letters of Colonel Collins to the Governor-General, Lord Mornington, in Calcutta. As a consequence of the Holkar-Scindia conflict, Colonel Collins's letter of 12 August 1801, outlining the military dispositions of Scindia's forces, amongst much else, informs us: 'Mr Perron and Begum Somru have been ordered to join him [Scindia] with the least possible delay, with their respective forces. It is not likely, however, that this order will be obeyed by the Begum.'[7]

Indeed, Perron himself kept out of this war, blaming his problems with George Thomas for his constant delays in joining his employer. With hindsight, it is easy to see that he was husbanding his resources and that, possibly, he underestimated the jealousy of the Maratha *sardars* as he sat in his palatial residence near the fortress of Aligarh. In 1801, Perron was appointed *subahdar* of Delhi,[8] which he exercised through

6 For an account of this war, see Copestake, *Their Infantry and Guns*, Chapter 10.
7 Sinh, *Poona Residency Correspondence*, vol.9 letter 27.
8 Sarkar, *Mughal Empire*, vol.4, p.208.

his subordinate, Captain – later Major – Drugeon,[9] a Savoyard mercenary who had served under de Boigne. Drugeon, therefore, had control of the emperor and the 5,000 strong garrison of Delhi, and he answered first to Perron.

This meant that Farzana had little or no access to Shah Alam and had therefore lost her once considerable influence with the emperor. However, the Somru Brigade was not directly part of the Army of Hindustan, as the *jaghirs* that supported it had come directly from the Emperor, 'There were, under the Delhi Empire, two other corps affiliated to Perron's command by virtue of Scindia being the official commander in chief (*bakhshi-ul-mamalik*) of the Emperor but they were paid and controlled independently of Perron. These were the brigades of Jean Baptiste Filose and the Begum Somru.'[10]

Payment for the Somru Brigade was, of course, raised from the land grants (*jaidad*) given by the emperor, first to Reinhardt and then confirmed by the emperor to Farzana. Nevertheless, Perron was now supreme in Hindustan, despite the jealousy of Ambaji Ingle and other Maratha *sardars*, so it behoved Farzana to tread carefully in the coming months as the whole edifice of the 'Maratha Empire' began to fall apart.

The Last Campaign of the Somru Brigade

Having successfully kept out of the Maratha civil war of 1801–1802,[11] Farzana now had only one real objective: to retain control of Sardhana. To do this, she needed allies. Perron, as we have seen, she could not trust. Thomas was now defeated and dispossessed and would die in August 1802. Daulat Rao Scindia, although not her enemy, could not be relied on for her security of tenure. To all intents and purposes, she was alone.

Her only recourse was the British.

Actual evidence for Farzana's contact with the British in the lead up to the Second Maratha War is scarce and circumstantial, especially as a contingent of her army was with Daulat Rao Scindia's army in the Deccan by 17 July 1803. At this time, the British envoy, Colonel Collins, and his assistant, Captain Paris Bradshaw, were both still in Daulat Rao's camp. Amongst other intelligence, Collins noted that: 'Scindia has, at present, with him no more than 11 battalions of sepoys (Colonel Dudrenec and Major Brownrigg being detached) seven under the command of Colonel Pohlmann and four in the service of Begum Somru, commanded by Colonel Saleur. The latter are reckoned very indifferent corps.'[12]

The Begum's troops were a long way from home and apparently none too well thought of, so one might wonder why they were there at all, other than to bolster Daulat Rao's forces. Perhaps – and this is speculation – they were there as some kind of counterbalance to Pohlmann's *compoo*. The Somru Brigade was not under Perron's command, while Pohlmann's battalions were originally de Boigne's First Brigade and so were now

9 Compton, *Particular Account*, p.347.
10 Sarkar, *Mughal Empire*, vol.4, p.217.
11 See Copestake, *Their Infantry and Guns*, Chapter 10, pp.141–156 for a narrative of this war.
12 Sinh, *Poona Residency Correspondence*, vol.9 letter 208.

ultimately part of the Army of Hindustan and therefore answerable to Pierre Cuillier Perron.

Colonel Collins, the ever-busy British resident with Scindia, once again providing intelligence to the Governor-General in Calcutta, tells us in a letter dated 6 May 1802: 'General Perron has of late assumed a high tone of authority at the Durbars of the Princes and Chiefs of Hindustan, By his advice or orders Begum Somru was induced to send four battalions of sepoys to Ujjain, in the vicinity of which city they are now encamped. These corps are commanded by a Frenchman named Saleur.'[13] So these four battalions had been away from home for over a year before the Anglo-Maratha war of 1803 began.

Whatever the reasons for their presence, they were part of the Maratha army that would fight the Battle of Assaye against Major General Arthur Wellesley, the future Duke of Wellington and the Governor-General's younger brother. However, as was usual in the hurly-burly of Indian politics at this time, it was not nearly as simple as that.

Sarkar gives us an impression of the 'secret' negotiations that must have ensued between Farzana and the British in 1803:

> The next step in Wellesley's scheme was to draw the allies and vassals of Scindia away from his side. This was a very easy task because Maratha rapacity and want of statesmanship had created a host of enemies among their agents and feudatories in North India. The first and foremost among these was the widowed Begum Somru of Sardhana. As an imperial fief-holder her army was legally under the orders of Scindia as the *Bakhshi* of the Empire. But she was eager to preserve her independent status in relation to Scindia's viceroy of Hindustan and her treasure, both of which had been threatened by Perron and Ambaji Ingle in concert in 1801. Moreover as a Christian she had long maintained friendly relations with the British ... More recently she had sent to Wellesley an application to be taken under British protection with a guarantee for her *jaghir*. The only question for the Governor-General was how to save her from Scindia's vengeance if she declared for the English or her treasonable correspondence was discovered before Perron's army had been defeated.[14]

Farzana, the Begum Somru, once a dancing girl and still the emperor's adopted daughter, was in a very delicate position, especially with most of her army many marches away from Sardhana.

Colonel Saleur, far away in the Deccan, was in an equally unenviable situation. We do not know if he was aware of his mistress's possible defection. In all probability, he was not so informed, lest the 'secret' became known.

Another problem arises as to actually how many battalions Saleur had under his command. 'Five of the six marched under Colonel Saleur to the Deccan with Scindia.

13 Sinh, *Poona Residency Correspondence,* vol.9 letter 58.
14 Sarkar, *Mughal Empire*, vol.4, pp.229–230.

They were in a state of mutiny the whole way, and utterly useless as auxiliaries as Saleur himself declared in many of his letters written in French to his mistress the Begum.'[15]

Sleeman was writing some 40 years later, but knew the Begum in her later years and may have had access to Saleur's letters. Compton also tells us that Saleur had five battalions,[16] but he may well have taken this from Sleeman's book. More recently, Simon Millar also sets Saleur's command at five battalions and 25 field pieces.[17]

Another more contemporary source, none other than Lewis Ferdinand Smith, also gives the strength of Saleur's command as five battalions. Smith had, of course, served with the Army of Hindustan for several years, and one would think he was in a position to know: 'It was present at the memorable and glorious battle of Assaye where it lost one battalion and its four guns the other four battalions having been left to guard the Maratha camp during the action. Five battalions had marched to the Deccan and one remained with the Begum Sombre at Sardhana.'[18]

Yet, conversely, Colonel Collins, who was actually in Daulat Rao's camp in the days immediately before the war began, sets Saleur's command at four battalions. Also, a report from 'Mr Stuart' – who served for a short time with the First Brigade, that is, Pohlmann's *compoo* – later reported that in the weeks before the war began he saw the following troops concentrated at Edilabad:

> 8 battalions of the 1st Brigade,
> 4 battalions of Begum Somru.
> 4 battalions of the brigade of the late Filose commanded by M. Dupont a person of Dutch extraction born in Ceylon.
> 4 or five battalions of the Fifth brigade commanded by Major Brownrigg.
> 6 or 7 battalions of the 4th brigade commanded by the Chevalier Dudrenec.

So, once again, only four battalions for Saleur's *compoo* are mentioned. The same report goes on to detail the artillery with this force: 'With the first brigade there were five guns to each battalion; besides a park to the brigade consisting of eight or 10 pieces 18 and 12 pounders. The ordnance of the other brigades was not quite so numerous, probably about three to each battalion.'[19]

Whatever the precise strength of Saleur's *compoo*, there was to be no glory for the Somru Brigade in this campaign. It appears that they were not completely trusted, and so four battalions were relegated to guarding Daulat Rao's camp and baggage, which was some distance away from the fighting at Assaye. This gave them ample opportunity to march away, with their guns, once the battle was lost.

15 Sleeman, *Rambles and Recollections*, p.610.
16 Compton, *Particular Account*, p.409.
17 S. Millar, *Assaye 1803: Wellington's First and 'Bloodiest' Victory* (Oxford: Osprey, 2006), p.27.
18 Smith, *Regular Corps*, pp.5–6.
19 A.S. Bennell (ed.), *The Maratha War Papers of Arthur Wellesley: January to December 1803* (Stroud: Sutton Publishing for the Army Records Society, 1998), pp.333–334.

If, indeed, five battalions were present, then the fifth battalion did fight in the line of battle against the British, possibly on the left of the Maratha line nearest to the village of Assaye, or perhaps as part of the village garrison.[20] If it was there, then the battalion was destroyed, as Compton rather wordily puts it when referring to Begum Somru's instinct for preservation:

> Amidst the kaleidoscopic changes of Hindustan she managed to preserve her power and independence intact, until her army, famous in peace if not in war, met the English on the plain of Assaye. But even here fortune favoured them, for four of her five battalions being left to guard the Maratha camp made good their escape and only one was destroyed.[21]

As Colonel Saleur and his four battalions made their escape in the confusion of the aftermath of the Battle of Assaye and began their march home, the Begum made a more open contact with the British.

Robert Skinner, the younger brother of James Skinner, of Skinner's Horse fame, had, after being dismissed from Maratha service, along with other officers of British descent by Perron, joined the forces of the Begum Somru. He was not with Colonel Saleur, but in Sardhana with that part of the Begum's army that remained at her capital. His brother's memoirs inform us of the course of events: 'When Lord Lake arrived at Secundra, my brother Robert was sent from the Begum Somru to make a treaty for her. His Lordship immediately sent him back with a treaty and directions to stand fast and not to move from Sardhana. In which case she should be treated favourably by the British Government.'[22]

Lake had, by this time, stormed the supposedly 'impregnable' fortress of Aligarh and defeated a Maratha army in the field at the Battle of Delhi,[23] capturing the city and the person of the emperor in late September 1803.

From Farzana's perspective, the British looked more than likely to win the war. It was important to be on the winning side. Losers rarely held on to their lands. To that end, she proceeded to meet with Lord Lake in an effort to secure her position:

> The overture made by that Lady to Lord Lake mentioned above, took place almost immediately after the battle of Delhi and it was not long before she came to pay her respects in person upon which an incident occurred of a curious and characteristic description. She arrived at headquarters it appears, just after dinner, and being carried in her palankeen, at once to the reception tent, his Lordship came out to meet and receive her. As the adhesion of every petty chieftain was, in those

20 J. Provan, *Bullocks, Grain and Good Madeira: The Maratha and Jat Campaigns 1803–1806 and the Emergence of an Indian Army* (Warwick: Helion, 2022), p.61.

21 Compton, *Particular Account*, p.408.

22 Fraser, *James Skinner*, pp.277–278.

23 For an account of Lake's campaign in Hindustan, see Copestake, *Their Infantry and Guns*, Chapter 12, and Provan, *Bullocks, Grain and Good Madeira*, Chapter 3.

General Gerard Lake, pictured here at the Battle of Laswari with his son. Lake, when 'elevated by wine', embraced the Begum Somru, thereby shocking her attendants. Nevertheless, this meeting went some way to concluding her alliance with the British. (Author's Collection)

> days, of consequence, Lord Lake was not a little pleased at the early demonstration of the Begums loyalty; and being a little elevated by the wine which had just been drunk he forgot the novel circumstances of its being a native female he was about to receive, instead of some well-bearded chief, so he gallantly advanced, and to the utter dismay of her attendants took her in his arms and kissed her. The mistake might have been awkward but the lady's presence of mind put all right. Receiving courteously the proffered attention, she turned calmly round to her astonished attendants – 'It is' said she 'the salute of a padre (*or priest)* to his daughter. The Begum professes Christianity, and thus the explanation was perfectly in character.[24]

In the coming months, there was to be some negotiation between Lord Lake and the Begum over the ownership of her various *jaghirs*,

> It was extremely important that the whole Doab, including the territory occupied by the Begum should come under direct British rule but how this was to be best effected was left to Lord Lake to decide. After a thorough study of the Begum's disposition and power she wielded in the province, Lake recommended that it would be better to propose an exchange of territories, which arrangement was sanctioned by Lord Wellesley.[25]

Colonel Saleur's battalions left Scindia's camp on 14 October,[26] beginning their march back to Sardhana. However, they did not get there, as they received orders from the Begum to proceed to Dieg and there they joined a British detachment, under a Colonel Ball at Kanund, on 15 December. The brigade served the British until the following May. Colonel Saleur retired in February 1804 due to ill health, and the command passed to Colonel Claude Pathod.[27] Once the service with the British was over, the brigade returned to Sardhana.[28]

However, despite these efforts, Farzana, the emperor's adopted daughter, still had more battles to fight, though not a shot was to be fired, and the enemy was Richard Wellesley, Lord Mornington, the British Governor-General in Calcutta. As Governor-General, Richard Wellesley's policy had been far more acquisitive and 'imperial' than other EIC governors. His primary concern had been to destroy the 'French State' of Hindustan, by which he meant the Maratha regulars and their French officers. His most telling blow in this regard had been the publication of an edict in August 1803 which allowed any European officer who resigned from Maratha service to continue to be paid by the British at the same rate. This had resulted in many of Scindia's European

24 Fraser, *James Skinner*, p.293.
25 Banerji, *Begam Samru*, p.86.
26 Banerji, *Begam Samru*, p.83.
27 Keay, *Farzana*, p.270.
28 Banerji, *Begam Samru*, pp.83–84.

officers either leaving his service or being dismissed by Perron.[29] The Begum's *compoo* does not appear to have suffered unduly in this regard, possibly due to previous secret correspondence with the British, which kept the majority of the brigade out of the fighting at Assaye.

Whatever the reasoning, Farzana perhaps hoped for some show of gratitude from the Governor-General for her service. However, in this, she was to be bitterly disappointed. Wellesley intended to dispossess her of all of the *jaghirs* she had striven to accumulate: 'Originally the idea was to 'commute her *Jaghir* for a suitable stipend the extent of which must be regulated by the profits which she actually derives from her territorial possessions, and by the importance of the services which the British Government may derive from the exertion of her aid and influence.'[30]

In other words, she was to be deprived of Sardhana and pensioned off, only being called upon by the British to exert her influence when it was to their advantage for her so to do. Wellesley saw it as vitally important that the whole of the Jumna Doab came under direct British rule. This included the territories occupied by the Begum for the payment of her troops and herself. Lake was the 'man on the spot', so to speak, and he proposed an exchange of territories. Farzana would give up Sardhana, and her other lands, in exchange for other lands which were not so vital to British interests and to their control of the lands around Delhi.

Although the Begum was amenable to the idea of an exchange of territories, nothing of the sort came to pass, despite the several letters that were exchanged between the Begum and Lieutenant Colonel David Ochterlony, the British resident in Delhi. The sticking point appears to have been the fact that the British appear to have expected Farzana to give up her territories before they gave her any specifics about which land she would receive in exchange.

Part of one of Ochterlony's letters reads,

> H.E. the Commander-in-Chief will adopt as soon as possible the necessary measures for transferring you to a portion of territory on the western side of the Jamuna equivalent to that which you have ceded in the Doab. I trust, however, that you will not delay the actual cession of your present jaghir to the authority of the British Government, until the assignment of the equivalent portion of territory, which must necessarily occupy some time before it can be effected.[31]

To Farzana, it seemed that the British simply might not keep their word and the wrangling and negotiation continued into 1804. Her enemies even went so far as to forge a letter implicating her in secret negotiations with Jaswant Rao Holkar, though the British, on acquiring this document, considered it a forgery.[32]

29 Copestake, *Their Infantry and Guns*, p.164.
30 Letter from Wellesley to Lake, 28 July 1803, quoted in Banerji, *Begam Samru*, p.86.
31 Letter from Ochterlony to the Begum, 23 December 1803, quoted in Banerji, *Begam Samru*, p.90.
32 Banerji, *Begam Samru*, p.93.

In the event, when Holkar began his war against the British in 1804, he did contact the Begum and try to persuade her to join his campaign. She prevaricated, trying to keep her options open. Despite her discontent with the British, she did not declare for either side, despite the initial success of Holkar and his allies. She was awaiting the British success or failure at the siege of Dieg. When that fortress fell to the British on Christmas Day 1804, Farzana saw that a British victory over Holkar had become a much more likely result.[33]

Even before this, the Begum had publicly supported the British. When a Sikh force took Saharanpur in October 1804, the EIC's Collector for the district, a Mr Guthrie, was captured by Sher Singh. The Begum arranged for that gentleman's release.[34] Further, Colonel Ochterlony in Delhi asked her to forward supplies from Sardhana to Saharanpur, under escort of her own troops, to which she consented her compliance.[35]

Yet, despite all of this, Wellesley still seemed determined upon depriving her of Sardhana and her other territories. However, Wellesley was not to get his wish, as the cost of his seemingly endless wars was causing sleepless nights for the EIC directors in London, and he was recalled in July 1805. His replacement was none other than Lord Cornwallis, whose instructions were simply to keep the peace. Wellesley's policy lapsed, and in August 1805, Begum Somru was confirmed in her possessions. Sardhana was to remain hers.[36]

Even in the times of relative peace which now ensued, the Somru Brigade continued to exist. It became, to an extent, part of the East India Company's irregular forces. Three battalions and some artillery were effectively under British orders.[37] Colonel Saleur had now retired and was living as one of the Begum's pensioners, and Colonel Claud Pathod, an Indian born officer whose father was Flemish, had taken over.[38] In theory, they remained to guard the new frontier of what was now British India, but in truth, there was little for them to do. The new overlord of the Sikhs, Ranjit Singh, did not want a war with the British, which he knew he could not win. It would be another 40 years before the Sikh Empire went to war with the British, by which time Farzana was dead and Sardhana absorbed into British India.

For the remaining years of her life, Farzana lived in peace, as did the Somru Brigade. The Begum thought it appropriate to make provision for her dependants: 'who attached themselves to her fortunes, at a time when her situation was precarious, and from their being the relatives of those who have fallen in her service, and the loss of whom deprives them of all support but what must be derived from her.'[39]

As she had no heirs, she was aware that her territories would be taken over by the British after her death, so she did her best to make sure her dependants and pensioners would continue to receive support. Lord Minto, now the Governor-General, wrote to

33 Banerji, *Begam Samru*, p.100.
34 Banerji, *Begam Samru*, p.98.
35 Banerji, *Begam Samru*, p.100.
36 Keay, *Farzana*, p.268.
37 Banerji, *Begam Samru*, p.150.
38 Keay, *Farzana*, p.270.
39 Banerji, *Begam Samru*, p.114.

the Begum in August 1807, 'I have great satisfaction in communicating to you my compliance with your wishes as described in your letter to Mr Seton.'[40]

The same letter also contained more than the usual effusion of flattery, showing how much relations between the British and the Begum had improved since Richard Wellesley had been recalled to London.

Indeed, as peace was restored to Hindustan, the Begum became something of a curiosity to the wealthy British travellers of the second decade of the nineteenth century. It was around this time that Sleeman visited Sardhana, and his *Rambles and Recollections of an Indian Official* gives us some contemporary insight into the financial workings of the Begum's state and her largesse to the Indian Christians and,[41] indeed, to other Christians in her domains.

Into the 1820s and 1830s, the Somru Brigade continued to exist, but it fought no more campaigns, and its only functions were as local security for the Begum's lands and properties. There was a tiny flash of the old style in 1826, when the Begum volunteered her army to join Lord Combermere's British Indian army at the siege of Bharatpur, which Lord Lake had so singularly failed to take in 1805.[42] However, the British commander for this new campaign against the great Jat city did not want the Begum's assistance.

Combermere's aide-de-camp, one Major Archer, remarked:

> When the army was before Bharatpur in 1826 the Commander-in-Chief was desirous that no Native chief of our allies would accompany the besieging force with any of his troops. This order hurt the pride of the Begum, who remonstrated. She was told that the large and holy place of Muttra was to be confided to her care. 'Nonsense' said she 'if I don't go to Bharatpur all Hindustan will say I am grown a coward in my old age'.[43]

But the old days were past, and there was no longer any need for the Begum to lead her troops into battle.

Farzana – once a dancing girl and an emperor's adopted daughter – died peacefully in her bed of a fever on 27 January 1836. She was approximately 86 years old.

40 Banerji, *Begam Samru*, p.116.
41 Sleeman, *Rambles and Recollections*, Chapter 75, pp.594–615.
42 Provan, *Bullocks, Grain and Good Madeira*, pp.137–166.
43 As quoted in Banerji, *Begam Samru*, p.146.

11

Uniforms and Organisation of the Somru Brigade and 'Mr Thomas's Party', 1760–1836

Of all the mercenary *compoos*, the Somru Brigade may have had the longest continuous existence of all the 'trained brigades' who fought in India from the second half of the eighteenth century. The largest, the 'Army of Hindustan', with five brigades, was destroyed by the British in the Second Maratha War. Others had only a fleeting existence of a few years. The *compoo* initially raised by Walter Reinhardt – 'Somru' – around 1760 or 1761 had a continuous existence from then until the death of his widow the Begum Somru in 1836, over 70 years, of which about half was spent in campaigning.

The strength of the *compoo* varied over the years from the small two battalion beginnings when Reinhardt, that is of course Somru, first began his career as a mercenary commander.[1]

For most of the *compoo*'s existence, the usual strength was four to six battalions of sepoys, a 'regiment' of cavalry and 20 pieces of artillery. This was the case when Thomas and the Begum almost went to war with each other in 1794: 'Her force consisting of four battalions of infantry 20 pieces of artillery and about 400 cavalry was commanded by officers of tried and acknowledged abilities.'[2]

Sleeman gives details of further battalions added to this force, 'Another battalion was added to the four in 1797 and another raised in 1798 and 1802; five of the six marched under Colonel Saleur to the Deccan with Scindia.'[3]

Sleeman's arithmetic is at fault here, as the three battalions added to the already existent four add up to seven battalions. Of course, Sleeman, although he met the Begum, was writing some 30 or more years after the event. However, in the list of units present at Sardhana on the Begum's death, we find a 'Bodyguard' of 266 men in existence, in addition to the six infantry battalions and the cavalry.[4] Could Sleeman have

1 See Chapter 3.
2 Francklin, *Military Memoirs*, p.32.
3 Sleeman, *Rambles and Recollections*, p.610.
4 Banerji, *Begam Samru*, p.149.

mistaken this unit for a seventh battalion? Or was the bodyguard a cavalry unit, which, to be honest, is probably more likely? That little mystery remains currently unsolved.

The table below gives the strengths of the individual battalions on the Begum's death in 1836.[5]

Begum Somru's Army in 1836

Unit	**Strength**
1st Infantry	507
2nd Infantry	504
3rd Infantry	504
4th Infantry	488
5th Infantry	481
6th Infantry	462
The Bodyguard	266
The Irregular Cavalry	245
The Artillery	1,007
Total	4,464

The strength of the artillery component would, like other Indian forces at this time, include such supernumeraries as bullock and elephant drivers, mahouts, 'beldars' to dig any fieldworks – in European terminology, pioneers – and other non-combatant but vital artisans such as carpenters, wheelwrights, and blacksmiths.[6] It is probable that these skilled artisans did most of the building and repair work around the fort and palace of Sardhana in the years of peace.

The table accords pretty well with the known totals for the Somru Brigade in its comparatively long existence, though Sleeman may be mistaken about the dates of augmentation of the force. Smith, for example, says, 'This party was augmented by the Begum in 1797 and 1798 to six battalions.'[7]

Smith mentions no additions in 1802, and six battalions does seem to be the 'optimum' strength of the *compoo* through much of its history with, as has been noted, a 'field force' of three or four battalions, with the remainder protecting their base at Sardhana.

At times, there were also numbers of irregular infantry, *seebundies* or *sehbandie*, 'whenever the need arose'.[8] Such troops were often used for revenue collection, or what might be termed 'policing', rather than strictly military duties. The 'need' would arise when the bulk of the regulars were away on campaign.

In the aftermath of the Second Maratha War, the Begum, now in alliance with the British, provided three battalions of sepoys and some details of artillery from her army

5 Banerji, *Begam Samru*, p.149.
6 Copestake, *Their Infantry and Guns*, p.63.
7 Smith, *Regular Corps*, p.5.
8 Banerji, *Begam Samru*, p.144.

for British use. They seem to have been used as garrison troops for internal security duties. In 1834, they were stationed as shown in the table below.

Unit and total strength	Number at each Station
2nd Battalion – 516 men	Rania 388
	Bhawani 128
3rd Battalion – 515 men	Meerut 259
	Muzaffarnagar 194
	Saharanpur 62
5th Battalion – 515 men	Karnal 250
	Gurgaon 265

The monthly pay for these troops was Rs 11,763 for the three battalions, plus another Rs 170 3 annas 8 pice for a detail of artillery stationed at Hansi – George Thomas's old capital.[9]

The army was paid off and disbanded barely a month after Farzana's death. Some, at least, 'sought a new master in Ranjit Singh of Lahore'.[10]

Uniforms

There is a description of the uniforms of the infantry by a Mrs Deane, the wife of a British officer, who visited Sardhana in 1810:

> We were escorted over the estate by her colonel commandant; a respectable old gentleman of the name of Peton, a Frenchman by birth but resident at her court for many years. She has a regular cantonment here for her troops, and a strong fort containing some good houses which are inhabited by the officers and their families. Her soldiers are tall stout men, with light complexions, hooked noses, and strongly marked features, being principally Rajputs who are the best soldiers but much addicted to chewing opium, generally proud, and often insolent. Their uniform is a dress of dark blue broad cloth reaching to the feet with scarlet turbans and waistbands. Her park of artillery seemed also in excellent order; most of the large guns stood in a line in front of the palace gates.[11]

There is also an Indian artist's painting 'Begum Somru and Her Army',[12] painted sometime between 1805 and 1836, which shows more details. The infantry are as in the description above, except that the waist sashes are yellow. Trousers are white. The

9 Details and table from British correspondence as quoted by Banerji, *Begam Samru*, pp.150–151.
10 Banerji, *Begam Samru*, p.154.
11 Banerji, *Begam Samru*, pp.146–147.
12 Available to view online <https://artsandculture.google.com/asset/begum-samru-and-her-army-unknown/iwEq5C-JbAC4Nw>

battalions march behind square, red standards, which appear to have an all-over pattern in a darker red – but this may be the artist's painting. Cartridge boxes appear black, with a white shoulder belt supporting them. Sword belts appear black or dark brown.

Cavalry are in red or scarlet coats, and their turbans are dark coloured, either brown or black. A very few men appear to have helmets. Sashes are light yellow and their trousers are white. Sword belts are black or brown. The troopers are armed with matchlock muskets in the Indian fashion, and a few men have shields on their backs. Saddle cloths are of various colours, with yellow and red being the most common, but blue and red, green and red, and yellow and green also appear. Boots are black. In amongst the cavalry is a triangular red standard. This unit may be the bodyguard, as it is shown in attendance on the Begum on her elephant. The cavalry has a kettledrummer in the same uniform. The drums have blue hoops and red drum banners.

Also shown is a group of camel guns, or *zambureks*. The riders have tan-brown coats, blue turbans, green waist sashes, and darker brown sword belts and scabbards. The troopers' saddlecloths are red, edged with green. What may be officers for the camel unit wear blue or pink coats, with a yellow sash on the blue-coated officer, and a white sash on the pink-coated one. Turbans in both cases are red. The blue-coated officer has a shield on his back. The officers' saddlecloths are yellow with a blue outer border and a pink inner border. The standard is again a triangular red one. This picture is the only evidence of camel-mounted *zambureks* that has come to light. They do not seem to be mentioned in the written sources.

The artillery appear in green coats with black turbans and dark blue or black sashes, though some appear to have blue coats, again with dark blue or black turbans and yellow or red sashes. These latter do not appear to be armed, unlike the gunners who have tulwars. The gun shown in the picture is limbered up and is a split-trailed piece. The carriage and limber are dark wood, and the cannon barrel is bronze. The team comprises six white oxen in three pairs. The 'driver' is in white civilian dress with a red turban. A second gun, although mostly the same, has only four oxen pulling the limber.

A European officer is shown mounted on a horse with a red and yellow saddlecloth. He wears a black round hat with a white plume at the front rising out of a red and gold plume holder. His open red jacket has a black standing collar, black lapels and cuffs, and short tails. His visible waistcoat is blue, worn with a white shirt and cravat. The coat has gold epaulettes. Nether wear consists of rather baggy, light reddish-brown trousers and black boots. Another European rides a grey horse and has a round hat with a white plume rising out of the left-hand side. He wears a dark blue, European-style open coat with red facings on the standing collar, lapels, and cuffs. His smallclothes are white and his boots black.

Not strictly military, but in this case probably part of the artillery, are a party of men carrying mattocks. In all probability these are beldars.

Indian officers of the Infantry are dressed individually and in richer style, though all have red turbans, their coats are patterned and sashes multi-coloured. *Bhistis* or water carriers are shown with their skin water bags. Gunga Din was not an invention of Kipling!

A group of armed men in non-uniform clothing, armed primarily with swords and shields, are probably *seebundies*. Those leading expensively saddled horses are more likely to be grooms and stable hands for the Begum's personal stables.

Other notes of the dress of the Begum's troops appear in Thomas Bacon's *First impressions and Studies from Nature in Hindustan*', where he mentions the following regarding the officers' dress: 'the most heterogeneous and varied possible being worn according to the taste or fancy of each without regard to uniformity of pattern or colour; but the troops are clad in vests of dark yellow cloth, with some attention to conformity of cut and they are all armed and appointed alike.'[13]

Quite what is meant by 'vests' is not made clear. Neither of the extant illustrations show troops dressed in yellow coats. The only yellow item in the troop's uniform is the waist sash.

Mr Thomas's Party

George Thomas's army was constantly at war. From the early service under Appa Khande Rao, to the time of Thomas's final defeat and the fall of Hansi, Jehazi Sahib was almost always fighting someone!

His force began as a single infantry battalion of roughly 700 men,[14] plus his cavalry, which usually numbered around 150–200 men, but sometimes fewer. He was often plagued by desertions, due to his frequent lack of the wherewithal to pay his men, but as his fame grew and his finances improved, he expanded the single battalion to a 'regiment' of two thousand men. He also added 500 irregulars, 10 pieces of artillery, and 200 cavalry.[15] This was in 1794–1795.

Later, during his involvement in the 'Widows' War' – operating against Lakwa Dada – Thomas had six battalions of sepoys 'much reduced by desertion', 300 Rohilla irregulars, 150 cavalry, and 22 guns.[16]

As we have already seen, by July 1800, Thomas disposed of a considerable force of seven infantry battalions, 500 cavalry, and 24 pieces of artillery.[17] This was perhaps the largest force that Thomas commanded before the war with Perron.

There seems to have been little time for the niceties of uniform or colours. Thomas's battalions certainly had their own standards or colours, but Thomas never describes them. Frustratingly, this is the same for whatever uniforms they may have worn, 'To deceive the enemy on this occasion, Mr Thomas was accustomed to change the uniforms and colours of his own people.'[18]

13 As quoted in Banerji, *Begam Samru*, p.147.
14 Francklin, *Military Memoirs*, p.14.
15 Francklin, *Military Memoirs*, p.32.
16 Francklin, *Military Memoirs*, p.155.
17 See Chapter 8.
18 Francklin, *Military Memoirs*, p.153.

But there is no hint of the type of uniforms or colours that Thomas's battalions may have carried. It is unlikely that they wore European-style uniforms similar to the 'Army of Hindustan', so uniforms of Indian-style, similar in cut to those of the Somru Brigade, are more likely, but there is no clue as to their colour. It is equally possible that some of Thomas's more hastily raised troops did not wear uniforms at all but only their civilian clothes with their equipment belts. Even this tentative conclusion is speculative.

Appendix

Known European Officers of the Somru Brigade and of 'Mr George Thomas's Party'

Commanding Officers of the Somru Brigade 1763–1836

Colonel Walter Reinhardt, alias 'Somru', German, 1763–1778. See Chapters 2, 3 and 4.

Colonel Pauli, German. Had been one of Somru's officers. Succeeded to the command in 1778, assassinated in 1783. See Chapter 4.

Major Baors. Possibly one of Somru's or Pauli's junior officers. French. In command 1783. Left the brigade in 1784 or 1785 and joined de Boigne's First Brigade. Killed at the Battle of Patan, 1790.

Major(?) Evans. English? Succeeded Baors in the command, which he held until 1789. Later in de Boigne's service as a captain.

Chevalier Dudrenec. French, born in Brest. A former midshipman in the French Navy. Began his mercenary service in 1780 as an officer in René Madec's *compoo*. In 1782, joined the Somru Brigade, succeeded to the command in 1790 or 1791, but left in 1793. Served Tukaji Holkar and fought against de Boigne at the Battle of Lakhieri, where his four-battalion *compoo* was destroyed. Later, commanded a *compoo* at the Battle of Malpura in 1800, where his command was roughly handled by Rathor cavalry. Would eventually command the Fourth Brigade of the Army of Hindustan under Perron. In 1803, he deserted his command and surrendered to the British.

Colonel Le Vaisseau. French. Succeeded Dudrenec in 1793 after being an artillery officer in the brigade for some time. Was noted as a cultured and able man. Married the Begum in May 1793, but in 1795 part of the brigade mutinied and Le Vaisseau and the Begum fled. Caught by the mutineers, Le Vaisseau committed suicide by blowing his brains out with one of his own pistols. See Chapter 6.

Colonel Saleur. French. Took over the brigade after Le Vaisseau's death in 1795 and would command it until February 1804, when he retired due to ill health.

Colonel Claude Pathod. Indian born, with a Flemish father. Took the command in 1804. Nothing else known.

Colonel Peton. French. Described by Mrs Deane, who visited Sardhana in 1810 as 'a respectable old gentleman of the name of Peton, a Frenchman by birth but resident at her court for many years'.[1] This may have actually been Colonel Pathod.

Other Officers who Served with the Somru Brigade

Captain Bernier. French. One of the witnesses at Le Vaisseau's wedding to the Begum. Later served with the Third Brigade of the Army of Hindustan and was killed at the siege of Hansi.

Captain (?) Liegeois. Possibly French. Known to Thomas, so in the brigade since sometime before 1787. Left Begum Somru's service. Nothing else is known.

Robert Skinner. Younger brother of Lieutenant Colonel James Skinner of Skinner's Horse. Joined after Perron dismissed his European officers at the beginning of the Second Maratha War in 1803. However, left soon after, and by 1805 was serving with his brother fighting for the British against Jaswant Rao Holkar. Died in 1821.[2] See Chapter 10.

John Thomas. A son of George is noted by Sleeman as serving in the brigade at the time of the Begum's death in 1836.[3]

And of course, George Thomas, 1787–1792.

Unusually, we have the names of two of the European gunners who served with the brigade, as they gave a statement when they 'came in' to the British as the Second Maratha War started, rather than fight their countrymen: John Roach, Englishman; George Blake, Scotsman.[4]

European Officers Serving Under George Thomas

1797 – Captain John Morris. Killed at the Battle of Fatehpur.

1801 – Captain Hopkins. Mortally wounded at the Battle of Georgeghur.

Captain Hearsey. Surrendered at the fall of Hansi. Perhaps later entered Maratha service and was one of the officers who took advantage of Wellesley's offer of a pension rather than fight the British in 1803.[5]

Lieutenant Birch. Surrendered at the fall of Hansi, but then seems to have entered Maratha service. Declined to fight the British in 1803 and took advantage of Wellesley's offer of a pension. May have been the same Captain Birch who commanded two

1 As quoted in Banerji, *Begam Samru*, pp.146–147.
2 Major A.M. Daniels, *Skinner's Horse* ([n.p.]: Published by the Regiment, 1924), p.7.
3 Sleeman, *Rambles and Recollections*, p.604.
4 Bennell, *Maratha War Papers*, p.262.
5 Compton, *Particular Account*, p.363.

battalions of Najibs defending Delhi. Fought against Bapu Scindia and later on the Punjab frontier, aiding Skinner against Sikh raiders.[6]

Indian Officers Serving Under Thomas

Unusually Thomas's memoir mentions several of his Indian officers by name:
Mortuza Khan. A regimental commander in 1801.
Afalut Khan. A native officer formerly in the service of the East India Company, possibly commanding a *rissalah* of Thomas's cavalry in 1801.
Shahtab Khan. *Killadar*, or governor of Thomas's fort of Georgeghur in 1801.

6 Compton, *Particular Account*, p.340.

Glossary

Beldars	Skilled labourers adept at digging earthworks and gun positions. In European terms, Pioneers or Sappers.
Compo, *compoo* or *Campoo*	A Brigade of trained battalions. Usually mercenaries, often but not always commanded by Europeans.
Gardi or *Gardis*	Term used by the Marathas to denote trained infantry. From Ibrahim Khan Gardi.
Golandauz	Trained artillerymen. Gunners.
Havildar	Indian NCO, equivalent to sergeant.
Havildar-Major	Senior Indian NCO, equivalent to sergeant major.
Hicarah	A mounted messenger or scout.
Jaghir	A grant of land in return for service, which was not always military. Not hereditary, though many became so in the crumbling Mughal Empire.
Jaidad	Grant of revenue or land specifically to support troops. Similar to, but distinct from a jaghir.
Jemadar	Indian officer, in the Army of Hindustan a platoon commander.
Jheel	A marsh or morass.
Kelasis	Skilled labourers who manhandled the guns in action after the gun had been unlimbered. Often rendered as clashies in European sources.
Killadar or *Khilladar*	Governor of a fortress.
Lascar	Term used by the British for a porter or labourer, often used to carry supplies or manhandle cannon.
Naik or *Naigue*	Indian NCO, equivalent to corporal.
Najib or *Nujib*	Semi-trained matchlock musketeer. Often a Rohilla.
Paltan	A battalion of trained infantry. Corruption of battalion. Several *paltans* make a *compoo*.
Rissalah	A body of trained cavalry with roughly 80–120 *sowars*, though sometimes stronger.
Rissaldar	Commander of a *Rissalah* of cavalry.

Rohilla	Tribesmen of Pathan origin who had settled in Hindustan. Fought both for and against the Mughals. Often found as mercenaries. In theory, specialised in the defence of fortresses.
Sardar	Generic term for chieftain or military commander.
Sepoy	Indian soldier, specifically a trained infantryman.
Sowar	A cavalry trooper.
Subahdar	Controller of a *subah* or district, which could be a single village or a whole province. De Boigne was subahdar of the whole of Hindustan under Madhaji Scindia.
Subedar	Indian officer rank, in the Army of Hindustan a commander of an infantry company.
Telinga	Term used to describe European trained infantry.
Top-Khana	Artillery park.
Zemindar	A landowner. The more powerful aspired to independent status. Much effort was expended in collecting taxes from 'refractory Zemindars' by the Army of Hindustan and by George Thomas. The British would have similar problems.

Bibliography

Primary Sources

Bennell, A.S. (ed.), *The Maratha War Papers of Arthur Wellesley: January to December 1803* (Stroud: Sutton Publishing for the Army Records Society, 1998)

Cormack, A.A., *The Mahratta Wars 1797–1805: Letters from the Front by Three Brothers, Nicholas, George and Thomas Carnegie* (Banff: Privately Published, 1971)

Corneille, John, *Journal of my Service in India*, edited by Michael Edwardes (London: The Folio Society, 1966)

Dundas, Colonel D., *Principles of Military Movements* (London: J. Walter, 1788)

Francklin, W., Capt, *The History of the Reign of Shah-Aulum, the Present Emperor of Hindostan* (Calcutta: Cooper and Graham, 1798)

Francklin, W., *The Military Memoirs of George Thomas* (Calcutta: Hurkaru Press, 1803)

Fraser, J.B., *The Military Memoirs of Lieutenant-Colonel James Skinner, C.B.* (London: Smith, Elder, 1851)

Joshi, P.M. (ed.) and J. Sarkar (trans.), *Persian Records of Maratha History*, vol.2: *Scindia as Regent of Delhi, 1787 and 1789–1791* (Bombay: Director of Archives, 1954)

Khan, Seid-Gholam Hossein, *The Seir Mutaqherin; or, Review of Modern Times: Being an History of India Containing in General the Reigns of the Seven Last Emperors of Hindustan*, 4 vols (Delhi: Low Price Publications, 1990)

Law de Lauriston, J., *A Memoir of the Mughal Empire: Events of 1757–1761*, translated by G.S. Cheema (New Delhi: Manohar, 2014)

Orme, R., *A History of the Military Transactions of the British Nation in Indostan* (London, 1758; repr. New Delhi: Today and Tomorrow, 1985)

Pester, J., *War and Sport in India 1802–1806: An Officer's Diary* (London: Alston Rivers, 1913)

Rawlinson, H.G. (ed.), *An Account of the Last Battle of Panipat and the Events Leading up to It* (London: Oxford University Press, 1926; repr. Milton Keynes: Lightning Source UK Ltd., [n.d.])

Sarkar, J. and G.S. Sardesai (eds), *English Records of Maratha History* (Bombay: Government Central Press, 1936–1953)

Shreeve, N., *The History of Zeb-ul-Nissa. The Begum Somru of Sardhana*, translated from the Persian of Lalla Gokul Chand (Crossbush. Bookwright, Convent of the Poor Clares 1994)

Sinh, R. (ed.), *Poona Residency Correspondence*, vol.9: *Daulat Rao Scindia and North Indian Affairs, 1800–1803* (Bombay: Government Central Press, 1943)

Sleeman, W.H., *Rambles and Recollections of an Indian Official* (London: Archibald Constable and Co., 1893)

Smith, Major L.F., *A Sketch of the Rise, Progress and Termination of the Regular Corps Formed and Commanded by Europeans in the Service of the Native Princes of India* (Calcutta: J. Greenway, 1805)

Thompson, J.P. (trans.), 'An Autobiographical Sketch of Louis Borquien', *Journal of the Punjab Historical Society*, vol.9, part 1 (Calcutta, 1923)

Thorn, Major William, *Memoir of the War in India Conducted by General Lord Lake, Commander-in-Chief...* (London: T. Egerton, 1818)

Tod, Lieutenant Colonel J., *Annals and Antiquities of Rajasthan* (London, 1829; repr. Delhi: Motilal Banarsidass, 1987)

Tone, William Henry, *Some Institutions of the Mahratta People* (London: [n. pub.], 1818)

Various, *The Asiatic Annual Register for the Years 1799–1805* (London: British Library, [n.d.])

Williams, Captain John, *The Bengal Native Infantry. An Historical Account From its First Formation in 1757 to 1796, with supplementary notes to 1814* (London: John Murray, 1817; facsimile repr. London: Muller, 1970)

Secondary Sources

Abbott, P., *Rivals of the Raj: Non-British Colonial Armies in Asia 1497–1941* (Nottingham: Foundry Books, 2010)

Athale, Colonel A., *The Legacy of Shivaji the Great: Military Strategy, Naval Supremacy and the Maratha Empire* (Mumbai: Indus Source Books, 2023)

Banerji, B., *Begam Samru* (Calcutta: M.C. Sarkar & Sons, 1925)

Barbé, Emile, *Le Nabab René Madec* (Paris: Felix Alcan, 1894), translated by Yog Mehta as *The Nawab René Madec* (Privately Published, 2023)

Bidwell, S., *Swords for Hire: European Mercenaries in Eighteenth-Century India* (London: John Murray, 1971)

Blackmore, D., *Destructive and Formidable: British Infantry Firepower 1642–1765* (London: Frontline Books, 2014)

Broome, A., *History of the Rise and Progress of the Bengal Army*, vol.1 (London: Smith, Elder & Co., 1850, repr. Legare Street Press, [n.d.])

Buckle, E. *Memoir of the Services of the Bengal Artillery* (London: W.H. Allen, 1852; repr. Uckfield: Naval & Military Press, 2021)

Cardew, F.G., *A Sketch of the Services of the Bengal Native Army to the Year 1895* (1895; repr. Calcutta: [n. pub.], 1971)

Chartrand, R., *Armies and Wars of the French East India Companies 1664–1770: European, Asian and African Soldiers in India, Africa, the Far East and Louisiana* (Warwick: Helion, 2024)

Compton, H., *A Particular Account of the European Military Adventurers of Hindustan* (London: T. Fisher Unwin, 1892; repr. Karachi: Oxford University Press, 1976)

Copestake, A., *Their Infantry and Guns Will Astonish You: The Army of Hindustan and European Mercenaries in Maratha Service 1780–1803* (Warwick: Helion & Company, 2021)

Cunningham, J.D., and H.L.O. Garrett, *A History of the Sikhs* (1849; repr. [n.p.]: Francklin Classics, [n.d.])

Dalrymple, W., *The Anarchy: The Relentless Rise of the East India Company* (London: Bloomsbury, 2019)

Dalrymple, W., *White Mughals* (London: Penguin, 2002)

Daniels, Major A.M., *Skinner's Horse* ([n.p.]: Published by the Regiment, 1924)

Deodhar, Y.N., *Nana Phadnis and the External Affairs of the Maratha Empire* (Bombay: Popular Prakashan, 1962)

Edwardes, M., *King of the World: The Life of the Last Great Moghul Emperor* (London: Secker & Warburg, 1970)

Fortescue, J.W., *A History of the British Army* (London: Macmillan and Co., 1910), vol.3

Grant Duff, J., *History of the Mahrattas* (London: Longmans, 1878)

Grey, C. and Garrett, H.L.O. (eds), *European Adventurers of Northern India, 1785–1849* (Lahore: 1929; repr. Delhi: AES, 1993)

Harrington, P., *The Battle of Plassey: Clive of India's Finest Hour* (London: Osprey, 1994)

Hennessy, M., *The Rajah from Tipperary: George Thomas* (London: Sidgwick & Jackson, 1971)

Holman, D., *Sikander Sahib: The Life of Colonel James Skinner, 1778–1841* (London: [n. pub.], 1961)

Holmes, R., *Wellington: The Iron Duke* (London: HarperCollins, 2001)

Hutchinson, L., *European Freebooters in Moghul India* (London: [n. pub.], 1964)

Kadam, V.S., *Maratha Confederacy: A Study in its Origin and Development* (New Delhi: Oxford University Press, 1993)

Keane, H.G., *The Fall of the Moghul Empire of Hindustan* (London: Leonaur, 2009)

Keane, H.G., *Hindustan under Free Lances* (London: Irish University Press, 1971)

Keay, J., *Farzana: The Woman Who Saved an Empire* (London: I.B. Tauris, 2014)

Klassens, J., *European Mercenaries in the Armies of Post-Mughal Successor States, 1775–1849* (Doctoral thesis, 2007)

Kulkarni, G.T. and Kantak, M.R., *Battle of Karda: Challenges and Responses* (Pune: [n. pub.], 1980)

Kumar, R. (ed.), *Military System of the Sikhs* (New Delhi: Commonwealth Publishers, 2004)

Lall, J., *Begam Samru: Fading Portrait in a Gilded Frame* (New Delhi: Roli Books, 1997)

Lang, J., *The Story of Lord Clive* (London: T.C. & E.C. Jack, 1906)

Lawford, J.P., *Britain's Army in India: From its Foundation to the Conquest of Bengal* (London: Allen & Unwin, 1978)

Madra, A.S., and P. Singh, *Warrior Saints: Four Centuries of Sikh Military History*, vol.1 (London: Kashi House, 2013)

Malleson, G.B., *History of the French in India* (Edinburgh: John Grant, 1909)

Malleson, G.B., *The Decisive Battles of India* (London: W.H. Allen, 1883)
Mason, P., *A Matter of Honour: An Account of the Indian Army, its Officers and Men* (London: Jonathan Cape, 1974)
Millar, S., *Assaye 1803: Wellington's First and 'Bloodiest' Victory* (Oxford: Osprey, 2006)
Mollo, B., *The Indian Army* (London: Blandford, 1981)
Parihar, G.R., *Marwar and the Marathas* (Jodhpur: Hindi Sahitya Mandir, 1968)
Pearse, H., *Life and Military Services of Viscount Lake* (Edinburgh: William Blackwood and Sons, 1908)
Provan, J., Bullocks, *Grain and Good Madeira* (Warwick: Helion, 2022)
Qanungo, K.R., *History of the Jats* (Calcutta: Sarkar & Sons, 1925)
Reid, S., *The Battle of Plassey 1757: The Victory that Won an Empire* (Barnsley: Frontline Books, 2017)
Roy, K., *From Hydaspes to Kargil: A History of Warfare in India from 326 BC to AD 1999* (New Delhi: Manohar, 2016)
Roy, K., *War, Culture and Society in Early Modern South Asia* (London: Routledge, 2011)
Roy, T., 'Rethinking the Origin of British India: State Formation and Military Fiscal Undertakings in an 18th-Century World Region', *Modern Asian Studies*, vol.47, no.4 (2013)
Sarkar, J., *The Fall of the Moghul Empire*, 4th edn (Hyderabad: Orient Blackswan, 1991)
Saxena, R.K., *The Army of the Rajputs* (Udaipur: Saroj Prakashan, 1989)
Sen, S.N., *The Military System of the Marathas*, 2nd edn (Delhi: K.P. Bagchi, 1958; reprint, 1979)
Sen, S.P., *The French in India 1760–1816* (Calcutta: [n. pub.], 1958)
Singh Mann, G., *The British and the Sikhs: Discovery, Warfare and Friendship, c.1700–1900* (Warwick: Helion & Co, 2020)
Singh Mann, G., *The Rise of the Sikh Soldier: The Sikh Warrior through the Ages, c.1700–1900* (Warwick: Helion & Co, 2022)
Singh, A., *A History of the Sikh Misals* (Croydon: OFI Group, 2024)
Singh, P. & J.M. Rai, *Empire of the Sikhs: The Life and Times of Maharaja Ranjit Singh* (London: Peter Owen, 2008)
Sykes, P., *A History of Afghanistan* vol.1 (London: Macmillan & Co, 1940), Indian reprint (New Delhi: Oriental Book Reprint Corporation, 1981)
Weller, J., *Wellington in India* (London: Greenhill, 1993)
Wilson, W.J., *History of the Madras Army* (Madras: [n. pub.], 1888)
Yule, H. and Burnell, A.C., *Hobson-Jobson: A Glossary of Colloquial Anglo-Indian Words and Phrases*, 2nd edn (London: Routledge and Kegan Paul, 1985)

From Reason to Revolution – Warfare 1721-1815

http://www.helion.co.uk/series/from-reason-to-revolution-1721-1815.php

The 'From Reason to Revolution' series covers the period of military history 1721–1815, an era in which fortress-based strategy and linear battles gave way to the nation-in-arms and the beginnings of total war.

This era saw the evolution and growth of light troops of all arms, and of increasingly flexible command systems to cope with the growing armies fielded by nations able to mobilise far greater proportions of their manpower than ever before. Many of these developments were fired by the great political upheavals of the era, with revolutions in America and France bringing about social change which in turn fed back into the military sphere as whole nations readied themselves for war. Only in the closing years of the period, as the reactionary powers began to regain the upper hand, did a military synthesis of the best of the old and the new become possible.

The series examines the military and naval history of the period in a greater degree of detail than has hitherto been attempted, and has a very wide brief, with the intention of covering all aspects from the battles, campaigns, logistics, and tactics, to the personalities, armies, uniforms, and equipment.

Submissions

The publishers would be pleased to receive submissions for this series. Please email reasontorevolution@helion.co.uk, or write to Helion & Company Limited, Unit 8 Amherst Business Centre, Budbrooke Road, Warwick, CV34 5WE

You may also be interested in:

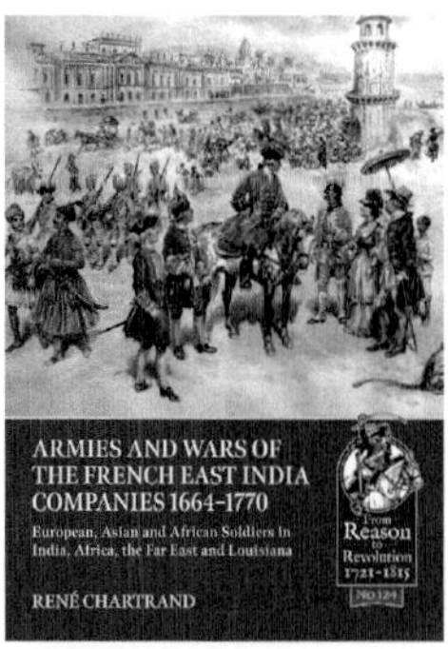

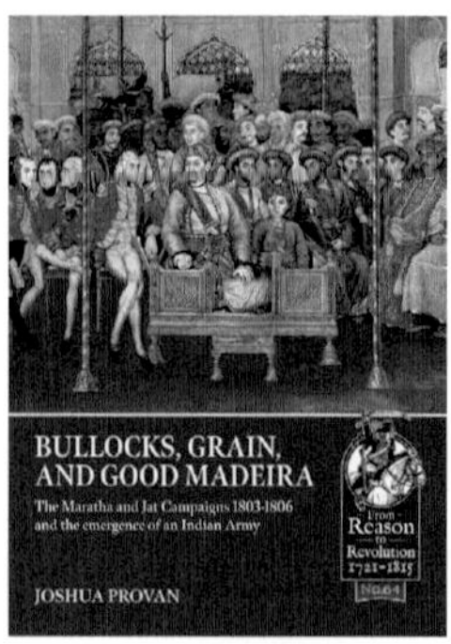

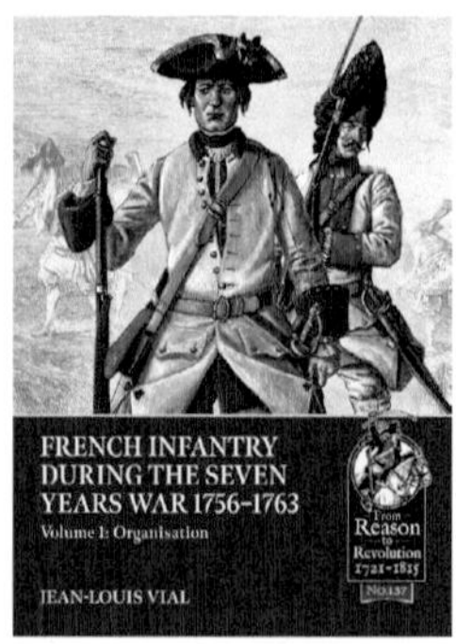

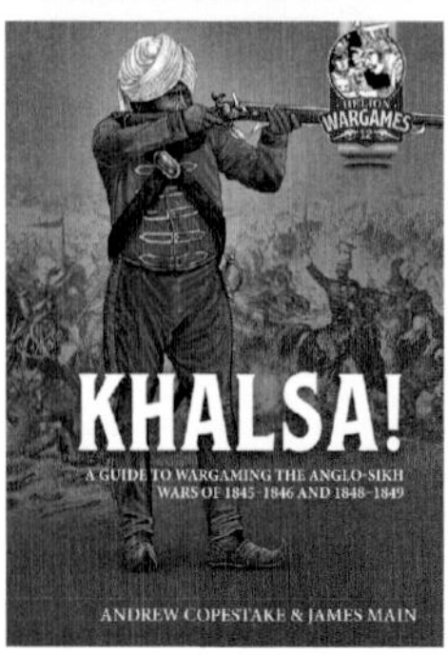

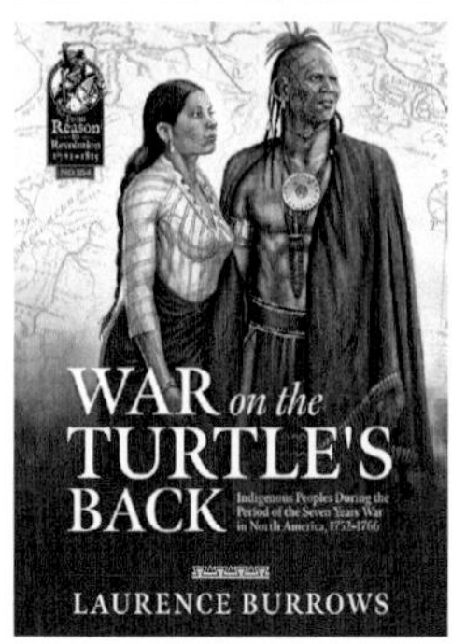